WEST COAST

ROAD EATS

WEST COAST
ROAD EATS

The Best Road Food from San Diego to the Canadian Border

ANNA ROTH

SASQUATCH BOOKS
SEATTLE

Printed in the United States of America
Published by Sasquatch Books
Distributed by PGW/Perseus
17 16 15 14 13 12 11   9 8 7 6 5 4 3 2 1

Cover photographs: © Corbis Photography/Veer, © Linda Bair / Dreamstime.com,
   © Peter Kim / Dreamstime.com, © Darryl Brooks / Dreamstime.com,
Cover and interior design: Anna Goldstein
Interior maps: Lisa Brower/GreenEye Design
Interior composition: Anna Goldstein
Interior photography and author photograph: Anna Roth

Library of Congress Cataloging-in-Publication Data

Roth, Anna.
 West Coast road eats : the best road food from San Diego to the Canadian border / Anna Roth.
    p. cm.
 Includes bibliographical references and index.
 ISBN 978-1-57061-690-7
 1. Restaurants--Pacific Coast (U.S.)--Guidebooks. 2. Pacific Coast (U.S.)--Guidebooks. 3. California--Guidebooks. 4. Oregon--Guidebooks. 5. Washington (State)--Guidebooks. 6. Pacific Coast (U.S.)--Description and travel. 7. Automobile travel--Pacific Coast (U.S.) 8. Pacific Coast (U.S.)--History, Local. I. Title.
 TX907.3.P33R68 2011
 641.5979--dc22
                         2011000593

Sasquatch Books
119 South Main Street, Suite 400
Seattle, WA 98104
(206) 467-4300
www.sasquatchbooks.com
custserv@sasquatchbooks.com

Contents

How to Use This Book

I know—99 percent of you have used a guidebook before, and you're pretty sure you know the drill. The basics are self-explanatory, but before you dive in, here's a guide to help you understand how to make the best use of this particular guidebook's information.

How The Book Is Structured

West Coast Road Eats follows major north-to-south highways from the Canadian border to San Diego. This includes everything west of the mountains, mainly focusing on Interstate 5, Highway 101, and Highway 1. California is broken into three regions—Northern, Central, and Southern—to account for the massive state's culinary, cultural, and geographic differences.

Routes were chosen based on road trip traffic more than mileage. For instance, I-5 in Washington is divided into two sections (north and south of Seattle), while I-5 Oregon has only one. Similarly, major culinary destinations like Napa and Sonoma Valleys and Santa Barbara Wine Country were given their own chapters, despite their relatively small geographic scope.

Region/Trip/City Stats boxes open most sections and provide need-to-know details about the region, road trip, or city. These include, when applicable:

DISTANCE: Length of road covered in the section, not counting detours.

START AND END POINTS: Where the coverage ends, not where the road ends (for instance, the Oregon chapter ends in Ashland, not the California border).

LOCAL FLAVOR: Food and drink the area is known for or does best. Region Stats go into detail, while individual chapters offer the Cliff's Notes. Refer to both for the greatest context.

BEST AND WORST TIMES: When to visit and when not to visit.

LOCAL FOOD FESTIVALS: Brief descriptions of notable food festivals.

WORD OF WARNING: Know-before-you-go info and things to watch for on the road.

MORE INFO: Further references; generally local tourism boards and chambers of commerce.

Introductions are short essays that put the region into culinary and historical context, provide detail about the road and landscape, and often include my first-person observations.

Establishments are divided into two sections. **On the Road** contains the establishments that you'll find on the highway or a short drive away. **Detours & Destinations**, included at the end of most regions, offers scenic routes, shortcuts, and destinations a little further off the beaten path.

Maps are provided for each region and meant to be approximate orientation guides. You should rely on paper maps, GPS devices, carrier pigeons, etc., for specific directions.

Sidebars are peppered throughout. These provide overarching context about the region or food, detail about a particularly interesting town or city, background on individual ingredients, global roundups of favorite spots, and general tips and advice.

The **Selected Bibliography** offers an abbreviated list of my major research references; I also relied on interviews, websites, stories in magazines and newspapers, and other sources. A detailed index is included at the end of the book.

Establishments

The establishments are the meat and potatoes of the book. I tried to answer these questions for each spot I included: What sets this place apart from the rest? And why is it worth getting off the highway?

Beyond those criteria, I loosely developed three basic guiding principals when it came to choosing which establishments made the cut:

1. Establishments needed to be wholly of their time and place, and mean something to the community. This could mean an oyster shack on the Oregon coast or a Basque restaurant in California's Central Valley—as long as it was authentic to the region and provoked a deeper understanding of the culture it came from. If I happened on a really good but totally random falafel stand, for instance, it didn't make it in—no matter how delicious.

2. "Authentic" didn't necessarily mean "hidden" or "hole in the wall." I get so tired of the food-snob attitude that a place stops being worthwhile after it's "discovered." Some locations are touristy for the wrong reasons, but most are touristy for the right reasons.

3. The food needed to be good. Reputation and location could recommend a place, but they couldn't be all it had to offer. All the critical accolades and salty breezes in the world couldn't save a seafood restaurant from day-old fish and rubbery calamari.

Anatomy of an Establishment Profile

Only applicable information is included—if a place doesn't have a website or phone number, those fact lines are omitted.

Name of establishment

Address

MILE/EXIT: The freeway exit where the place is found, or the approximate highway mile where you'll find the location. (Note: California highways are organized by county; MO-44 is for Monterey County, for instance.)

DISTANCE: Distance of establishment from driving route, if more than five miles.

Phone number (if applicable)

Website (if applicable)

OPEN: Specific operating hours; if they vary, it's noted in the text and readers are advised to call ahead.

Cash only (if applicable)
Most profiles end with at least one of the following "extras":

KNOW: Insider information that didn't fit into the main body of text or deserved to be called out separately.

TOURS: More detail on tours of wineries, breweries, factories, etc. Prices and hours are reflective of publication date and could change.

VARIOUS LOCATIONS: Lists other cities where establishments can be found. It was tricky to figure out where to place chains in the text. For the most part, I chose the original location, though there are exceptions like In-N-Out, where I chose the location farthest north.

Icons

Icons shown to the left of the establishment name are intended as directional. Many establishments fit under more than one category—e.g., specialty food stores that also have delis, wineries with on-site restaurants, and burger shacks with killer ice cream.

🍸 **DRINKS:** Breweries, wineries, dive bars, and other watering holes.

🍔 **BURGER:** Mainly burger shacks and other spots that specialize in hamburgers.

🍴 **RESTAURANT:** Cafes, diners, coffee shops, delis, ethnic restaurants, etc.—basically all dining establishments that don't fall under another category.

🐟 **SEAFOOD:** Oysters, fish and chips, chowder, seafood shacks, and fancy restaurants specializing in seafood.

🥛 **FARM STAND:** Farmers markets, family farms, and other agricultural establishments.

(🏠) **SWEETS:** Bakeries, ice cream, chocolatiers, taffy shops, doughnuts, and all things sugary.

(🛍) **SHOP:** Grocery stores, specialty food shops, artisans like cheese-makers and olive oil producers, and other places to stock a picnic basket or larder.

(🏛) **EXPERIENCE:** Food factories, farm tours, museums, picnic spots, scenic drives, and everywhere else that offers exploration and adventure.

The Usual Disclaimers

My goal with this book was to offer the greatest hits of every location, but there are certainly worthy destinations that I left out. And though I vouch for the deliciousness of these places at the time of publication, I can't promise that every meal will be a home run.

As they say in all guidebooks, establishments evolve over time. Management changes hands, chefs move on, kitchen fires happen, and new spots open down the street. I tried to pick established locations that had weathered these storms before, but dining out is always a roll of the dice—and food is, after all, a matter of taste.

Throughout my research I strived to maintain an objective professional distance, but I'm only human. My impressions, both good and bad, were informed by what I ordered, who was serving me, and the mood I was in at the moment. You might have a totally different experience. That's the nature of the road: personal, tactile, nostalgic. It only makes sense that the establishments you discover will mirror your surroundings.

Acknowledgments

Whenever I mention that I wrote a culinary guidebook, one question inevitably comes up: "How did you find the locations you included?" The answer is simple: I found them everywhere. Naming and thanking all the sources for this book would fill another, but I owe it to everyone who contributed to try.

First and foremost, this book's existence owes a great deal to the kindness of strangers. Hundreds of people I didn't know contributed their favorite places—bartenders and waitresses, people I met on the road, anonymous contributors to message boards, Twitter followers, Yelp reviewers . . . the list goes on and on. Thank you all for your selfless recommendations, motivated only by the need to share good food with the world. May you live and prosper.

My parents Rick and Sheila played an integral role of support and assistance, as they have so often in my life, and now that I'm old enough to appreciate their efforts I'm deeply thankful for them. Also, a big thanks and hug to family friends for sharing their favorites: Alison Miller, Molly Hashimoto, Molly Anderson, Melanie Perez, and Jim and Anna Airy.

I wrote this book in nine months while maintaining a full-time editorial job, and I could not have done it, let alone kept my sanity, without the help of my smart and supportive Demand Media colleagues. Jeremy Reed, Robyn Galbos, Soren Bowie, Joey Campbell, Emily Faget, Marie Horrigan, Charley Daniels, Dan O'Brien, Joe Crosby, Sarah Metzger, Andrew Lawton, Steven Kydd, and the entire editorial team—I benefited more than I can ever say from your unwavering encouragement, detailed feedback on early drafts, and professional consideration during the month I stopped sleeping. Also thank you to Remi Guyton and Mike Cowan, who not only helped me navigate the waters of self-marketing over many happy hour drinks, but also, at least in Mike's case, lent me access to a Palm Springs house as a writerly retreat.

My writing has been shaped by great editors in the past who taught me much about the craft of food writing and the responsibilities of service journalism. Many come to mind, but especially Jill Lightner, Jonathan Kauffman, and Peter Behle—since editors so often work behind the scenes, I want to thank you publicly for the role you've played in making me the writer I am today.

A big thanks and bottle of Pepto Bismol to everyone who came along with me on research trips. Helen Freund, Gina Goff, Angela Ashe, Marie Horrigan, Quinn O'Toole, Charley Daniels, Mary Kosearas, and Johan Mengesha—you are true road food warriors, and I hope I did justice to our adventures in the following pages.

Thank you to my sisters, Cat and Alice, and to all my friends who let me disappear into the book for nine months and were still there for me when I emerged.

My love to the supportive and caring Seattle food community: Jill Lightner, Maggie Savarino, Kim Ricketts, Lisa Simpson, Jess Thomson, Steven Blum, Jon Rowley, Rebekah Denn, Jess Voelker, Chelsea Lin, Ali Scheff, Jacob Meyer, Myra Kohn, Lorna Yee, Henry H Lo, and dozens of others. I miss you every day.

Finally, thank you to everyone at Sasquatch Books, especially Kurt Stephan, for his endless patience with my questions and minute edits; Anna Goldstein, for her amazing design; and above all, to my editor and partner-in-crime Whitney Ricketts, for dreaming big and changing my life with an email in January 2010: "So I want to do a Road Food book for WA/OR/CA. And I need an author. Whatcha think? You up for the challenge?"

Introduction

My introduction to road food came at the age of 10, on a cross-country road trip from New York to Seattle. I don't remember much about the landscape or events therein, but I do remember the food. Chili for breakfast in a dark Cincinnati chili parlor. Three barbecue lunches on one unforgettable afternoon in Kansas City. A late-night cheeseburger in Salina. And so it began: a lifetime chasing the thrill of eating a meal that exists only at that time and that place. The thrill of eating in the moment.

I owe it all to my food-obsessed parents, of course, who opened my eyes to new cuisines and flavors on every trip we took thereafter. And they in turn owed a great deal to Jane and Michael Stern, whose groundbreaking 1978 culinary guidebook, *Roadfood*, was always stowed in our glove compartment. *Roadfood* introduced the country to the eccentricity and diversity of American roadside cooking, and remains the inspiration for, and foundation of, this book you hold in your hands.

When my editor first approached me about writing a guidebook on West Coast road food, I went immediately to my bookcase and pulled down my own dog-eared copy of the Sterns' seminal work. I'd been enthralled with it for years; what could I possibly presume to contribute? But, when reading *Roadfood* in this new context—not as a fawning fan but with the cool eye of a critic—I was struck by three things.

First, the Sterns include the West Coast almost as an afterthought. Washington, Oregon, and California are the last chapters in the book and allocated a mere 45 pages; New England alone gets 76. The locations the Sterns chose along the West Coast are fine, but there is the sense of something missing: a lack of overall cohesion, an air of incompleteness and arbitrary randomness. The West Coast has waves and vibrations that the Sterns, two Easterners, simply did not see or decided not to include.

To be fair, this omission isn't entirely due to editorial oversight. Thirty years ago, there just wasn't a cohesive West Coast cuisine to write about. It was only "ingredients in search of a cuisine," as notorious gastronome Jeffrey Steingarten wrote in *Vogue* in 1990. We have come far over the past quarter century to realize that the ingredients *are* the cuisine. The West Coast is blessed with incredible bounty and diversity—and the much-discussed "local food revolution" led by Alice Waters, Michael Pollan, and countless others is only the dawning comprehension that our ingredients speak for themselves.

The second thing I noticed: for a book called *Roadfood*, it contains very little about the road itself. This exclusion is especially glaring to a Westerner, because the open road is the most enduring image of the American West. We are a people who followed the road until it ran out, then farmed around where we landed because it was as far as we were going to get.

But though the road ended, we never stopped believing in its possibilities. Ours is a story about people inventing, reinventing, ripping out unproductive crops and planting others, experimenting with new ways to use old ingredients and old ways to use new ones. To Westerners—who have never put much stock in the past, anyway—this tinkering comes naturally. The West's inherent capacity for invention and reinvention is the engine driving this food revolution and the continuing creation of new technology for better farming and earth stewardship.

If the road trip symbolizes the possibility of the West, then the food of a road trip is that same possibility made tangible and sensory. The thrill of road food—the good fortune of finding a fantastic burger in a roadside diner chosen at random, or discovering a charming small winery 10 minutes from the California freeway—infuses the journey with a sense of adventure. It turns an excursion into a treasure hunt. Road trips can be revelatory, but so can a single good meal.

The last thing I noticed upon rereading was that *Roadfood* is a vestige of a world that no longer exists—a time before Starbucks and smartphones, when it was still possible to stumble upon local delicacies whose reputations had not extended beyond county lines. With *Roadfood* and its 2009 companion, *500 Foods to Eat Before It's Too Late*, the Sterns declared themselves culinary archaeologists, documenting small-town restaurants now overlooked in favor of the endless corridors of drive-thrus and quickie marts.

I saw another view through my windshield. I saw a culinary world that was expanding, not contracting. A cuisine that isn't disappearing, but evolving. And that's when I knew I had something to bring to the table.

Though this is a guidebook, it is also in many ways a very personal text. I've spent my entire life on the West Coast, bouncing between Seattle and Los Angeles like a pinball, but the past year of on-the-ground research taught me that there was much to be discovered in places I hadn't thought to look.

It also taught me that road food is as much a state of mind as a physical entity. Its taste is affected not only by its ingredients, but also by where you are, how far you've come that day, how far you still have to go. As travel writer Paul Theroux once put it, *The traveler invents the place.*

And I think that's why we take road trips—we want to participate in the journey; we want the freedom to make it our own. Social lines are drawn in restaurants in every town, but on a trip their cultural demarcations don't affect you. You can be whoever you want to be, and if that means all-you-can-eat biscuits and gravy, so be it. The open road awaits.

Washington

During their first weeks on the Sound, they studied the settlement as sightseers, and said to each other wonderingly, "Look at these people: they just live here on salmon and clams, as their children will too, for whole ages; they live and die on this isolated coast like gulls, as if there were no other place in the world."

—ANNIE DILLARD, *The Living*

LOCAL FLAVOR:

- **Seafood:** The state's icy waters and Seattle's status as a trading center make fresh seafood not only a basic right, but a necessity. Mark the seasons by the fish in the market: spring brings fresh halibut, summer brings extra-oily Copper River salmon from Alaska, and when the weather turns cold, it's oyster season again.

- **Coffee:** Dark roasts and artisan beans dominate the coffee scene, and locals are fiercely loyal about their allegiances. Nearly every town has at least one good coffee shop (and there's probably one on every commercial block in Seattle).

- **Beer:** Washingtonians love their microbrews. The two dominate local ales are the slightly sweet, malty Mac & Jacks African Amber, brewed in Redmond, and Manny's Pale Ale from Georgetown Brewing Co. in Seattle. But the state has more than 100 breweries, so it's best to just check out the taps and get what sounds good.

KNOW: Rest stops have free coffee.

W ashington was a late bloomer—it didn't have gold or readily accessible farmland to lure travelers, and so it remained untamed and unsettled for much longer than its southern siblings. The state only had 1,049 residents when the Census of 1850 was taken (Oregon had 11,873; California 92,597), and these were mostly fur trappers and lumbermen, ambitious visionaries who could see the uncivilized land's enormous potential.

The state's most distinctive feature—its magnificent geography—was also the cause of its isolation for so many years. The rugged mountains with snowcapped volcanic peaks; the deep forests of old-growth cedar; the frigid waters of glacier-carved Puget Sound; the savage coastline . . . these features presented a challenge that only the most driven and resourceful would take on.

What European settlers didn't realize was that these wild elements hid a treasure trove of foraged foods—found edibles that had long been celebrated by indigenous people, who lived so effortlessly off the land that they could form a complex culture without developing agriculture. The

Native Americans celebrated these natural gifts at potlatch, a ceremonial feast and gift exchange that highlighted the best of the region. Seafood was the star—salmon, trout, oysters, geoducks—supplemented by wild game and foods plucked from the forest—fiddlehead ferns, nettles, morel mushrooms, dandelion greens.

It was the Native Americans who showed European settlers the lay of the land. They taught early pioneers how to farm oysters in Willapa Bay and catch salmon in present-day Bellingham. Soon agriculture and seafood bypassed fur and lumber to became the major players in the local economy—fed by rich soil, deepwater ports, and the close proximity to Asian markets.

These days, Washington is second only to California in total number of agricultural commodities produced. It leads the nation in total production of berries, apples, grapes, and seafood. And the indigenous presence is still alive and seen in everything from the state's motto ("Alki," a Chinook word for "by and by") to the number of places that retain their tribal names—Nisqually, Puyallup, Duwamish.

Washingtonians haven't lost sight of their tremendous culinary good fortune. It's celebrated in harvest festivals and salmon cook-offs, but also appreciated every day throughout the year at restaurants that serve the best of what's in season. Better to bloom late than never. It just took a while for the settlers to develop the local knowledge necessary to harvest and sustain nature's bounty.

Trips in Washington

I-5: Canadian Border to Seattle
Travel through the fertile Skagit Valley and sample fresh produce, artisan cheese, and oysters straight from the source. (Page 5)

In and Around Seattle
Spend an hour or a day visiting the biggest metropolitan area and learning what makes it tick. (Page 25)

I-5: Seattle to Portland
A utilitarian strip of highway puts you in touch with the state's pioneer past. (Page 37)

Highway 101: Southern Washington Coast
Visit the "Oyster Capital of the World" and eat plenty of fresh seafood while enjoying the windswept scenery of the coast. (Page 47)

I-5: Canadian Border to Seattle

Trip Stats

START: Blaine

END: Seattle

LENGTH: 110 miles

LOCAL FLAVOR: Fresh oysters, seafood shacks, farm-to-table cooking, dramatic picnic spots.

BEST TIME: Spring and summer, especially April during the Skagit Valley Tulip Festival, when fields blaze with tulips. Peak berry season comes in late July and August.

WORST TIME: Winters in northern Washington are dark, damp, and involve a lot of root vegetables.

WORD OF WARNING: Prepare for traffic starting just north of Everett, which can last all the way through Seattle during the morning commute. Watch out for black ice on winter roadways, especially through the Lookout Mountains south of Bellingham.

MORE INFO: Skagit Valley Tourism (www.visitskagitvalley.com), Slow Food Skagit (www.slowfoodskagit.org)

My editor, Whitney Ricketts, and I set off into the great unknown one early April morning, armed with maps and notebooks and coffee, determined to conquer whatever was out there to conquer. Both of us were harboring a hunch that the thesis on which we'd pitched the book would hold true—that good food can be found nearly everywhere, if you just know where to look for it.

What we discovered that day put any lingering doubts to rest. We marveled at Edison, a town with no stoplight but three good bakeries. We found local, small-batch microbrews on tap at even the diviest of Bellingham dive bars. We tasted our way through working dairies and farm stands, and gained a deeper appreciation for the relationship between the land and its cuisine. I grew up traveling this stretch of I-5 and thought I knew it like the back of my hand, but I had no idea of

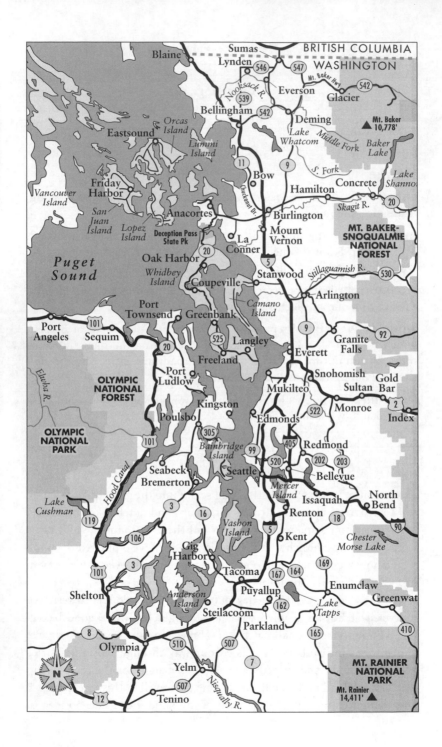

the culinary bounty that lay within 10 minutes of the freeway exits. The region is a showcase of farm-to-table cuisine that rivals anything Europe has to offer. It helped that it was a gorgeous day and the Skagit Valley was in the throes of the first flush of spring. The annual Tulip Festival was under way, and the fields were bright stripes of bold pinks and deep purples and vibrant reds. Everywhere we looked held some new delight: horses grazing in pastures, daffodils and apple blossoms, tree-covered hills where the pale green of new leaves stood out brightly against the dark evergreens.

Above everything loomed the snowy, conical peak of Mount Baker.

Back in Seattle later that night, Whitney and I took Skagit bread, fresh butter, hard cider, and tales of our discoveries to a dinner party at the house of a food-writer friend. Eventually we all ended up at the bar at Spring Hill, a West Seattle restaurant that's garnered tons of accolades since day one for its inventive approach to Northwest cuisine.

Mark Fuller, the hot young executive chef and owner, fed us drinks and laughed for a while when he heard that we'd skipped oysters at Taylor Shellfish because we didn't know how to shuck one. Mark had recently been photographed in *GQ* shucking an oyster with a screwdriver, and proceeded to give us a late-night lesson neither of us would soon forget.

The energy in the room that night was palpable. The local food revolution was under way, and our adventure was just getting started. It was a most auspicious beginning.

ON THE ROAD

Bob's Burgers and Brew

8120 Birch Bay Square St, Blaine
MILE/EXIT: 270
360.366.3199
www.bobsburgersandbrew.com
OPEN: *Mon–Thu 8a–9p, Fri–Sat 8a–11p, Sun 9a–9p*

Bob Kildall grew up near the Canadian border, put in time at various fast-food joints across Skagit and Whatcom counties, and watched his eponymous burger chain grow from one Lynden stand into something of a local institution. A Bob's burger probably won't change your life, but it will make you happy—it's properly juicy, slathered with secret sauce, set on a sturdy bun, topped with crisp lettuce and ripe slices of tomato, and is everything a person could ask of a hot meal on the road. Bob's also offers a longer-than-usual list of chicken and veggie burgers, along with a dozen variations on the original involving bacon, mushrooms, barbecue sauce, and so on. Throw in a decent selection of microbrews, an unobtrusive sleek black interior, friendly service, and a choice of fries, onion rings, or Jo Jos with every order, and you have no reason on earth to ever go back to Applebee's.

VARIOUS LOCATIONS *in Bellingham, Burlington, Tulalip, and Everett*

Haggen

1815 Main St, Ferndale
MILE/EXIT: 262
360.380.9000
www.haggen.com
OPEN: *24/7*

Fifty years before Whole Foods there was Haggen, a Bellingham-based grocery chain that's been committed to stocking local producers since 1933. Haggen carries products from nearly 300 Washington and Oregon suppliers, from big names like Nancy's Yogurt and Bob's Red Mill to small mom-and-pop operations that have personal relationships with store managers. Haggen sealed its place in local history in 1989, when it became the first grocery store in the country to open an in-store Starbucks. Today, it's a reliable refueling stop on the I-5 corridor, offering a good deli, clean restrooms, strong coffee, and a nondepressing dining area if you need a break.

VARIOUS LOCATIONS *in Bellingham, Burlington, Mount Vernon, Stanwood, Arlington, Marysville, Lake Stevens, and Portland*

Boundary Bay Brewing Co.

1107 Railroad Ave, Bellingham
MILE/EXIT: 253
360.647.5593
www.bbaybrewery.com
OPEN: *Daily 11a–midnight*

Boundary Bay is your textbook Northwest brewpub, with a line of bicycles outside, a dozen house beers on tap, and relics of wholesome outdoorsy pursuits on the walls (in this case, a mountain bike suspended from the ceiling, though the brewery also sells branded Frisbees along with tees and hoodies). The former garage setting also lends itself to conviviality—the bar and main dining room have big windows and high ceilings, and there's a patio for sunny afternoons—and the beer certainly helps things along. The light, flowery Bellingham Blonde hits the spot on a sunny day; fans of big brews will appreciate the extra-hoppy Bellingham Bay IPA. Order a six-beer sampler to taste it all. Food is playful (a popular choice is the "Great Northwest Pizza," which has a basil pesto base topped with smoked salmon, roasted garlic, goat cheese, tomatoes, and Parmesan), and many dishes incorporate beer and local ingredients.

KNOW: *Hit the brewery for a midday pick-me-up after the Saturday farmers market, held in the parking lot of the train station. It's one of the best in the region and a good glimpse into Bellingham's emerging food culture.*

TOURS: *Available upon request. Call ahead to gain access to the brewing area visible through a window next to the bar and learn about the brewing process.*

⌂ Mallard Ice Cream

1323 Railroad Ave, Bellingham
MILE/EXIT: 253
360.734.3884
www.mallardicecream.com
OPEN: *Sun–Thu 11a–10p, Fri–Sat 11a–11p*

To make good ice cream you need to start with good ingredients. Owners of this family-friendly shop go out of their way to use local, organic products for their ice creams, even when it means inventing entirely new flavors like sea berry and aronia berry to meet the needs of available ingredients. And therein lies the secret to Mallard's success—the ice cream is good, but innovation makes it great. Ice cream pushes the boundaries with flavors like cayenne pepper and chocolate Earl Grey, which make you question all you thought you knew about sweet and savory. Mallard also spotlights the best of the region's produce, sourcing local ingredients like raspberries, strawberries, huckleberries, figs, and more. The community seems to agree—the Ikea-furnished room is

---
Essential Car Picnic Kit

Take a page from the Boy Scout manual and keep an easy picnic kit in your car so you're always prepared for an impromptu feast. Eco-friendly napkins, plates, utensils, and cups help cut down on waste.

Corkscrew	Plastic cups	Salt and pepper
Wet naps	Plastic wineglasses	Can opener
Paper towels		Oyster shucker
Picnic blanket	Bread knife	Candles and matches (if you're setting a mood)
Napkins	Wooden cutting board (useful for serving, too)	
Paper plates		
Utensils	Paring knife	

---

filled with a mix of parents trying to clean up after their toddlers, restless teenagers looking for something to do, and adults just hanging out—and everyone has a big smile on their face.

KNOW: *Basil is a favorite flavor in the summertime; cardamom, chili-lime, and cayenne pepper are a few of the more popular eccentric choices.*

The Beaver Inn

1315 N State St, Bellingham
MILE/EXIT: 253
360.733.3460
OPEN: *Daily 11a–last call (usually around 1a)*

If there are proven litmus tests of a dive bar's authenticity (world-weariness of regulars, bathroom cleanliness, cocktail strength, kitchen's reliance on deep fryer), the Beaver passes them with flying colors. The place's dim dinginess and strong presence of unironic trucker hats gave me early hope—and that was before I saw the bathroom stalls—but the Beaver's fried pickles are the reason it's a top contender in my Dive Bar Hall of Fame. A specialty unique to the South, a deep-fried dill pickle spear dipped in ranch dressing sounds kind of gross until you've tried one, but then you realize that a fried pickle is exactly what you want after a few stiff drinks. The vegetable melts down just enough in its crispy batter shell to become a warm, salty treat with an appealingly succulent texture. They should be mandatory in every dive bar on earth. As it is, they make the Beaver the just-right local dive, the kind of place that exposes the lumberjack roots beneath Bellingham's steel-awning-and-organic-ice-cream veneer. The fact that there are also a half dozen small-batch microbrews on tap is just further proof of the place's exceptionalism.

Rhododendron Café

5521 Chuckanut Dr, Bow
MILE/EXIT: 231
360.766.6667
www.rhodycafe.com
OPEN: *Wed–Fri 11:30a–9p, Sat–Sun 9a–9p (note: the cafe is closed annually from the Sunday before Thanksgiving to the end of January)*

It's a food writing cliché, but in this case it's the truth: You haven't had cocktail sauce until you've had the blood-red, clear-your-sinuses slurry that accompanies oyster shooters at the Rhododendron Café. The first tip that you're entering uncharted territory is the texture, not mechanically pulverized but studded with visible chunks of garlic and horseradish. Then you take it down and understand the good cop–bad cop complexity of an oyster shooter: a spicy, citrusy kick tempered by the cool, metallic creaminess of the oysters. The sauce's aggressiveness is all the more jarring because of the dowdiness of the cafe's interior—all teal and dusty rose, with wicker lampshades and a clock shaped like a teapot—and the incongruousness is as disorienting as the time my mother told me about a night in her twenties when she took five vodka shots and danced on a table in Krakow.

KNOW: *Despite its stubborn homeliness, the place gets so crowded on weekends that there's a special waiting room in back overlooking a seasonal patio and organic garden. To pass the time, peruse the only provided reading material: a Classic Wines of the World box set from 1990.*

# Samish Bay Cheese

15115 Bow Hill Rd., Bow

MILE/EXIT: 231

DISTANCE FROM HWY: 7 miles

360.766.6707

www.samishbaycheese.com

OPEN: *Hours vary; call ahead for details*

At the turn of the twentieth century there were 900 producing dairies in the Skagit Valley, a number that has since dwindled considerably, but the region still boasts a handful of the state's finest artisan creameries. Samish Bay Cheese is one of them. The dairy produces handcrafted, certified-organic cheeses from owners Roger and Suzanne Wechster's 150-acre Rootabaga Country Farm at the base of the Chuckanut Mountains. Cows graze on natural clover and grass pastures and only feed on organic grain, resulting in a purity of flavor that's hard to find at larger-scale operations. You can actually taste the seasons change if you visit often enough. The dairy makes a rotating stable of cheeses, including Mont Blanchard, a cheddar named after a nearby mountain, and the fresh, crumbly Ladysmith, but it's known for its aged Gouda. Great on its own, the cheese pops with added flavors like nettle, cumin, caraway, and herb variations that are hard to find outside the tiny, unadorned retail store.

KNOW: *Someone is usually on-site during the day, but call ahead to make sure—and to request an in-depth tour of the farm.*

Golden Glen Creamery

15013 Field Rd, Bow

MILE/EXIT: 231

DISTANCE FROM HWY: 5 miles

360.766.6455

www.goldenglencreamery.com

OPEN: *Mon–Sat 10a–4p*

I swear I am not making this up: the man behind the counter at the dairy's retail store/office was watching YouTube tractor videos on the office computer when we walked in. He was friendly enough and answered all our questions, but it was obvious he wanted to get back to the business at hand. I didn't blame him—this dairy is not about the show or

Local Flavor: Nettles

It took me a long time to get over the deep-seated fear that a nettle would hurt me if I ate it—painful encounters on childhood camping trips taught me to keep my distance from the stinging plant. But it turns out that a quick bath in boiling water renders a stinging nettle as harmless as spinach (foragers and chefs still need to wear heavy gloves to protect their skin). The leafy green has long been a staple of Asian and European cuisine, and is finally catching on in the states. Nettles are only available in March and early April, when the shoots are still young, and are worth seeking out for a subtle, woodsy flavor that adds an herbal earthiness to everything from soups to cheeses.

bending over backward for the customer, it's about dairy farming as a livelihood. That's just fine with me, because Golden Glen Creamery produces ambrosial butter and impossibly creamy milk sold in glass bottles. The efficient family-run business isn't without its own eccentric charm; a hand-lettered signpost declares the population of the farm: "62 cows, 65 calves, 16 steers, 5 turkeys, 3 pigs." Tours of the cheese production line are available upon request.

KNOW: *You'll recognize the retail store by the large fiberglass cow out front.*

Snow Goose Produce

15170 Fir Island Rd, Mount Vernon

MILE/EXIT: 221

DISTANCE FROM HWY: 5 miles

360.445.6908

www.snowgooseproducemarket.com

OPEN: *Daily 8a–6p, mid-Feb through mid-Oct*

Ice cream bar is cash only

True-blue Northwesterners are hard-core about braving the elements, which is why I'm never surprised to find a line for ice cream cones at this open-air farm stand, even when the outside temperature isn't much higher than the inside of the freezer case. The line isn't only because of the ice cream itself, though it's drippingly delicious and made from local cream and berries; nor is it the portions, which large signs modestly describe as "immodest." It's not even the house-made waffle cones, which you smell baking as soon as you get out of the car. It's something deeper, more ephemeral—it's almost spiritual to eat your cone under the rusty eaves of this reclaimed granary, gazing over lush farmland with the snowy Cascades in the distance, feeling for a second like you are utterly part of this place. One sunny morning in April, a flock of real-life snow geese took flight all at once from a field across the road, and it was the only time in my life I've actually pinched myself to make sure I wasn't dreaming.

KNOW: *Snow Goose is also a local grocer and a good place to stock a picnic. Pack your basket with a variety of local cheeses, fresh loaves from Breadfarm, Washington wines, fruit preserves made in-house from Skagit berries, oysters from Taylor Shellfish, and produce from the owners' organic garden.*

Biringer Farm

4625 40th Pl NE, Everett
MILE/EXIT: 208
425.259.0255
www.biringerfarm.com
OPEN: *Hours vary by season; call ahead for details*

Biringer Farm has been a Washington state institution for more than half a century, most famous for its strawberry shortcake booth at state fairs and festivals. But many natives, myself included, have fond memories of childhood day trips to the original Marysville farm, where we slathered on sunscreen, rode the open-air trolley into the dusty strawberry fields, and happily crouched in the dirt for hours, hands stained red from the juice, picking the bounty of midsummer. The farm now has two outposts—both within a few minutes of the highway—offering flats of fresh berries in season and acres of U-pick fields for those who feel like working for their reward. In autumn, families will also enjoy the corn maze and pumpkin patch.

KNOW: *Call the farm to get the latest update on crop conditions; the dedicated "berry line" is updated daily in season.*

🍩 FROST Doughnuts

15421 Main St, Suite H102, Mill Creek

MILE/EXIT: 183

425.379.2600

www.frostology.com

OPEN: *Mon–Fri 6a–8p, Sat 7a–8p, Sun 7a–7p*

I don't know how to feel about fancy doughnuts. Cupcakes: fine. Ice cream: often much improved. But a doughnut, to me, is the ultimate in democratic breakfast pastries, favored by cops and best dunked in coffee, so to elevate it to gourmet status seems somehow wrong, the same way $15 hot dogs are wrong. That said, FROST Doughnuts are pretty incredible, despite the cringe-worthy tagline of "Doughnuts evolved." They're not too doughy, but not all air like Krispy Kreme, and bursting with so much flavor you can tell it didn't come from an extract. The salt in the salted caramel is present, but not overpowering; the blueberry bismark tastes like real blueberries, only better, because sugar and fat are involved. Red velvet is like red velvet cake in doughnut form, which is to say, awesome. Also—and you might want to sit down for this—the maple bacon bar is topped with *actual bacon*. Like, at least one strip, chopped into bite-size hunks. It's the love child of my two favorite breakfast foods, and it possibly brought me over the edge into the gourmet-doughnut dark side.

DETOURS & DESTINATIONS

Chuckanut Drive

MILE/EXIT: 250

LENGTH: 21 miles

www.chuckanutdrive.com

If it's a sunny day and you've got an extra half hour on your hands, you're a fool to choose I-5 over Chuckanut Drive—a 21-mile stretch of Highway 11 between Bellingham and the Skagit Valley, universally acknowledged as one of the most scenic in the country. It's one of those roads that will stick with you forever: a two-lane highway winding its way along a rocky cliff blanketed with moss-covered evergreens, affording incredible views of Samish Bay and the San Juan Islands. It's awe-inspiring, especially if you have the good fortune to hit it at sunset. Chuckanut Drive also happens to be one of the best places in the state for fresh oysters, thanks to the shallow, sandy bottom of Samish Bay. Have a DIY picnic at the industrial Taylor Shellfish Farms, or go the classy half-shell-and-bubbly route at fancier stops like Chuckanut Manor or the Oyster Creek Inn. The best part? When the drive is over, you're nestled deep in the agricultural food heaven of the Skagit Valley, where you can hop from farm stand to farm stand all the way back to the interstate.

Taylor Shellfish Farms

2182 Chuckanut Dr, Bow
MILE/EXIT: 231
DISTANCE FROM HWY: 7.4 miles
360.426.6178
www.taylorshellfish.com
OPEN: *Daily 10a–6p*

Taylor Shellfish has been in the family for five generations and is one of the biggest suppliers in the state. Over the past century, the company has done an admirable job adapting to the ups and downs of the storied shellfish industry in the region. Not far from the Skagit Valley, nestled in a wooded bend on Chuckanut Drive, you'll find the oyster shell–lined driveway down to this shoreside shellfish operation. After a short jaunt down a road lined with mossy evergreens, you emerge from the woods onto a Puget Sound beach, empty save for Taylor Shellfish Farms and a railroad track with a lonely sign that says, simply, "Samish." Nose your car past the shipping pallets and shellfish cages and park in front of the storefront, which sells whole cooked and live crabs, bags of mussels and clams, and of course, oysters. After you choose from the bevy of oyster varieties, get them packed in ice for travel or fresh for you to shuck and eat right there. The shop also stocks cocktail sauce from Rhododendron Café, Ritz crackers, lemons, Tabasco, and all the oyster-eating fixings imaginable, including oyster-shucking knives. Gather your purchases and head out to the communal tables next to the shell-strewn beach for an impromptu picnic. As you look out at Puget Sound and the same ocean water that grew the oysters in your hand, you know that seafood can hardly get any fresher than this.

KNOW: *Brush up on your shucking skills before you go—the staff is not sympathetic to newbies.*

Oysters in Washington State

The Washington State oyster industry started out with the native **Olympia** oyster, a very small, sweetly metallic bivalve native to the region. Olympias were mostly shipped to the oyster-hungry San Francisco market, until overharvesting and pollution from pulp mills almost made them locally extinct. Attempts to transplant oysters from the East Coast failed, and the oyster industry floundered until 1919, when a shipment of **Pacific** oysters arrived from Japan. They were pronounced dead on arrival and unceremoniously dumped into Samish Bay, where they shocked everyone by flourishing in Washington waters. Pacific oysters proved to be resilient to pollution and much larger than Olympias, and were transplanted to Willapa Bay, which, thanks to its miles of exposed tidal flats, became a giant player in the oyster scene. Today, Washington exports mostly Pacifics, but there are a few favorites among half-shell enthusiasts: the **Kumamoto** imported from Japan in the 1940s, which is revered for its sweetness and attractive, deep, moss-green shells; and the **Penn Cove Select**, classically handsome oysters with a light, cucumbery taste.

KNOW: *Oysters differ by region because they assume the characteristics of the water and growing conditions—like wine, the* terroir *matters. Unless you're a connoisseur you may never be able to tell in a blind taste test, but you naturally gravitate to some oysters more than others for a reason.*

Skagit Valley

When I picture the afterlife, it looks an awful lot like the Skagit Valley. Just an hour north of Seattle, this lush farming region has scenery that will take your breath away—pastoral farmland that runs up and into the snowy Cascades in a dramatic contrast of tamed and wild. The Skagit Valley is also a must-stop for anyone who likes to eat. An edible fairyland where everything is served fresh from local producers, here the quality of ingredients and the quality of life go hand in hand. The region owes its agricultural success to the first settlers of La Conner back in 1863, who built a series of dikes along the Skagit River and turned the formerly useless wetland into viable farmland. Today, the county's constant temperatures, rainfall, and rich soil make it one of the most profitable farming regions in Western Washington, and the cooperative relationship among its inhabitants—manure from the dairy and cattle farms fertilizes the produce fields, and farmers often swap land to rotate crops—ensures the valley stays that way. I cannot imagine a place I'd rather spend eternity.

KNOW: *You can't drive more than a few miles in the summer without hitting a farm stand. They range from the established to the makeshift (sometimes out of the backs of pickups), but the berries and produce are uniformly good, and all come from family-owned farms that need your support.*

Edison

MILE/EXIT: 236

DISTANCE FROM HWY: 5 miles

Any town with a main drag called "Farm-to-Market Road" seems too good to be true, and I still kind of can't believe that the town of Edison is real and not some culinary Brigadoon that we somehow had the happy fortune to stumble into. Edison's main street is less than a mile long, but this small strip of restaurants offers a wealth of cuisine that challenges food scenes in cities ten times its size The town has not one but *three* incredible bakeries, a sturdy dive bar, and many patios made for lounging in the sun. It's also the birthplace of Edward R. Murrow. What more do you need out of life?

KNOW: *Very few local businesses take credit cards, but there is an ATM in the Longhorn Saloon.*

Longhorn Saloon

5754 Cains Ct, Edison

MILE/EXIT: 236

DISTANCE FROM HWY: 5 miles

360.766.6330

OPEN: *Sun–Thu 11:30a–midnight, Fri–Sat 11:30a–2a*

Don't be intimidated by the line of Harleys out front—this dive is a stop on the biker's shellfish pilgrimage known as the Oyster Run, and even tattooed dudes in leather have a hard time looking tough while slurping down raw shellfish. The weird and wonderful thing about the Longhorn is that it defies all categorization: It's full of bikers, but it's not a biker bar; there's a flat-screen TV showing college basketball, but it's not a sports bar; hard-to-find microbrews dominate the taps, but it's not a beer bar. It's just a bar, in the feel-good, *Cheers*-y sense of the word, and one Saturday afternoon the communal vibes were contagious. Retirees lunched in a sunny booth by the window. Barely legal youths pounded vodka tonics and played Big Buck Hunter. A large middle-aged group sat at a long table and commemorated some sort of monumental life occasion. Community gathering places like this can make an outsider feel even more alienated, but though we were strangers we felt wholly welcome to sip a beer and observe the natives. The only disappointment was the Longhorn Amber house brew made by Seattle's Pyramid Brewery. It started with a promising maltiness that dissipated before we had a chance to swallow.

 Breadfarm

5766 Cains Ct, Edison
MILE/EXIT: 236
DISTANCE FROM HWY: 5 miles
360.766.4065
www.breadfarm.com
OPEN: *Mon–Fri 11a–7p, Sat 9a–7p, Sun 10a–7p*
Cash only

If someone ever holds a gun to my head and forces me to choose between pastries and bread for the rest of my life (such scenarios are common in my imagination, which may be part of the reason I don't have a boyfriend), there's no question: I could happily live on bread alone. Which is why I'm predisposed to like a place called Breadfarm. This is one of the largest suppliers of bread in the region, for local groceries like the Store Bakery in Anacortes and the Skagit Valley co-op, and, like most of its neighbors, it is wholly dedicated to local, sustainable, mostly organic ingredients for its hand-formed loaves. Breadfarm breads begin life from the same sourdough starter, but morph into individuals depending on the ingredients: Skagit Valley potatoes for the Samish River potato bread; stone-ground Fairhaven Mills cornmeal for the Chuckanut Multigrain; spring onions from a local farmer for the seasonal Allium Loaf, which came about one day when the farmer asked if the owners would take the onions off his hands. The bakery also makes pastries that lean toward the bready side, including the popular chocolate babkas, sweetened yeast bread traditional in Poland.

KNOW: *You don't see many peanut butter and jelly sandwiches outside the kids' menu these days, but this bakery features the grown-up version: house-made peanut butter and preserves from local berries, on the bakery's simple white Farmer Bread.*

Slough Food

5766 Cains Ct, Suite B, Edison
MILE/EXIT: 236
DISTANCE FROM HWY: 5 miles
360.766.4458
www.sloughfood.com
OPEN: *Wed–Sat 11a–6p, Sun 11a–5p*
Cash only

Specialty food stores are like designer boutiques for the foodie set: places that inspire longing, envy, and dreams of fabulously epic dinner parties that go far beyond one's reach as chef and host. Such browsing is a pleasure in this amazingly well-stocked shop—made all the more amazing by its location, which is more or less in the middle of nowhere. Owner John DeGloria grew up in the area and, after spending time working at Whole Foods and the well-known Pike & Western Wine Shop in Seattle, he moved back to the region and opened a store to bring his urban favorites to the country. The inventory is just the right mix of imported goods and local foods: honey from a nearby beekeeper, olive and truffle oils imported from Italy, jars of sea salt, Skagit Valley cheese, Theo chocolate, cured Salumi meat. The store even encourages lingering: after a half hour on the back patio next to the improbably scenic backwater of Edison Slough (hence the name), savoring a cheese plate with a glass of Washington wine, you'll be willing to quit your job and move to Edison, too.

Tweets

5800 Cains Ct, Edison
MILE/EXIT: 236
DISTANCE FROM HWY: 5 miles
OPEN: *Breakfast and lunch, Fri–Sun (no set hours)*
Cash only

Were it to open in Seattle or Portland next week, Tweets is the kind of studiously casual, pitch-perfect coffee shop/bakery/cafe that foodies would have conniptions about and then later deem overrated when popular attention made them wait an hour for a table. Luckily it's in Edison, where it can simply exist without falling victim to the relentless hype machine. The artful shabby chic interior decor is a mix of reclaimed wood fixtures, succulent plants, and playful just-for-the-heck-of-it elements—like baskets full of vintage blocks—all of which make it look like a spread from *Dwell* magazine. The chalkboard menu features a daily rotation of satisfying, intriguing dishes, all improbably made from a scant kitchen equipped with only a burner and convection oven. We tried the house-made nettle and goat cheese ravioli, in a sort of *puttanesca* sauce with a good amount of spice, and drooled over the stuffed French toast at another table. Enjoy your food on the communal table inside or on the back deck, which affords a view of Farm to Market Bakery's organic garden and Edison Slough. If anything, Tweets' only fault is that it's too friendly—your coffee might take a few extra minutes because the owner wants to chat about a coffee bean–roasting competition he's in with the owner of Slough Food next door—but didn't you come to the country to let go of that fast-paced urban mind-set?

KNOW: *Try something from the bakery case—the Tweets take on almond roca, with its sweet-salty-chocolaty crunch, is out of this world. There's also a surprising number of vegan options.*

🍽 Farm to Market Bakery

14003 Gilmore, Edison

MILE/EXIT: 236

DISTANCE FROM HWY: 5 miles

360.766.6240

OPEN: *Wed–Sun 9a–4p*

Cash only

Sometimes it's okay to judge a book by its cover. I wanted to like this cozy bakery before I even went in. An appealingly overgrown front yard with a couple of attractively rusting tables, a lopsided hopscotch drawn in sidewalk chalk on the front walk, a hand-lettered sign pointing to the bakery's organic garden next door—it had to be good, or else I didn't know what was right in the world. But, from the moment I entered, I only had eyes for the bakery case. Piles of rustic cookies, fruit pies stuffed to almost bursting, bready sticky buns dotted with glazed pecan—this is the mother lode to a carbohydrate freak. And that was all before I tried the lime-polenta cake, a toothsome single-serving cornmeal cake soaked in just-sweet-enough lime syrup that was reminiscent of Native American honey cake and stayed fresh for days. It was a baked-good revelation. I'd drive any distance to have it again.

KNOW: *Farm to Market is also a good, quick lunch option, with soups and sandwiches featuring ingredients from its own garden.*

SIDE TRIP: Anacortes

MILE/EXIT: 230

DISTANCE FROM HWY: 16 miles

Most people know Anacortes only from long lines at the ferry dock, waiting to catch a boat to the serene San Juan Islands. Few people know that Anacortes is actually located on the easternmost San Juan Island, Fidalgo, and has a cute downtown with historic murals and a few good places to eat if you want to grab a bite before or after the ferry. Named in 1896 after the town promoter's wife, Anna Curtis, Anacortes was primarily a fishing and lumber center until the 1950s, when oil companies started building refineries on the Swinomish Channel. Oil is still the city's biggest industry, and the two biggest refineries can be seen from nearly every vantage point in town, adding a *Twin Peaks*–esque industrial edge to the raw beauty of the region. The town also retains a sizeable fishing fleet, and has become a destination for boaters, kayakers, and whale watchers, along with visitors from nearby Whidbey Island Naval Air Station.

Bob's Chowder Bar

3320 Commercial Ave, Anacortes

MILE/EXIT: 230

DISTANCE FROM HWY: 16 miles

360.299.8000

www.bobschowderbar.com

OPEN: *Daily 11a–7p*

Certain foods have evolved to maximize their consumability while you pilot 4,000 tons of steel down the highway: the fast-food burger, the chicken nugget, the Crunchwrap Supreme. To attempt a bowl of clam chowder while driving, on the other hand, is to play road food roulette—one wrong move and you've got a ruined T-shirt, third-degree chest burns, and a car that smells like old milk. It's a bizarre flaw in this drive-thru seafood shack's business model, though it's a flaw that's easy to overlook because the place is downright adorable. For starters, it's painted fire-engine red, bringing a cheerful vibe to an otherwise gray town. There are recyclable utensils and Dry Sodas. And the house-specialty chowder is tasty: appropriately herbal, chunky with potato and clams. The corn flour–breaded fish is so fresh it was probably alive the very same morning, comes in cute sizes like Nemo, Gilligan, and Ahab (the largest; named for the immensity of his obsession, I assume), and is infinitely easier than chowder to eat on the go, though you might grease up the steering wheel.

KNOW: *If you do choose to eat there, the picnic tables in the parking lot have a million-dollar view of Mount Baker and the Swinomish Channel, if you can edit out the rather depressing industrial foreground.*

 Adrift

510 Commercial Ave, Anacortes
MILE/EXIT: 230
DISTANCE FROM HWY: 16 miles
360.588.0653
www.adriftrestaurant.com
OPEN: *Mon–Thu 8a–9p, Fri–Sat 8a–10p*

This friendly cafe feels like a second living room. It's instantly likeable and hip in a way you do not expect from the generic exterior—there are copper tabletops and rolling leather library chairs, the Flaming Lips' *The Soft Bulletin* is playing on the stereo, and a line of bookcases against a wall offers interesting, dusty volumes to read for free or buy for five bucks a pop. The place also nods to Anacortes's fisherman roots with the blue ceiling covered by blue sailcloth, gray-washed concrete floors made to look like the ocean, model ships on every surface, and a map of old Anacortes dominating one wall. Service is slow, but the food is surprisingly sophisticated and locally sourced whenever possible. A meaty crab cake melds with a sweet chili sauce and avocado mayonnaise into something extraordinary, and the lamb burger has just the right bouquet of herbs and spices to tone down the meat's natural gaminess.

 SeaBear Smokehouse

605 30th St, Anacortes
MILE/EXIT: 230
DISTANCE FROM HWY: 16 miles
360.293.4661 ext. 3001
www.seabear.com
OPEN: *Mon-Fri 8:30a–5:30p, Sat 11a–4p, Sun 10a–4p*

With its long shelf life and local cachet, vacuum-packed smoked salmon has been a go-to hostess gift, thank-you present, and stocking stuffer for out-of-towners for years. Get it straight from the source at this Anacortes factory, which started in 1957 as a backyard salmon-smoking operation by a local fisherman and his wife, and has grown into one of the largest salmon packagers in the country. Take the free 20-minute tour of the factory floor if you're interested in the 15-step, hands-on process for curing wild Alaskan salmon, from hand-filleting the raw carcasses to loading them into a traditional alder smoker—it's all very maritime and industrial, and you'll learn everything you ever wanted to know about the different oil contents and smoking methods of salmon varieties. Or, skip the tour and head directly to the gift shop, where prices can be significantly lower than the online store and the staff is forthcoming with free samples. You can even get your picture taken with a giant salmon. Score.

KNOW: *The factory is located among the marinas and warehouses of the Anacortes waterfront, but is clearly marked by a sign.*

TOURS: *The best time to tour is between 9:15 and 10:45 weekday mornings, when the salmon is filleted. But tours are available anytime, provided you call ahead.*

In and Around Seattle

City Stats

LOCAL FLAVOR: Coffee, microbrews, seafood, farm-to-table dining.

BEST TIME: In July and August, cafes spill out onto sidewalks, menus and farmers markets are filled with local produce, and a general summertime joie de vivre pervades the city.

WORST TIME: December is the wettest and coldest month on average, but all the better to appreciate the city's coffee shop culture.

WORD OF WARNING: Bring a good map if you plan to do much city driving. Seattle is divided in half by a shipping canal, and even locals sometimes have a hard time navigating their way to one of the four bridges that span it.

MORE INFO: Seattle Convention & Visitors Bureau (www.visitseattle.org)

There's something about the gray weather that encourages people to sit around a dark bar or bright warm restaurant for hours, shooting the breeze. On a rainy day, you'll find Seattleites at their favorite haunts, plugging away on their laptops to a soundtrack created by the tattooed baristas, who moonlight in rock bands and make every macchiato into a masterpiece. The chains are local, the cuisine is seasonal, the farmers markets are exceptional. It's just how things are. Seattleites have high standards.

I spent the first eighteen years of my life in the Emerald City, and three more after I moved back from college, and I find it difficult to describe my hometown with any sort of objectivity. It's one thing to write about what you know; it's quite another to write about something that's so much a part of you that it's influenced your deepest idiosyncrasies, prejudices, tastes, and world views. To live in Seattle is to take fresh seafood, community coffee shops, local restaurant chains, farmers markets, stellar microbrews, and a supportive, laid-back culinary culture for granted. Through my experience elsewhere, I've since learned that my hometown is exceptional.

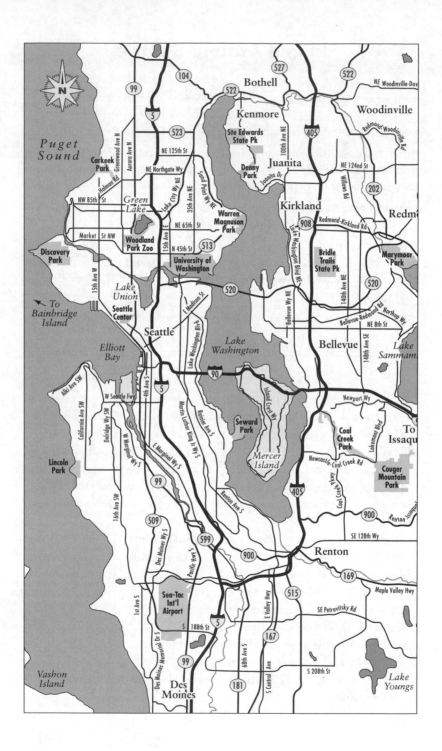

Seattle hasn't always been the economic and cultural powerhouse it is today. It's a relatively new city—the founding Denny party only landed at Alki Beach in 1851, three years after the California gold rush, and the city stayed in relative anonymity until the 1890s, when the Great Northern Railway connected it to the rest of the country and the Yukon gold rush transformed it into the "Gateway to the Gold Fields."

It's still evolving, even over my relatively short lifetime. I was born into a city that had just gone through a depression so bad that there was a famous billboard on the highway outside of town that said: "Will the last person who leaves Seattle please turn out the lights?" Then came Microsoft and Amazon and the rest of the Silicon Forest, and the success of Nordstrom and Starbucks, and the blue-collar town I once knew suddenly grew up.

Microsoft money transformed Belltown from a derelict neighborhood to a prosperous one; Capitol Hill went from a grungy hang for starving artists to a hip, commercial area with cupcake and ice cream shops; and everyone is saying the same may happen soon to South Lake Union. Even through the recent economic downturn, restaurants keep getting built. Maybe they're just as much a part of the city's identity as the Space Needle. Try creating one of those L.A. lounges with house music and bright lights and mod furniture and Seattleites will put you out of business in a month.

They say you can't go home again, but when I moved back to Seattle after college graduation I gorged myself on summertime Copper River salmon washed down with local brews I'd been too young to appreciate the first time around, and I was deliciously, deliriously happy. I'm back in Los Angeles these days, but I'd be lying if I said I didn't miss the stately mountains and culinary delights of my hometown every day.

(Ⓧ) University District Farmers Market

Corner of University Way and NE 50th St, Seattle
MILE/EXIT: 169
206.547.2278
www.seattlefarmersmarkets.org
OPEN: *Sat 9a–2p*
Cash only

See Seattle's vibrant foodie scene at its most primal at this bustling farmers market. Here, locavores shop the farm stands toting wicker baskets and shopping lists, frequently stopping to greet friends and neighbors in the aisles and say hello to farmers who have made their acquaintance. It's not Europe, but it's not far off. The University Farmers Market is one of the oldest and biggest in the city; with more than 50 local producers, it provides a comprehensive overview of the region's culinary riches. Much of the produce is so seasonal it's only available for a few weeks, and local dairies, shellfish farms, and bakers are also well represented. There are also cooking demonstrations and live music. And how great is a place where the question "What should I do with squash blossoms?" will likely get you a dozen answers from growers and fellow shoppers?

KNOW: *Read the signs carefully before you park. The University District is a popular shopping area and student hangout, and parking on side streets can be restricted to residents.*

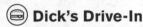 Dick's Drive-In

111 NE 45th St, Seattle
MILE/EXIT: 169
206.632.5125
www.ddir.com
OPEN: *Daily 10:30a–2a*

Once, in a former life, I was on KOMO radio doing a monthly slot on local restaurants and said, as loudly and earnestly as I could muster, "I *love* Dick's." I didn't think anything of it until months later, when I found out that particular audio clip had circulated around the KOMO offices for weeks, and I was widely known as the "Dick's girl." Awesome. The point is, the fact that I said such a thing so innocently on the radio only shows how much Dick's Drive-In is part of the local lexicon. Dick's opened in 1954 at this Wallingford location (burgers cost 19 cents), and is still known today for its burgers, hand-dipped cones, cheap prices, and famously rigid substitution policy (as in, there are none). Whether it's lunchtime or last call, the classic Seattleite order is a Dick's Deluxe (a burger with cheese, lettuce, and tomatoes; the regular burger comes naked), fries, and a shake. Dick's fries are a hot-button issue in the city, a more polarizing subject than politics in certain circles. They're sliced from real potatoes, cooked in 100 percent vegetable oil, and are more greasy than crisp. I love them, but then again, I love everything about Dick's.

KNOW: *If you want ketchup or tartar sauce, you need to order them at the counter. Both cost 5 cents.*

Farmers Market Shopping Tips

- Walk through the market before you commit to a stand. It's good to get the lay of the land.

- Bring lots of small bills and change. Most farmers won't take credit cards, and there's not usually an ATM around.

- Have a shopping bag handy. Some farmers provide plastic bags; some don't. A reusable bag will save you multiple trips to the car, also.

- Don't try to bargain, unless you're buying in bulk.

- Ask if you have questions on preparation or how to use an ingredient. If the farmer can't tell you, chances are another customer can.

- Only take one free sample. (Come on. This isn't Costco.)

(a) Theo Chocolate

3400 Phinney Ave N, Seattle
MILE/EXIT: 169
206.632.5100
www.theochocolate.com
OPEN: *Daily 10a–6p*

This delightful chocolate factory in Seattle's quirky Fremont neighborhood is like something out of a storybook. Start in the gift shop at the corner of 35th Street and Phinney Avenue, where the friendly staff of "Theonistas" is happy to explain the factory's fair-trade policy and will guide you through their dazzling array of bars and filled confections (hint: they aren't stingy with the samples). Flavors run the gamut from pure dark chocolate to exotic flavors like coconut curry, lavender caramel, and pearl jasmine. To see the factory in action, call in advance to reserve a spot on the public tour, where a few bucks gets you a comprehensive overview of the history of the cacao bean, a peek at the process from bean to bar, and more chocolate than you can handle. (Seriously; you'll be begging for mercy. Death by chocolate doesn't seem so far-fetched.)

KNOW: *Cacao nibs—unrefined, roasted cacao beans—are fairly bitter and can be an acquired taste, but make great road snacks and are good to incorporate into trail mix. They are sold in the gift shop.*

TOURS: *Offered daily at regular intervals; $6 per person. Call for tour schedule and to make reservations (encouraged on weekdays, required on weekends).*

Capitol Hill Coffee Culture

Much is made of Seattle's coffee shop culture, and I never understood why until I went away to college and realized that the rest of the world wasn't like Seattle. Where were the cafes where I could spread out my books and stay the afternoon on the price of a single latte? (These were the days before free Wi-Fi.) Where was, in fact, the good coffee? In most of the world, Starbucks is the best option. Though the coffee megalith started here, Seattle has plenty of other places to take your business, where baristas treat each cup as a work of art (expect a leaf or other design on the foam of your cappuccino). And many local coffee shops are working with growers to develop small-batch blends and sustainable business practices, which is leading to a new renaissance in boutique coffee.

To really immerse yourself in the coffee shop scene, check out two Capitol Hill coffeehouses. They tell a tale of two Seattles, and though there are certainly more, these are as good a start as any to understand how the city has evolved over the past quarter century. **Bauhaus Books & Coffee** (301 E Pine St; 206.625.1600; www.bauhauscoffee.net) has been around since Seattle's grunge heyday. It's got strong coffee, but it's best for people watching—snag a seat on Pine Avenue and watch Capitol Hill's hipster scene pass by. Around the corner in a remodeled 1920s auto shop, **Victrola Coffee** (310 E Pike St; 206.624.1725; www.victrolacoffee.com) represents the new Seattle, specializing in small-batch beans and taking their drinks very seriously indeed. Other beloved standbys include **Caffe Vita** (1005 E Pike St; 206.709.4440; www.caffevita.com) and the walk-up **Espresso Vivace** (532 Broadway E, 206.860.5869; www.espressovivace.com).

 Pike Place Market

85 Pike St, Seattle
MILE/EXIT: 166
206.622.6198
www.pikeplacemarket.org
OPEN: *Mon–Sat 10a–6p, Sun 11a–5p; however, vendors set their own hours*

Fish-tossers, fresh produce, peekaboo views of the snow-capped Olympic Mountains, and ferries gliding across Puget Sound. Pike Place Market is *so* Seattle and so packed with dawdling tourists most of the time that it's impossible to get from one end to another. Despite being full of out-of-towners, especially in the summer, this permanent farmers market continually draws locals—but they pick their shopping times carefully. The best time to hit the Market is around 9 am, before the crowds take over, when the farmers and fishmongers are still setting up their stands. Skip the crowds surrounding the original Starbucks and head instead to **Le Panier**, a fragrant French bakery with sensuous chocolate croissants and espresso from local roaster Caffe Umbria.

If you go at lunchtime, avoid the Market's Main Arcade building on the west side of Pike Place (pedestrian gridlock can resemble Los Angeles freeways at rush hour), and head to **Jack's Fish Spot** in the Sanitary Market across the street—a stainless steel lunch counter with super-fresh and affordable oysters, fish-and-chips, and steamed Dungeness crabs with melted butter. (The exception to this rule is the **Market Grill**'s craveable blackened salmon sandwiches, worth any amount of hustle.) Fancier meals can be had at **Matt's in the Market** and the **Steelhead Diner**, both with ever-changing menus highlighting seasonal ingredients. Also worth a stop is **Pike Brewing Company**, one of the city's older breweries with a back room full of beer memorabilia.

KNOW: *Parking at the Market presents its own special challenge, especially during July and August. Every local has his own survival strategy—some park further afield and take advantage of downtown Seattle's free ride zone on public transportation; others troll for meters on Western Avenue. If neither sounds appealing, the Market-provided parking lots have fairly reasonable hourly rates (enter on Western).*

TOURS: *Stroll through the Market with a local expert on a Market Heritage walking tour. Requires advance reservations; call for details.*

 Salumi Artisan Cured Meats

309 3rd Ave S, Seattle
MILE/EXIT: 154B
206.621.8772
www.salumicuredmeats.com
OPEN: *Tue–Fri 11a–4p*

Salumi looms large on every serious carnivore's bucket list, and it's one of those rare instances where the food actually lives up to the hype. One trip will change the way you think about pork forever. The long line starts well before opening and lasts into the afternoon, but it moves faster than you think, and gives you ample time to make the extremely important decision: what to order. Daily specials are displayed on the chalkboard as you enter the narrow shop, and range from the usual cold salami offerings (regular, oregano, and the chocolatey, slightly spicy mole salamis are favorite choices) to hot sandwiches that depend on the day (the pork-a-riffic porchetta and lamb sandwiches are always available, and always delicious). If you're visiting this meaty mecca with a vegetarian in tow, the caprese sandwich is everything it should be, and though I have never personally ordered the pasta specials (something compels me to say "porcetta sandwich" every time I visit), I have it on good authority that they are quite tasty.

KNOW: *The communal tables in the back are charming, but fill up quickly. If the weather cooperates, take your sandwich a block away to the peaceful Waterfall Garden Park (219 2nd Avenue) or a bench in Occidental Square (2nd Avenue and Main Street).*

Elysian Fields

542 1st Ave S, Seattle
MILE/EXIT: 154B
206.382.4498
www.elysianbrewing.com
OPEN: *Daily 11a; closing times vary depending on stadium events*

Since opening the doors of its flagship Capitol Hill brewpub in 1994, Elysian Brewing Company has been pushing the boundaries to define what Northwest breweries are capable of producing. This is the largest of Elysian's brewpubs, and because it's got the roomiest brewing room, the brewmasters have much more leeway to experiment with new flavors of beer that challenge the established flavor profiles. Sometimes results are unsuccessful (a pomegranate beer had a weird bitterness), but sometimes they are outstanding, like the popular Jasmine IPA, a flowery brew that was once only available during springtime but is now found at all Elysian locations year-round. Perseus Porter and the Immortal IPA are all favored standbys, along with fall's Night Owl Pumpkin Ale. The Pioneer Square brewpub has plenty of seats at the long bar and booths for dining; it fills up during Mariners home games (it's right near the stadium), so plan in advance.

KNOW: *If you're not planning a trip to Pioneer Square, check out the other Elysian locations in Capitol Hill (1221 E Pike St; 206.860.1920) and near Green Lake (2106 N 55th St; 206.547.5929).*

 **Uwajimaya**

600 5th Ave S, Seattle
MILE/EXIT: 154B
206.336.2796
www.uwajimaya.com
OPEN: *Mon–Sat 8a–10p, Sun 9a–9p*

Seattle's significant and varied Asian population is on display at this massive supermarket in the heart of the International District. In the age of globalization it's hard to come across foods you've never encountered before, but one trip to Uwajimaya—an Asian specialty food store—reminds you that there are whole new frontiers to conquer. Browse the aisles that are filled with packages of mysterious-sounding products with indecipherable labels, gawk at the tremendous array of soy sauces, cruise the impeccably fresh and huge fish selection, or spend some time in the produce section to encounter fruits and vegetables you never before knew existed. Pick up some Botan rice candy (with edible rice paper labels; you'll find it in a pink-and-green box near the registers) and rice crackers for the road, or grab lunch in the international food court. The east side of the building has the entrance to Samurai Noodle—one of the best Japanese ramen spots in the city. Uwajimaya also has a great selection of Asian gifts and a bookstore with weird and wonderful discoveries to be made. It's the perfect place to kill an afternoon.

DETOURS & DESTINATIONS

Woodinville

MILE/EXIT: 182
DISTANCE FROM HWY: 8 miles

The wine scene in Washington State has exploded over the past decade—in 2000, there were 145 wineries in the state, today there are more than 600—and the majority of them are located in the arid climate and volcanic soil of Eastern Washington, a few hours' drive over the mountain passes. Many of these wineries have opened satellite tasting rooms in Woodinville, a quasi-rural area 15 miles north of Seattle, and provide a taste of the state's vinicultural offerings. Woodinville tasting rooms range from the opulent, like Chateau Ste. Michelle's massive French-style chateau and peacock-friendly grounds, to literal warehouses that offer little more than storage and a tasting counter.

Chateau Ste. Michelle

14111 NE 145th St, Woodinville
MILE/EXIT: 182
DISTANCE FROM HWY: 8 miles
425.488.3300
www.ste-michelle.com
OPEN: *Daily 10a–5p*

Sure, it's cheesy to visit this sophisticated winery—established in 1976, which makes it the oldest in the state—and truth be told, the tour does feel a bit corporate. But, the tour is also free, which is the right price in my book, and it includes four tastings, which is basically a gratis glass of wine. No complaints here. The tour also provides a comprehensive breakdown of the white wine making process that you don't get at some of the smaller tasting rooms, and also helps you understand what makes the Columbia Valley such a special place for grape-growing. The tasting room in the winery's faux-French main building can be crowded, but if you want to stick around after your tour, buy a bottle of wine and head into the romantic, lushly landscaped 87-acre grounds, which are tailor-made for picnics. Be on the lookout for the peacocks that roam the grounds.

TOURS: *Offered daily from 10:30a to 4p and last about a half hour.*

 Novelty Hill Winery

14710 Woodinville–Redmond Rd NE, Woodinville
MILE/EXIT: 182
DISTANCE FROM HWY: 8 miles
425.481.5502
www.noveltyhillwines.com
OPEN: *Daily 11a–5p*

If Chateau Ste. Michelle is the grande dame of the Woodinville wine scene, then Novelty Hill down the street is the quietly rebellious little sister. Those in the know considerate it a must-visit stop on the Woodinville Wine Country trek. The experience starts with the building itself, a contemporary blend of wood and concrete that is far from the traditional stylings of the other winery. The modern theme continues in the airy, state-of-the-art tasting room, a casual triumph of light wood and clean lines. Don't leave without touring the gardens in back, where a series of terraces has been designed to emulate the agrarian rhythms of the wine-making process in Eastern Washington.

KNOW: *Winemaker Mike Januik sometimes cooks up wood-fired pizza or other gourmet snacks for tasting guests.*

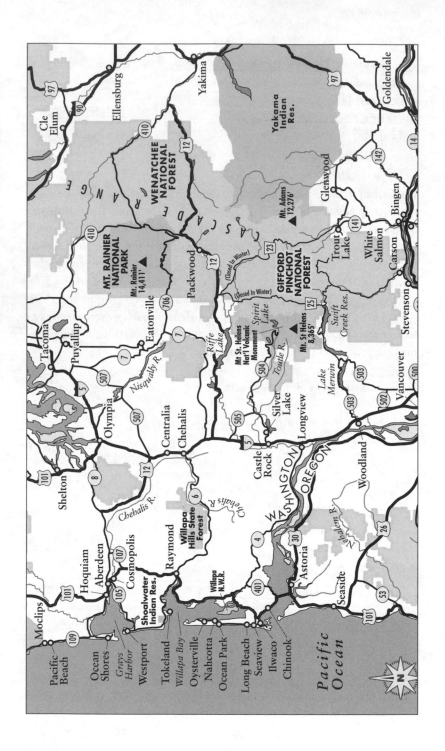

I-5: Seattle to Portland

$$\textit{Trip Stats}$$

START: Seattle

END: Portland

LENGTH: 174 miles

LOCAL FLAVOR: Burgers and diners—this is a commuter route, and many of the businesses cater to travelers looking for quick road food classics.

MORE INFO: Southwest Washington Convention & Visitors Bureau (www.southwestwashington.com)

I've probably been down this road a hundred times or more, but when I sat down to write about it I found I couldn't remember a single thing. This is a pleasantly dull landscape of forest and pastureland, not so much boring as it is forgettable.

It must have been exciting once, at the turn of the twentieth century when the land was developed in a feverish speculation rush in the name of progress. This is one of the oldest settled parts of the state, but the freeway isolates you from most of its history—most of which played out over the course of the last century. Whether its most exciting times are behind it or not, for now southwestern Washington seems content with existing as it is.

Men ventured in the wild country north of the Oregon Territory on the prowl for fur trapping and lumber to fuel the frenzied building spree in post–gold rush San Francisco. Sawmills sprung up everywhere, and an infrastructure of waterways and roads and railroads were built around getting the logs south. Papermills gave towns a sweaty stench (Tacoma only recently lost the moniker "Tacoma Aroma" when the sawmill closed its doors). Down by Longview a faint papermill belch still permeates downtown and the road meets up with the mighty Columbia River, loaded with logs stockpiled on their way to market.

Tacoma, 30 miles south of Seattle, was the seat of the powerful Hudson's Bay Company and the town that for a long time everyone thought would be the biggest in the region. It was built almost too quickly, "staggering under a boom of the boomiest" as Rudyard Kipling wrote in 1889, then a 24-year-old British journalist. The city thrived, then choked. Seattle yanked the state's gravitational center upward when it became the terminus for the Great Northern Railway and the stopping-off point for Klondike prospectors. Tacoma settled into relative obscurity.

The road passes through forest and suburbs until Olympia, where Puget Sound meets the flat fields of the south. You pass the neoclassical state capital dome on your right followed by the end of Puget Sound. After Olympia, the scenery turns to repetitious prairieland. And then you finally reach Vancouver, Washington, the oldest continuous settlement in the Northwest, set on the dramatic Columbia River Gorge. Pass over the river and you're in Oregon.

As for road food, there's not much here. It's a region developed almost entirely around the lumber trade; industry never revolved around agriculture. You're always within 90 minutes of culinary powerhouses Seattle and Portland. Unless you're peeling off for a day trip to the coast or visiting the destruction wrought by the now-dormant Mount St. Helens there's no reason to dawdle along the way.

ON THE ROAD

Pick-Quick Drive In

4306 Pacific Hwy E, Fife
MILE/EXIT: 137
253.922.5599
www.pick-quick.net
OPEN: *Mon–Sat 10a–8p, Sun 11a–6p (closed Dec 1–Feb 1)*

Fife's barely kept secret is out. Those in the know were already willing to brave the line at this retro burger stand, no matter the weather, for pitch-perfect hamburgers and shakes. Then *USA Today* let the cat out of the bag by naming it the best burger in the state in 2010. Nothing this good can stay a secret forever, I suppose, though this one lasted longer than most—Pick-Quick has been serving the same burger since it opened in 1949. It's a simple masterpiece of thin grilled beef patties and American cheese oozing in its nooks and crannies, and a reminder that well-executed classics don't need culinary bells and whistles to shine.

Don't miss the milk shakes, made with fresh fruit and local ice cream. Pick-Quick has no inside seating—order at the counter, and take your food to the pleasant grassy area behind the stand, where there are picnic tables, shady trees, and pots of flowers.

KNOW: *Decide what you want before you get to the counter—the seemingly all-female staff run the whole operation with remarkable efficiency and do not tolerate dawdlers.*

 Tacoma Boys

7320 6th Ave, Tacoma
MILE/EXIT: 132
253.756.0902
www.tacomaboys.com
OPEN: *24/7*

There's something about road trips that enables you to indulge in snacks like Combos and Cheetos from gas stations, but this 24-hour Tacoma shop gives you no reason to give into all those chemical-laced options. Tacoma Boys specializes in products made and grown locally, from produce, cheese, wine, and beer, to a giant selection of dried fruit, snack mixes, old-fashioned candy, and other road-worthy nibbles—real, recognizable food that will do your body good. The shop started in 1985 selling produce from a red-and-white-striped awning by the side of the road, and still retains the original farm-stand feel despite its expansion to three locations in Western Washington. Indulge in handmade fudge concocted daily on-site, which comes in a rainbow of flavors from cherry walnut to mint cookie. The store also makes its own corn tortilla chips, and—even better—a range of salsas to accompany them.

VARIOUS LOCATIONS *in Puyallup, Longview, and Lakewood*

The Spar

114 4th Ave E, Olympia
MILE/EXIT: 105
360.357.6444
www.mcmenamins.com
OPEN: *Sun–Thu 7a–midnight, Fri–Sat 7a–1a*

The Spar was once a smoke-filled den of iniquity frequented by lumberjacks, longshoremen, and other blue-collar workers (no women were allowed inside back then). Over time, Olympia's population morphed into a mix of politicians, hippies, and college kids from nearby Evergreen State, and the Spar's dingy, cafeteria-like atmosphere was embraced by hipsters and other local eccentrics. Then it was bought in 2007 by McMenamins and transformed into a family-friendly brewpub. The bar's original mid-century wooden fixtures are all still in place—though now so polished you can practically see your reflection in them—and colorful murals and blown-glass accents mask the establishment's unsavory past. History hasn't been completely erased, however. McMenamins hung black-and-white prints from the town's logging past (the bar was named for the "spar trees" loggers used to anchor their cables and pulleys), and the logging spirit lives on in the hugely caloric breakfasts. Try the "4th Avenue Mess"—a pile of hash browns topped with country gravy, Tillamook cheddar, and sausage links.

KNOW: *Olympia used to be the home of Olympia beer—known locally as "Oly"—a working man's lager with the well-known slogan, "It's the water." McMenamins kept up the tradition with its Spartesian IPA, a special brew made with local artisan well water.*

Lattin's Country Cider Mill

9402 Rich Rd SE, Olympia
MILE/EXIT: 102
DISTANCE FROM HWY: 5.7 miles
360.491.7328
www.lattinscider.com
OPEN: *Mon–Sat 9a–5:30p, Sun (June–Dec) 11a–4p*

To call the Lattin family's livelihood a mere "cider mill" is misleading, because 77-year-old Carolyn Lattin and her two daughters run nothing less than a homespun farm-industrial complex. In addition to producing six flavors of apple cider, the mill's 25 acres also house a working farm, petting zoo, commercial bakery, and vegetable garden. A few years ago, I spent a day with the Lattin women for a story I was writing for *Edible Seattle* and was blown away by their friendliness, commitment to their land and customers, willingness to work hard for little profit, and incredibly flavorful apple cider. One year later, news of a tragic shooting of one of their employees in the main retail store—witnessed by Carolyn Lattin herself—touched me deeply, because it's the textbook example of how bad things happen to the very best people. Lattin's continues to produce award-winning cider in flavors like blackberry and strawberry, along with incredibly moist, perfectly spiced apple cider doughnuts. I make it a point to stop by when I'm in the area; you should too, if only to support the steady production of quality products from steadily good people.

KNOW: *Saturday mornings bring legendary apple fritters—basically fried chunks of cinnamon roll tossed with apple chunks. The last weekend in September, the ladies host Applefest, a community fair for the whole family, featuring live bluegrass, wagon rides, apple bobbing, and more.*

(¶) Northwest Sausage & Deli/ Dick's Brewing Company

5945 Prather Rd, Centralia
MILE/EXIT: 88
360.736.7760
www.nwsausage.com
OPEN: *Mon–Wed, Sat 9a–5p; Thu–Fri 9a–9p*

It was nine in the morning and we were buying sausages and a sandwich to go when the very friendly woman behind the counter asked us if we wanted to try some beer from the on-site microbrewery. We glanced at each other—why not? After pouring five or six sample shots of the many varieties on tap (the IPA, Irish, and Danger ales were the stand-outs; smooth, not too sweet, a little bitter in all the right places), the woman mentioned that she hadn't tried the latest batch of the signature Dick Danger Ale. "Don't tell anybody, but I'm going to have a little taste too," she said, and we toasted this small rebellion. I've never met the man, but based on his reputation, it doesn't seem like owner Dick Young would mind too much. He's based his career on making his own rules, from the meat he buys at nearby farms and smokes himself on the premises, to the small-batch microbrewery he started running for fun as a side business. The black pepper–seasoned pepperoni is the best of the bunch—spicy and supple—but Young also smokes turkey, beef jerky, and more. Order and consume a sandwich on the funky patio (its location on overgrown old Route 99 makes it seem tucked-away and secret), or get it to go. This is an especially good stop for picnic fare if you're headed to Mount St. Helens.

 **Country Cousin**

1054 Harrison Ave, Centralia

MILE/EXIT: 82

360.736.2200

www.ramblinrestaurants.com/country-cousin-restaurant.html

OPEN: *Sun–Thu 5:30a–9:30p, Fri–Sat 5:30a–10p*

Call me a snob, but I'm generally prejudiced against restaurants with gift shops—especially if the gift shop stocks cutesy kitsch like wooden roosters and other old-timey knickknacks. Country Cousin is the restaurant that called my bluff. It might not be the most sophisticated restaurant in the world, but it also doesn't pretend to be anything it's not, and sometimes a self-consciously "country" place like this—tricked out with wooden barrel chairs and lamps sporting cowboy prints and fringe—is just what the doctor ordered. The breakfast country-fried steak is locally famous, and the 150-mile breakfast, "guaranteed to last a minimum of 150 miles," delivers exactly what it promises (one egg, pancake, sausage, and bacon, or you can double-down with the "300-mile breakfast"). Country Cousin calls itself the "Home of the Old-Fashioned Pot Roast" for a reason, but, beyond that succulent specialty, everything on the menu is well executed, and the staff is so genuinely warm and down to earth that you can forget your road exhaustion.

 **La Tarasca**

1001 W Main St, Centralia

MILE/EXIT: 82

360.736.7756

OPEN: *Sun–Thu 11a–8p, Fri–Sat 11a–9p*

La Tarasca is like that gorgeous girl in your high school who, upon venturing into the larger world, realized she was no longer the shining star of existence, but merely one of the crowd. Among foodies traveling on I-5 between Seattle and Portland, La Tarasca is that girl. The restaurant would just be one of many in a Mexican food mecca like Los Angeles, but its location in downtown Centralia ensures that it's the best Mexican food for miles. The space started life as a diner, from the looks of it, but a healthy dose of Mexican kitsch and bright paint transformed it into a cheery dining room. The first clue that the food is above ordinary comes

How to Find a Good Local Restaurant

You're tired, hungry, and flying blind in a strange town. It's easy to find the best road food with a few simple tricks of the trade.

1. Ask the locals: gas station attendants, baristas, bartenders, grocery store checkers, and other natives are a goldmine of information. (Be as specific as you can. A broad question like "What's the best restaurant in town?" can elicit mild panic, whereas "Where can I find a good burger around here?" lets them know exactly what you're looking for.)

2. Consult the Internet: If you have a smart phone, a quick peek at a local review website like Yelp or Chowhound can give you all the info you need. Many also have mobile apps.

3. Query your social networks: You'd be surprised how many people come out of the woodwork to answer the most esoteric questions. Use geo-specific hashtags on Twitter; for example, "Looking for a modestly priced dinner in Santa Cruz. Any recommendations? #santacruz"

4. Check the parking lots: Places crowded with local cars—even better, police cars or semi trucks—are usually local favorites. Avoid places with empty lots during peak hours like breakfast and dinner.

5. Consider the location: Seek out seafood on the coast, not 300 miles inland. Eat tacos in a town near the border or with a large migrant worker population, not one high in the mountains. (There are exceptions to every rule, such as the totally delicious aberration of Buz's Crab Shack in landlocked Redding, CA.)

6. Go with your gut: Sometimes it comes down to instinct, and the more road food you eat, the better your "spidey sense" will be. Maybe it's the charmingly homemade sign, maybe it's the planters outside the window, maybe it's the people walking in . . . when all else fails, take a chance on the place that appeals to you the most.

when you sit down and the waitress delivers tangy marinated carrots and jalapenos instead of the usual chips and salsa. The owners are from the Mexican state of Michoacan, which is known for its corn dishes among other things, and the house-made tamales are a definite thing to order (if the kitchen hasn't run out). Also worth seeking out are the carnitas, spicy little strips of pork on soft, warm homemade corn tortillas.

John R. Jackson House

275 Jackson Hwy, Chehalis

MILE/EXIT: 68

OPEN: *Daily 8a–dusk*

Built in 1845, this tiny log cabin is one of the oldest pioneer structures north of the Columbia River, and was an important stopover for early travelers on the Cowlitz Trail, a northern spur of the Oregon Trail that went up to south Puget Sound. Rumor has it that Isaac Stevens, Washington State's first governor, spent the night here, as did Ulysses S. Grant. Today, the wooded park has a few picnic tables and restrooms and is as good a spot as any for a picnic. The house itself is closed up, but there is some dusty furniture in there that you can see if you peek through the windows. Interpretive signs explain the history of the region.

KNOW: *A few miles south of the cabin is Lewis and Clark State Park, which has a short nature trail if you feel like stretching your legs.*

Cedar Creek Grist Mill

43907 NE Grist Mill Rd, Woodland

MILE/EXIT: 21

DISTANCE FROM HWY: 10.4 miles

360.225.5832

www.cedarcreekgristmill.com

OPEN: *Sat 1–4p, Sun 2–4p*

The next time you find yourself frustrated with the inconveniences of day-to-day life, imagine what life was like back in 1876, when this grist mill was the only place for miles for farmers to grind their grain into flour, cornmeal, and animal feed. Early Washington pioneer George Woodham chose the location for the year-round water flow on Cedar Creek, but it was at least a two-day wagon journey from the fertile plains where grain farmers harvested their crops. (Talk about inconvenient!)

The mill's remoteness turned out to work against Woodham, and when the mill flooded three years later he packed up and moved to Centralia. His mill gradually fell into disrepair for nearly a century until 1980, when a group of local residents decided to fix it up themselves. Now restored to its former glory, the mill is one of the oldest surviving structures in the state and a National Historic Landmark. It's also a working grist mill once again. On weekends, volunteer docents give an overview of the mill's history and take you inside to see the old-school stone milling process in action—samples of milled grain are available for a donation. The peaceful Cedar Creek setting is a scenic spot for a picnic—tables are thoughtfully provided overlooking the mill and a nearby covered wooden bridge.

KNOW: *Go on the last Saturday in October for the Annual Apple Pressing, where volunteers press more than 8,000 pounds of Washington apples into cider.*

Burgerville

307 E Mill Plain Blvd, Vancouver
MILE/EXIT: 1C
360.693.8801
www.burgerville.com
OPEN: *Mon–Sat 7a–10p, Sun 9a–8p*

With all the anti-fast-food evangelizing that's gone on over the past decade, it's about time someone came up with a socially conscious fast-food restaurant. Enter Burgerville, a Northwest burger chain that has been committed to local ingredients and sustainable methods since 1961. We'll start with the "local" part. On the chain's website, you can view every one of their producers, from antibiotic- and hormone-free Oregon beef, to buns from Portland's Franz Bakery, cheese from Rogue Creamery and Tillamook, onion rings from Walla Walla onions, pickles from Pleasant Valley Farms in Mount Vernon, ice cream and milk from Sunshine Dairy in Portland, and many, many more. Then there are the seasonal items, which have something of a cult following: fried asparagus, strawberry shortcake, sweet potato fries, blackberry lemonade, and milk shakes made with fresh berries, pumpkins, or hazelnuts, just to name a few. And finally, the sustainable business practices: the company is dedicated to utilizing wind power, composting its waste by using eco-friendly packaging, and recycling its cooking oil into biofuel. Oh yeah, and the burger is above average too. The only thing Burgerville hasn't done yet is convert water into wine, but I imagine when they do, they'll do it with social responsibility.

KNOW: *This is actually the second Burgerville location—the original is only a few miles away—but it's the only one still housed in its original 1962 building.*

VARIOUS LOCATIONS *throughout southern Washington (Centralia, Kelso, and Battle Ground) and northern Oregon (greater Portland, Oswego, Newberg, Monmouth, and Albany)*

Highway 101: Southern Washington Coast

Trip Stats

LENGTH: 133 miles

LOCAL FLAVOR: Fresh DIY seafood, especially oysters; cranberries.

BEST TIME: July and August are your best bets for good weather, but blustery winter storms have their appeal too.

WORD OF WARNING: The speed limit can vary every few miles on the highway, and there are many traffic cops watching.

Despite the fact that I know hordes of food writers throughout Washington State, no one had an answer to what I thought was a fairly simple question: "What's good to eat on the Washington Coast?" Not Jon Rowley, the oyster king of Seattle who spends more time than most out on the Willapa Bay tidal flats; not the voracious legions on Chowhound, who can scare up good food in the unlikeliest of places; not even the cop who pulled me over 10 miles outside of Aberdeen for going 71 in a 60 mph zone, and who chuckled when I told him I was writing a book about West Coast road food, but grew serious when I asked him for recommendations. "That'll be quite a book," he said, in an amused, indulgent way that haunted me for the rest of the afternoon.

"We're a fishing community out here. Plenty of places to buy fish to cook at home. Not so many restaurants," he told me. I told him I'd heard Westport had good clam chowder, the same way certain girls mention how good their friends looked at a party to surreptitiously gauge their boyfriend's reaction. "Clam chowder's okay," my cop said. "You'll find much better up in Seattle." He let me off with a warning, but not before cautioning me to watch my speed on the narrow coastal highways.

I was barreling down the road alone, and not by my own choosing. I was convinced that I could pull myself out of the quicksand of self-pity with one amazing meal (not to mention make everyone who ditched me jealous when I got back to Seattle)—but the cop's attitude hadn't exactly stoked my confidence in accomplishing this goal. As it turns out, the Washington Coast is the right place to go when you're feeling blue,

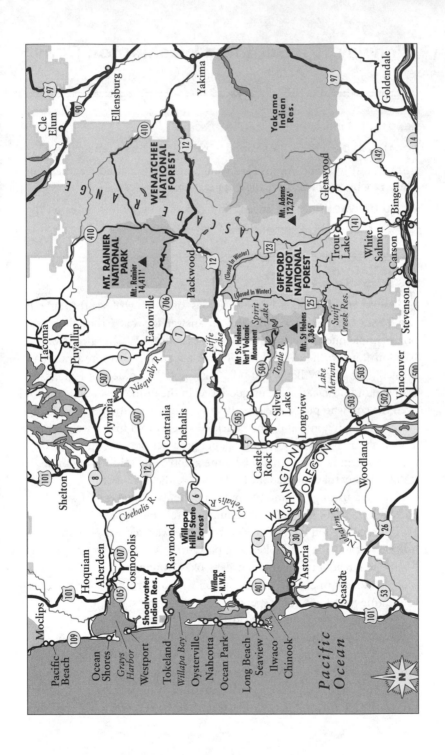

because there's something downright desolate about it. It has all the loneliness of an area left behind; a once-thriving logging and fishing epicenter later forsaken by the changing tides of industry. Piles of sun-bleached oyster shells abandoned on the shore, boarded-up fireworks stands on the Shoalwater Bay Indian Reservation, roadside fields of former old-growth forests reduced to tree stumps—each of these scenes stands as a relic of a time long since past.

Every so often, a round blue sign points to a tsunami evacuation route—inland to higher ground—suddenly making you aware of the place's impermanence, vulnerability, and ultimate insignificance.

As it turns out, my sources were mostly right: there just isn't much good food out there on the southern Washington Coast. But somewhere on the Long Beach Peninsula, after a day of driving down mostly deserted highways, it all ceased to matter if there was good food out there or not. I sat on the hood of my car and stared out over miles of exposed muddy tidal flats, my back to the preserved and empty nineteenth-century ghost town of Oysterville, my eyes trained on the evergreen-covered Willapa Hills in the distance. Higher ground. The thunderheads above them looked like freshly whipped meringue, and suddenly I realized I was hungry. I no longer cared if the next meal changed my life; I just wanted a full stomach.

Serendipitously, my next stop was Jimella's Seafood Market & Cafe, the newest endeavor from a pair of women who practically invented local Washington cuisine with their former Nahcotta restaurant, The Ark. I had run out of the energy it took to get my hopes up, even when presented with a fresh-from-the-oven sourdough roll with sweet local butter and a fantastic glass of Washington chardonnay. Then came the succulent fried oyster appetizer, the best thing I'd eaten in weeks. Later, the unstinting friendliness and garlicky-creamy Dungeness crab mac and cheese at The Depot in Seaview nearly made me weep with appreciation. Graded on a curve or not, these were meals to remember.

On the drive back to Seattle I blasted ABBA's *Gold* and sang along at the top of my voice and remembered that there are upsides to road tripping alone.

ON THE ROAD

 Estrella Family Creamery

659 Wynoochee Valley Rd, Montesano

MILE/EXIT: 12 miles from Aberdeen on Hwy 12 E

360.249.6541

www.estrellafamilycreamery.com

[Editor's note: Estrella Family Creamery was shut down by the FDA in December 2009. At press time, it's uncertain whether the creamery will open its doors again. But as an homage to the Estrella Family's efforts, an encouragement to independent dairy farmers everywhere, and a reminder that things do not last forever, we wanted to keep it in the book for posterity. Please call before visiting.]

It's only a little disconcerting to look out the window while you're tasting cheese and see the cows it came from. You start to think about things like udders and chewing cud and manure; things that never cross your mind while perusing the fancy cheese aisle at Whole Foods, and that signify the kind of city-mouse squeamishness that drives us to seek out farm stands and producing dairies in the first place. I mention this to the woman behind the tasting counter, and she starts to riff on the relationship of cheese to the land and the seasons. "We are one removed from what we eat," she says, helping me to a slice of Black Creek Buttery, the dairy's smooth, six-month aged cheddar. "It used to be that you made dinner from what you could bring into your home. Something has been lost."

That "something" can be found at places like this family-owned creamery, which makes nearly 20 seasonally rotating varieties of cheese from the cows and goats that roam the farm's 164 acres. All production is done on-site in stainless steel vats visible through a window in the tasting room, and aged in a homemade cave a couple hundred yards beyond the gravel parking lot. It's rural in the most engaging sense: You get out of your car and the gravel and mud driveway crunches under your feet. A rooster crows. A barn cat comes to investigate the new visitor. The air smells like cows and sweet grass, and gets you in the mood to taste the fruits of the farm's labor.

Bruce Port Historical Marker

MILE/EXIT: 490.5

There's no road food worth mentioning on the highway between Westport and Long Beach save for a few industrial fishing operations with storefronts where you can buy seafood to go, but the area has a rich legacy of oyster cultivation. Willapa Bay is historically one of the country's biggest oyster-producing regions because nearly half of the bay is exposed twice a day at low tide, which makes for easy harvesting; then the beds are flooded at high tide, which feeds and protects the oysters. This historical marker a few miles south of South Bay, the self-proclaimed "Oyster Capital of the World," commemorates the spot where the survivors of the *Robert Bruce* schooner from San Francisco came ashore after their ship burned and sank in the bay thanks to the meddling of an unhappy cook. They started their own settlement, Bruceville, and their own oyster business, known as the The Bruce Boys.

 **The Depot**

1208 38th Pl, Seaview

MILE/EXIT: 460

360.642.7880

www.depotrestaurantdining.com

OPEN: *Dinner only; hours vary by season—call ahead for details*

This Seaview restaurant has the rare knack of making guests feel welcome from the moment they walk in. With its high ceilings, checkered floor, and convivial vibe, the space is instantly appealing—and though I was sitting alone at the bar, I wasn't lonely. Nearby tables housed a meet-the-parents dinner, a couple on a date, and a family of four. On the wall hangs an old-timey photo of the train that used to be parked in the restaurant's namesake depot—the same train credited with bringing commerce to the region. (Its history is printed on the back of the menu.) The Dungeness mac and cheese is a heaping creamy, cheesy, garlicky concoction, with huge chunks of crabmeat and visible strings of cheese. The modern plating seemed like it was trying too hard, and I could have used some bread to sop up the sauce, but I washed it all down with a Black Butte Porter and was satisfied.

KNOW: *Wednesdays the kitchen departs from the regular menu for burger night—your choice of organic, grass-fed beef, Portobello mushroom, or buffalo burgers, with an eclectic mix of 14 toppings.*

DETOURS & DESTINATIONS

Scenic Route: Highway 105

MILE/EXIT: 530

LENGTH: 50 miles

From Aberdeen you can hop on Highway 101, which will take you down to Raymond in 40 minutes, or you can take Highway 105, which hugs the shore and gives you a glimpse into life on the coast—groups of quaint houses interspersed along the two-lane highway, makeshift stands by the side of the road selling whirligigs and chainsaw art, RV parks, and motels with vaguely nautical names like "Surf Spray" and "Sand Castle." Drive through Westport, the surfing capital of the Washington Coast, and past the vast tidal flats on the Shoalwater Bay Indian Reservation and beaches where you can go razor clamming in season. (See page 53.) The highway meets up with 101 in Raymond, a depressed logging town with a giant Weyerhaeuser plant—and not much else.

 Westport Winery

1 South Arbor Rd, Aberdeen

MILE/EXIT: 15 miles from Aberdeen on WA-105 S

360.648.2224

www.westportwinery.org

OPEN: *Daily 11a–6p*

It seems negative, somehow, to say that the best thing about a place is that it doesn't totally suck—but in this case it's honestly meant as a compliment. Westport Winery & Vineyards-by-the-Sea is located on the marshy coastal highway between Aberdeen and Westport, a strange location for a vineyard (wine grapes like dry places with big fluctuations in daily temperatures and well-drained soil; Aberdeen offers none of these things). Inside the twee shop, the perimeters painted with vines furled around quotations about wine from famous people, taken out of context ("Wine is the most civilized thing in the world"—Ernest Hemingway). I was pleasantly surprised when the wine itself wasn't bad at all—Pinot Noirvana turned out to be a light, fruity red good for a hot summer night, and the popular Jetty Cat Red goes down easy and would be fine with cheese. As I tasted, I learned that the winery gets most of its grapes from the Columbia Valley, and donates a portion of the proceeds from every bottle to a different charity.

Razor Clamming

About 15 to 35 days a year, usually in the spring and fall, the Washington Department of Fish and Wildlife deems it okay to go razor clamming out on certain intertidal coastal beaches, and dozens of people go out every day to try their hand at catching razor clams. Access is available at the state parks, but many folks just pull over to the side of the highway. Do get a license and pay attention to the restrictions: You can only get 15 clams a day, and consequences range from heavy fines to jail time.

KNOW: *Westport Winery is best for picnic supplies—the shop features lots of local cheeses and meats, along with jars of olives and other snacky items. Stop here and stock up on your way out to the coast, because this is the best gourmet bet for miles.*

Bay City Sausages

2249 SR 105, Aberdeen
MILE/EXIT: 17 miles from Aberdeen on WA-105 S
360.648.2344
OPEN: *Daily 9a–6p*

This highway sausage place's eye-catching black-and-white cow-spotted exterior got my attention, but it would have anyway because I'm on for a semipermanent quest for the best pepperoni in the world. This was not it. A good pepperoni stick is an amazing thing: a tough casing that snaps as you bite into it, the melting give of the inside meat, a heat that's almost too much to bear. Bay City's pepperoni's flavor is all in the casing, which houses a somewhat bland sausage stick. I did not try what I later discovered was their specialty, a pineapple variety that allegedly balances the spice with the sweetness of the fruit. Made fresh on the premises, Bay City's products surely best any vacuum-packaged meat product found at nearby gas stations. They also offer beef jerky and more than a dozen flavors of fresh sausages, which the brochure proudly announces are produced "the old fashion way like grandpa use [*sic*] to make," including a version studded with sliced cranberries in a nod to the area's deep history with Ocean Spray.

How to Drive on the Beach

Try something new and take the beach route up the Long Beach Peninsula. It's disorienting at first, seeing locals drive their SUVs out onto the sand and proceed to camp out right next to their ride. But when in Long Beach, do as the locals do—just exercise caution while you're doing it. Always bring a jack and a shovel with you, as well as the number of a good towing company, and remember to watch the tides.

1. Decrease the air pressure in your tires to 20–25 pounds. Think back to high school physics: increased surface area.

2. Drive at a slow, steady pace, like driving in snow. Beach speed limit is 25 mph, and it is possible to get a speeding ticket.

3. Try to drive in the ruts made by other drivers, or, if there are none, on hardpack sand. Avoid "sugar sand," which is like quicksand.

4. Don't turn, accelerate, or stop too quickly, especially in softer sand. Light, deliberate movements are the way to go.

5. Know where you can and can't go. Some places have seasonal restrictions. There are hefty fines for these and your license can be revoked.

6. Watch for children, sunbathers, animals, beach debris, and other vehicles. Pedestrians aren't used to looking both ways to cross a beach.

7. If you do get stuck, don't spin your wheels. You will only dig yourself deeper into the sand. Put the car in a low gear and try to back up slowly, using the ruts you already made.

8. Reinflate your tires as soon as you hit the pavement again, and rinse the corrosive sand and salt from your car's undercarriage as soon as possible.

 **Brady's Oysters**

3714 Oyster Pl E, Aberdeen

MILE/EXIT: 17 miles from Aberdeen on WA-105 S

360.268.0077

www.bradysoysters.com

OPEN: *Daily 9a–6p*

Brady's was the only recommendation I managed to worm out of the kindly traffic cop, who said it was where locals got their fresh seafood. You'll see the oyster-shaped wood-painted signs before you see the place itself, an unassuming seafood shack with a corrugated metal roof, set in the shadow of a bridge over South Bay with its protected oyster fields. Brady's is a fourth-generation family business, locally famous for figuring out how to raise oysters in a way that kept them out of the mud, and is *the* place to get fresh and smoked seafood, cooked Dungeness crab, and the usual fixings. But the real reason to visit to Brady's is the merchandise, which takes up the entire south wall. I was especially attracted to the bumper stickers, which had delightfully bawdy slogans like "Shuck Me, Suck Me, Eat Me RAW," "I Got Crabs at . . . Brady's Oysters," and "Forget Viagra, Eat Brady's Oysters." The memory of a great meal is always a good trip souvenir, but a local bumper sticker or T-shirt.

Westport

Maybe it's my mental association with the well-to-do Connecticut town of the same name, but Westport, Washington, population 2,500, located 21 miles from Aberdeen on WA-105 S, seems like it should be nicer than one-story tract homes and empty lots stacked with used shipping pallets and castaway fishing nets. The town is set in a scenic spot at the tidal flats where Grays Harbor meets the ocean, and you can see the snowy Olympic Mountains in the distance. It's also one of the biggest surfing meccas in the state, and it's right where the fishing fleet comes in; you want it to be better than a run-down fishing village fallen on hard times, but so it goes. Expect wide, empty streets and a boardwalk with fading paint and souvenir shops half-heartedly selling saltwater taffy. If you're starving, there are a few places that will fill you up without letting you down.

🍴 Mermaid Deli & Pub

200 E Patterson, Westport

360.612.0435

www.mermaiddeli.com

OPEN: *Sun–Thu 11a–8p, Fri–Sat 11a–9p*

Westport is a surfer town, when the tides are right, and the Mermaid is where beach bums gather after hours. They congregate in the restaurant's back room—a space decorated with surfing memorabilia, teal blue cement-brick walls covered with decidedly homemade undersea murals, and a bar backed with a giant photo of a palm tree silhouetted against a tropical sunset. Often the party spills out to the backyard, which looks like the set of an MTV reality show: a fire pit with benches next to a giant stack of wood, a volleyball court and basketball hoop, and a stage that features live music on weekends. By day, Mermaid Deli is a sandwich shop that offers thoroughly mediocre hoagies and surprisingly good clam chowder, chock-full of herbs and chunks of clam.

🧁 Little Richard's House of Donuts

2557 Westhaven Dr, Westport

360.268.9733

OPEN: *Weekends only; hours vary by season—call ahead for details*

There is nothing exceptional about this doughnut and fish-and-chips shack on Westport's faded boardwalk—the fried fish is perfectly decent, enhanced somewhat by the salty breezes coming off the ocean, and the doughnuts are certainly a step up from the type you buy in the grocery store. It might be the best place to stop for lunch in Westport, however, and gets major props for its name (which I'd rather assume is a kick-ass rock 'n' roll allusion than find out it's the name of the owner's son or something). Go in with low expectations, and they will be more than met.

Long Beach Peninsula

MILE/EXIT: 355.5

LENGTH: 17 miles

Cranberries and oysters are the two main cash crops on this 28-mile spit of land that separates Willapa Bay from the Pacific Ocean. It's a friendly, close-knit community, the kind of place where you see a dozen eggs in a basket on the side of the road with a basket of cash next to it and a sign that says "$1/dozen." Because you've been driving on empty highways for a while in a strange and lonely state of mind, you might start to marvel that such trusting places still exist. They do. And the peninsula is one big study in contrasts—the land is wild and pastoral at the same time, with the untamed ocean on one side and the quiet bay on the other, and even in late May, spring is still raw and new.

When the piles of oyster shells start to appear by the side of the road, you know you're approaching Oysterville. Oyster production used to be the main focus, thanks to the enormous appetites of forty-niners in San Francisco who were used to oysters from back east. Willapa Bay was the closest place to San Francisco with open access to the ocean, and oyster farmers took full advantage, until overharvesting nearly wiped out production for good. Oysterville today is a well-preserved ghost town with whitewashed buildings, an interesting cemetery, and a storybook schoolhouse—get a walking map in the church—but with a lingering spooky vibe about it.

Cranberry Museum & Research Station

2907 Pioneer Rd, Long Beach
360.642.5553
www.cranberrymuseum.com
OPEN: *Daily 10a–5p, Apr 1–Dec 15*

I know: this sounds like the kind of place your parents dragged you on family vacations, an outing they pitched as "fun," but the sulky teenager in you knew it was actually a thinly veiled "educational experience." The weird thing is, this stuff turns out to be pretty interesting as an adult. The museum is dowdy, no doubt about it, but in a charming way—it's just a collection of old tools and photos and machinery with homemade-looking plaques, providing a comprehensive glimpse into the history of cranberry production. Also, there are these rad cranberry bog shoes that look like space boots with spikes on them. Take the self-guided walking tour to get up close and personal with the museum's cranberry bogs, set up by the Pacific Coast Cranberry Research Foundation operated by Washington State University, to give you an idea of the different varieties of berries, irrigation techniques, and harvesting methods. Or, just hit the gift shop, which has every cranberry product you can possibly imagine

Washington State Cranberries

Cranberries are kind of a big deal on the Washington Coast. If the huge mural in downtown Long Beach about the Ocean Spray harvest of 1920 didn't tip you off, a trip out the peninsula will. Chinook Indians harvested wild cranberries that grew in bogs until an entrepreneurial visitor decided that the regional similarities to Cape Cod meant he could make his fortune in cranberry pickings. It worked for a while until blight set in, and bogs lay dormant until Ocean Spray, a co-op owned by cranberry farmers, came to the region in the 1930s and revived the industry. All along the peninsula you see signs with the Ocean Spray logo and the names of the people who own the farm. Still, a series of rough harvests and a bad market almost spelled disaster for cranberry farmers, until fairly recently when Ocean Spray branched into juice blends (cran-apple, etc.) and built on the public's antioxidant craze with Craisins, which make up most of the Washington crop. Today, Willapa Bay produces 1.5 million pounds of cranberries—the most of any region in the state, which is the country's fifth-largest producer, growing about 3 percent of the nation's total output.

and then some: relish, wine, candles, syrup, baked goods, cookbooks, shower gel, etc.

KNOW: *During the annual October harvest, one weekend is given over to the Cranberrian Fair, which celebrates, well, everything cranberry. October is also the month when you can watch cranberry harvesting in action.*

(🍴) Jimella's Seafood Market & Cafe

21712 Pacific Way, Klipsan Beach
360.665.4847
OPEN: *Wed 11a–2:30p, Thu–Sat 5a–8:30p, Sun 11a–2:30p*

There are days when the pleasures of adulthood seem few and far between, but one such pleasure is a restaurant like Jimella's, which is grown up in all the right ways: the interior is all antique mirrors and subtle sage-colored walls, jazz standards play low in the background, and the wine list is extensive and mostly local. But this isn't just any restaurant—it's the latest venture from Jimella Lucas and Nanci Main, the duo who opened The Ark in 1980 and quietly led the local, organic, fresh-food revolution in the Northwest from a tiny cafe perched on a dock in nearby Nahcotta. (They sold the original restaurant in 2004, and it has since closed.) Half of their new place is a market, but such a market—hand-lettered signs give you the name of the oysterman who caught the oysters, along with their variety and price—that you might be tempted to forgo the restaurant and get a picnic instead. I can't advise either way, except that the fried Pacific oysters are some of the best I've ever eaten, and I am a dyed-in-the-wool raw-on-the-half-shell girl, so that's saying a lot. They were warm, tender, barely breaded, with an amazingly meaty texture—not rubbery at all—and were so creamy and yielding I almost felt dirty eating them in public. The house salmon, in a creamy Drambuie sauce with candied citrus and brown rice, is also good, but after the high of the oysters it was hard to compare. Jimella does the cooking, but Nanci's desserts should not be overlooked; they're one of the things this place is known for.

KNOW: *The market is open Wed–Sun 10a–5p.*

🏠 Bailey's Bakery & Café

26910 Sandridge Rd, Nahcotta
360.665.4449
www.baileysbakerycafe.com
OPEN: *Thu–Mon 8a–3p, Sun 9a–3p*
Cash only

Nothing more, or less, than it should be. A low-key local hangout in the old Nahcotta post office (built in 1858), this is a place to stop for a coffee, cranberry scone, soup and sandwich, or, on weekends, savory breakfast pastries. Much is made of the unfortunately named Thunder Buns, sticky buns filled with currants and pecans with a honey-butter glaze, only available on Sundays. The north side of the building has a display with an original timetable of the Ilwaco railroad, which terminated in Nahcotta and was an instrumental transportation link in shipping oysters to San Francisco.

Oysterville Sea Farms

1st and Clark, Ocean Park
360.665.6585
www.willabay.com
OPEN: *Daily 9:30a–5p*

"When in Honolulu take home pineapples, when in Oysterville take home oysters," orders a sign in front of this weathered wooden seafood shack in a historic cannery on the shore of Willapa Bay, and thanks to the salty breezes and piles of oyster shells lying around, you are more than happy to oblige. This is the last oyster farm left in the historic town of Oysterville, and it's worth a stop in homage to the area's rich past, if for nothing else. If you don't like fresh oysters on the half-shell, try smoked oysters from Ekone Oysters in Westport, which come in all sorts of unconventional flavors like habanero and chili pepper. Oysterville Sea Farms also supports the peninsula's other industry by selling local cranberry products.

Know Your Capitals

South Bay, WA: Oyster Capital of the World

Kelso, WA: Smelt Capital of the World

Astoria, OR: Salmon Capital of the World

Corning, CA: Olive Capital of the World

Patterson, CA: Apricot Capital of the World

Gilroy, CA: Garlic Capital of the World

Castroville, CA: Artichoke Capital of the World

Oregon

That was my first real sense of the Northwest coast: driving through dense green woods along a road that traced the rim of a bowl-shaped curve, then suddenly below us, a sweep of ocean rolling out in a great skirt of water laced in foam. It was love at first sight.

—COLLEEN MCELROY,
Edge Walking on the Western Rim

Region Stats

LOCAL FLAVOR:

- **Beer:** Oregon's the second-largest producer of craft beer in the United States, with more than 75 operating breweries. The state's also the country's second-largest hops producer. Oregon brews are usually floral and hop-heavy, though nothing like NorCal über IPAs.

- **Wine:** Pinot noir from the Willamette Valley is some of the best in the country. The cool region's also known for pinot gris and chardonnay, to a lesser extent.

- **Seafood:** The coast is one long line of seafood shacks. Local specialties: fish-and-chips (albacore or cod, usually), clam chowder, fried razor clams, hot Dungeness crab sandwiches, oysters.

- **Hazelnuts:** The official state nut, accounting for 99 percent of the commercial US crop. Groves of hazelnut trees share space with vineyards in the Willamette Valley, and the nut shows up in everything from beer to baked goods.

- **Marionberrys:** A hybrid of a raspberry and a blackberry, this sweet-tart berry makes excellent pies, jams, and syrups.

KNOW: It is illegal for motorists to pump their own gas.

Congress created the Oregon Territory the same year that gold was discovered in California. The year was 1848, and from then on the American population followed the oft-quoted dictum popularized by newspaper editor Horace Greeley: "Go West, young man, and grow up with the country."

The vast majority went to California, chasing get-rich-quick dreams of fame and fortune. But many took the northern route to Oregon, where there was good farmland available to the first takers. Both were gambles, but those who chose Oregon knew that they had a long trail ahead of them, and when they reached the end they would have to work for their rewards. Oregonians knew more than anyone else that if you want something done, you need to do it yourself.

They still do—and that DIY ethos translates to a food culture on the cutting edge of the locavore revolution. It's a state of aging hippies who pick up local produce from their bountiful farmers markets; foodies who can recite whole Michael Pollan paragraphs from memory; energetic young hipsters who experiment with new cooking styles and ingredients; and working-class farmers and fishermen who operate much the same as their families have for generations.

Oregon was built by people taking a risk for reinvention, the people who lit out for the territory ahead of the rest. Many of its towns are named for places "back home": Portland, Salem, Newport, Ashland, McMinnville. But here they had a chance to make the world anew. And this time, they did it right.

Trips in Oregon

In and Around Portland
Discover what makes this the country's most exciting food city. (Page 65)

Willamette Valley
Pinot noir–tasting at mountaintop wineries puts you on top of the world. (Page 73)

I-5: Oregon
Lush valleys and surprising finds a few minutes off the busy interstate. (Page 85)

Highway 101: Oregon Coast
Wind your way down the coast on this beautiful drive, and eat plenty of local seafood along the way. (Page 99)

In and Around Portland

City Stats

LOCAL FLAVOR: Beer (Portland has the most microbreweries of any city in the nation), street food, coffee.

LOCAL FOOD FESTIVALS:

- **Oregon Brewers Fest** (July). Try suds from more than 80 breweries at this long-running celebration in Tom McCall Waterfront Park.

MORE INFO: Portland Convention & Visitors Bureau (www.travel portland.com)

For a while in 2007 and 2008, you couldn't open the *New York Times* without running into a story about Portland's culinary and cultural renaissance. The story of Portland's rise to foodie heaven has lost its newsworthiness, but this doesn't change the fact that exciting things are still happening daily in the City of Roses.

The truth is, Portland is probably one of the most exciting food cities in America. It's still cheap, for one thing—which has drawn a crowd of culinary artists and dreamers who have no interest in the heat of Manhattan and opened their own kitchens 3,000 miles away. They draw on the agricultural bounty of the Tualatin and Willamette valleys and the seafood from the Pacific, and don't worry as much about the old ways as they continually invent new ones.

Portland was originally settled in an area formerly known as "the clearing" at the confluence of the Willamette and Columbia rivers, halfway between Oregon City and Fort Vancouver. It had a population of 800 in 1851, which swelled to 17,000 by 1879. It was the most important port in the Northwest for most of the nineteenth century, until the railroad came to Seattle and ships no longer had to navigate the treacherous Columbia River. But the seedy roots of the rough-and-tumble port town still remain, even though the economy evened out.

The town is divided by the Willamette River, a major waterway, and the usual logic is that west Portland is more gentrified than hipster east

OREGON

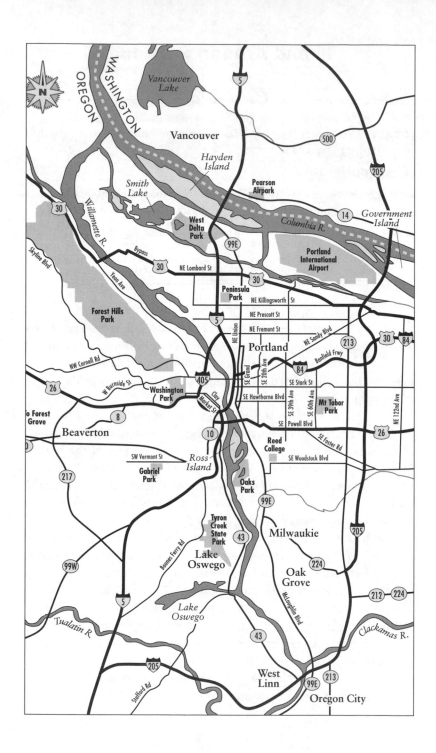

Portland. It's a town of bike paths and Olmsted-designed city parks; sidewalk cafes and microbreweries; North Face fleeces and Nalgene bottles. It's been named, at one time or another, one of the country's greenest, fittest, most sustainable, cleanest, artist-friendly, and all-around-best cities in America. It's a lovely place to visit.

 Voodoo Doughnut

22 SW 3rd Ave, Portland
MILE/EXIT: *302A*
503.241.4704
www.voodoodoughnut.com
OPEN: *24/7*
Cash only (but ATM on the premises)

It's gotta be some form of black magic that caused the owners of this colorful doughnut shop to create their crazy concoctions. Because how else could anyone conceptualize a bacon-maple bar—a normal maple bar literally covered in slices of crispy bacon—years before bacon (and bacon doughnuts) became trendy? Or a raised vanilla doughnut coated in Cap'n Crunch, appropriately called Captain My Captain? For a humble doughnut shop, Voodoo has garnered plenty of accolades for reinventing a treat best known as the domain of nighttime cops and Homer Simpson. The doughnuts have appeared on *Good Morning America*, *The Tonight Show*, Anthony Bordain's *No Reservations*—and, in 2008, Portland mayor Tom Potter declared Voodoo's Portland Crème the official "Doughnut of the City." Luckily, national press hasn't affected the bakery's fundamental quirkiness. The flagship store has brightly painted walls and eclectic decor, including a massive fiberglass doughnut mounted on the wall. It's a momentary trip into a funhouse, and immediately after you exit you see a large mural across the street echoing a common slogan: "Keep Portland Weird." Mission accomplished, guys.

KNOW: *The Texas Challenge doughnut—six times the size of the others—is free if eaten in 80 seconds or less.*

VARIOUS LOCATIONS *in northeast Portland (1501 NE Davis St; 503.235.2666) and Eugene (20 E Broadway; 541.868.8666)*

OREGON

 Pearl Bakery

102 NW 9th Ave, Portland
MILE/EXIT: 302B
503.827.0910
www.pearlbakery.com
OPEN: *Mon–Fri 6:30a–5:30p, Sat 7a–5p, Sun 8a–3p*

"Honest ingredients" is a phrase that's bandied about so much in West Coast foodie circles that it hardly has meaning anymore, but the Pearl Bakery is its embodiment: a bakery with integrity. It's an easy stop off I-5 if you're just passing through town, and a great place to refuel for the drive ahead (I'm a big fan of the espresso cookies, which will rocket you down to Ashland in no time). The bakery case is a gorgeous display of rich, French-inspired pastries and rustic loaves. The ingredients are local and sustainable. The ceilings are high, with the wrought-iron reinforcements that characterize Northwest architecture. Big windows let in light and look out on the Pearl District, a triumph of urban revitalization. Simply put: unless you're some sort of misanthrope, you'll leave the Pearl Bakery in high spirits.

The Ace Hotel

1022 SW Stark St, Portland
MILE/EXIT: 302B
503.228.2277
www.acehotel.com/Portland
OPEN: *Hotel open 24/7, hours for restaurants vary—call for details.*

If I ever become rich, famous, and eccentric enough to take up residence in a hotel, I'm going straight to the Ace. The chain of hipster hotels has been wildly successful because they give customers exactly what they want: stylish surroundings and good food. Room service at the Portland location is from Clyde Common, an excellent Northwest-cuisine restaurant off the lobby that mixes a mean cocktail as well as makes a great burger. At the other end of the lobby sits Stumptown Coffee, the best wake-up call possible. Finally, at the corner is Kenny & Zuke's Delicatessen, and old-world deli that has outsized pastrami sandwiches and large breakfasts. The whole complex radiates an aura of cool that's contagious.

PDX Food Pods

The pod people are everywhere, taking over empty parking lots in Portland's downtown. The food pods are semipermanent communities of food carts that band together to form a sort of mobile food court, and offer some of the best inventive and international cuisine in the city. Portland has more than 500 of these restaurants on wheels, representing practically every type of cuisine in the world. Some are broad (Mexican, Thai, Czech), some are super-specialized (grilled cheese, dim sum), but all offer restaurant-quality food at dirt cheap prices. The Internet is the best place to get the latest on the mobile kitchens—there are tons of blogs, websites, and even apps devoted to them—but if you want to ramble, the best pods downtown are at 10th and Alder, 5th and Stark, and 3rd and Ash.

 **Stumptown Coffee**

4525 SE Division St, Portland
MILE/EXIT: 301
503.230.7702
www.stumptowncoffee.com
OPEN: *Mon–Fri 6a–7p, Sat–Sun 7a–7p*

This is the original location and main roasting plant of the famous Portland coffee chain, which pretty much revolutionized the Northwest's coffee shop scene when it opened in 1999. Coffee shop culture in the early '90s was all about quality beans and skilled roasters, but a good cuppa wasn't enough for Stumptown owner Duane Sorenson. He wanted to know where his beans came from, and led a new vanguard of roasters committed to sustainable business practices and direct relationships with the growers themselves. Sorenson still travels around the world to visit his producers and work with them one-on-one, often paying more than market rate for the beans to ensure that he's getting the highest quality and also giving the growers the best deal. Back in Portland, the beans are vetted in a cupping laboratory, lovingly roasted to Stumptown specifications, and then delivered to the cafe, where each cup of coffee is made to the customer's specs. A simple drip coffee can run up to $4, but this particular cup of coffee will

OREGON

Portland Brewery Pub Crawl

Portland's a beer town, no doubt about it. It has more breweries per capita than any other city in the country—since it's impossible to try them all, here's an abbreviated pub crawl to sample the best of the best. Start in the Pearl, in the five-block area known as the Brewery Blocks because it was built on the former site of Blitz-Weinhard Brewery. Don't miss **Rogue** (try inventive brews like Chipotle Ale), **Deschutes** (known for its creamy Black Butte Porter), and **BridgePort** (don't miss the crisp Blue Heron Pale Ale). Then head across the river. **Amnesia Brewing** is my favorite brewpub in Portland, just because I like the casual, backyard barbecue feel and the just-hoppy-enough IPA. **Widmer Bros.**, an Oregon institution, has an enviable location on the water and a fantastic hefeweizen. **Lucky Labrador** is dog-themed, dog-friendly, solar-powered, and offers the popular, citrusy Hawthorne's Best Bitter.

change the way you look at the beverage forever. All Stumptown locations are incredibly, almost painfully hip, with clean modern lines and a chalkboard menu displaying the day's coffee menu.

KNOW: *Before it was a coffee shop, this location was a hair salon called Hair Bender, a name that now graces a strong espresso blend.*

VARIOUS LOCATIONS *in downtown Portland (128 SW 3rd Ave; 503.295.6144), southeast Portland (3356 SE Belmont St; 503.232.8889), Portland's Pearl District (see Ace Hotel, page 68), and Seattle's Capitol Hill neighborhood (1115 12th Ave; 206.323.1544 and 616 E Pine St; 206.329.0155)*

 Pok Pok

3226 SE Division St, Portland

MILE/EXIT: 301

503.232.1387

www.pokpokpdx.com

OPEN: *Daily 11:30a–10p*

In a town full of Thai restaurants, this popular spot sets itself apart from the pack by what's not on the menu. Instead of the usual Thai standards like pad thai and chicken curry, Pok Pok has gathered tons of accolades for featuring the pub and street food of Southeast Asia, most notably northern Thailand, where the owners hail from. Challenge your palate with signature items like Kai Yaang, a roasted game hen rubbed with lemongrass, garlic, pepper, and cilantro, with a spicy sweet-and-sour dipping sauce. Another crowd-pleaser is the Vietnamese Fish Sauce Wings, from the daytime grill cook's family recipe—chicken wings marinated in fish sauce, garlic, and sugar, deep fried, tossed in a caramelized fish sauce, and served with a salad. Pok Pok is located in a small converted house, and the dining room and heated patio can fill up quickly. While you wait, try a signature cocktail at the Whiskey Soda Lounge across the street.

KNOW: *The water's supposed to taste like that. The grassy flavor comes from pandanus leaf floating in the pitcher—a Thai tradition.*

Bob's Red Mill Whole Grain Store

5000 SE International Way, Milwaukie
MILE/EXIT: 300B
DISTANCE FROM HWY: 7.1 miles
503.607.6455
www.bobsredmill.com
OPEN: *Mon–Fri 6a–6p, Sat 7a–5p*

Grains are milled here the same way they were hundreds of years ago, thanks to the relentlessness of owner Bob Moor. In the late 1970s, Moor became interested in historic flour mills, and traveled around the country with his wife, Charlee, to defunct grain mills to get his hands on authentic French millstones from the 1800s. He succeeded, and grinds grain for his mostly organic products using old world techniques. See the millstones in action during the hour-long tour of the mill, or just walk around the grounds yourself to view the 18-foot waterwheel, displays of historic milling equipment, and the working stone mill. The retail store carries the full line of Bob's Red Mill's 300-plus products, and an on-site cafe serves breakfast and lunch made with BRM ingredients. The cafe doubles as a savvy marketing ploy—after a delicious, restorative plate of flapjacks, grits, or steel-cut oats, all you'll want to do is buy a bag so to re-create your meal at home.

TOURS: *Offered weekdays at 10a (free, one hour)*

McMenamins Hillside Brewery & Public House

1505 SW Sunset Blvd, Portland

MILE/EXIT: 297

503.225.0047

www.mcmenamins.com

OPEN: *Mon–Thu 11a–12a, Fri–Sat 11a–1a, Sun 12–11p*

When brothers Mike and Brian McMenamin opened this brewpub in southwest Portland in 1985, they had little idea that it would expand to an empire of more than 50 breweries, hotels, and movie theaters. We'll start with the brewery part: McMenamins is, in many ways, just another Northwest brewer, with a strong presence throughout Washington and Oregon, turning out fine beers (I'm partial to the raspberry-flavored Ruby on a hot day in the summer—it was the first fruit beer in the United States) and excellent burgers (get the Communication Breakdown with cheddar, mushrooms, and peppers). Then the brothers decided to stretch the boundaries of the basic pub concept of a communal gathering place by opening hotels and movie theaters under the McMenamins name. These feature McMenamins brews on draft, and are beloved by locals for their laid-back atmosphere and cheap prices (especially during happy hour). Though every location is unique—the brothers have a weakness for buildings on the National Historic Register—McMenamins pubs and gathering places have an overall vibe and consistency that can, at times, make them feel like a larger corporate entity. But at their core, the value proposition is the same: you know exactly what you're getting when you walk into a McMenamins, and that's definitely not a bad thing.

KNOW: *The original Hillsdale location is filled with McMenamins history. The bowl-shaped planter by the bar once held the mash for the brothers's first on-site brew, and the original, handwritten brew sheet is framed near the front door.*

VARIOUS LOCATIONS *in Oregon (greater Portland, McMinnville, Salem, Eugene, Roseburg, Lincoln City, Gearhardt) and Washington (Seattle, Olympia, Centralia, Vancouver)*

Willamette Valley

Trip Stats

START: Portland

END: Salem

LENGTH: 47 miles

LOCAL FLAVOR: Wine (Pinot noir is king, but chardonnay and pinot gris are close runners-up).

BEST TIME: All wineries open their doors on Memorial Day and Thanksgiving weekends—it's crowded, but there's a festival vibe in the air.

LOCAL FOOD FESTIVALS:

- **International Pinot Noir Celebration:** McMinnville (July). Join West Culinary luminaries for a three-day event celebrating the temperamental grape.

WORD OF WARNING: Most wineries don't have regular tasting room hours—you'll need to call for an appointment at the smaller ones.

MORE INFO: Willamette Valley Visitors Association (www.oregonwine country.org)

OREGON

It's impossible for me to think about the Willamette Valley without thinking about Oregon Trail, the vaguely educational computer game that most of us born in the early 1980s had on our rudimentary elementary school computers. The premise was to survive a wagon train from Independence, Missouri, to the Willamette Valley and navigate all the struggles one would encounter along the way.

Though most of us only played it to hunt buffalo and see who would die from dysentery, the game perhaps served a higher purpose I wasn't capable of seeing at the time. When you reached the end, a tinny victory tune played over a shot of pixilated paradise: pine trees, green pastureland cut by a river, purple mountains rising in the distance. This is my vision of the Willamette Valley, a prosperous, fertile wonderland

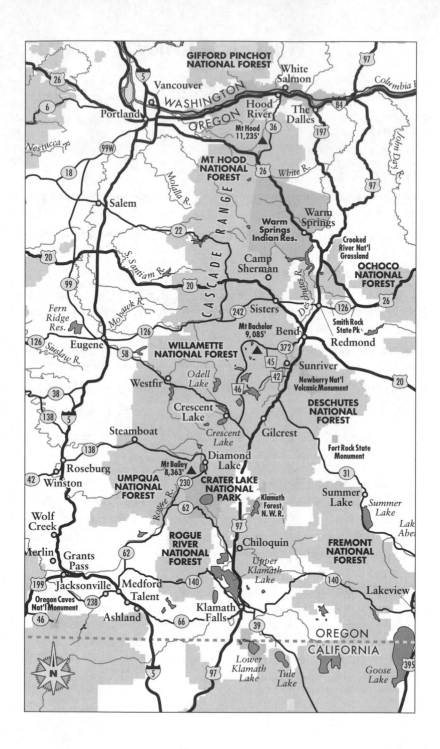

that must be what many of the early settlers dreamed of finding on their arduous wagon trains out West.

It seems a miracle that anyone went to Oregon at all. Stories reached the Midwest and East about an available land so fertile you barely had to touch a plow to produce a banner crop yield. An estimated 53,000 settlers emigrated over to the Oregon Trail between 1840 and 1860—a pretty astonishing number considering the journey was fraught with danger and the promise of a better life was based on nothing but rumors, stories, and a couple rudimentary maps.

But go West they did, and out in the fertile Willamette Valley they tended crops and created their own paradise. Today the valley is home to hazelnut groves, Christmas tree farms, hop vines, and nurseries, but wine is by far its biggest agricultural output. The mineral-rich soils turn out to be perfect for the vine, and the cool climate echoes that of Burgundy. Some of the world's best pinot noirs come from Oregon, and have an earthiness and elegance that separates them from their California counterparts. You can taste the moody weather and rich soil in each sip. It's a temperamental wine patiently coaxed to its own potential.

The tasting rooms at these wineries have a haunting beauty all their own. Many are located up gravel roads at the top of Douglas fir–lined hillsides, and command expansive views of the valley and snowy mountains in the distance. Some of these wineries are only 20 minutes from downtown Portland, but you'll feel like you've truly escaped into the clouds. You've made it to the territory. You feel like you're on the top of the world.

ON THE ROAD

Penner-Ash Wine Cellars

15771 NE Ribbon Ridge Rd, Newberg

MILE/EXIT: 23

DISTANCE FROM HWY: 6.5 miles

503.554.5545

www.pennerash.com

OPEN: *Wed–Sun 11a–5p*

A short drive up a gravel road takes you to this modern winery carved into the hillside. The tasting room is all blonde wood and wraparound windows, which let in natural light and afford panoramic views of the surrounding vineyards and Chehalem Valley. On a clear day, you can see Mount Hood and Mount Jefferson. Penner-Ash is known for its well-structured, earthy pinot noirs and syrahs—taste your way through them guided by the friendly, helpful tasting room staff. Windows into the wine-making space give you a view of the gravity-flow process winemaker and founder Lynn Penner-Ash employs, a three-level approach that utilizes gravity to minimize the damage from forceful pumping of wine from stage to stage. A lovely terrace features a pretty garden with sunflowers and the same million-dollar views.

TOURS: *Sat & Sun, 10a (call for reservation)*

Duck Pond Cellars

23145 Hwy 99W, Dundee
MILE/EXIT: 25
503.538.3199
www.duckpondcellars.com
OPEN: *May–Sept daily 10a–5p, Oct–Apr daily 11a–5p*

Wine tasting novices should stop here—the tasting is free, the wines are approachable and affordable, and the laid-back vibe puts you instantly at ease. Duck Pond has nearly 900 acres of vineyards in the Willamette Valley and the Columbia Valley in Washington State, and the geographic diversity allows the winery to produce a wide range of vintages. The Willamette pinot noir is a classic, and the Washington reds—cabernet sauvignon, merlot, sangiovese, and syrah—are earthy and fruit-forward. Grab your glass and ramble on the lushly landscaped grounds, which include a tranquil duck pond and a large patio offset with hanging baskets of flowers. There's also a gift shop with wine accessories and kitchen goods, and a deli for picnic supplies. Congratulations, you've officially outgrown your training wheels.

Argyle Winery

691 Hwy 99W, Dundee
MILE/EXIT: 26
888.427.4953
www.argylewinery.com
OPEN: *Daily 11a–5p*

Argyle is one of the most well-known and best Willamette Valley producers, declared "Oregon's premier winery" by *Wine Spectator* in 2000. Founders Rollin Sotes and Brian Crosser started the winery in 1987 after a quest to find the best cool-weather wine-growing area in the New World. They were the first to use Dijon-clone chardonnay and pinot noir grapes produce the nuanced sparkling wine they're now known for. Today Argyle operates four vineyards around the region, and has earned LIVE certification for its commitment to sustainability and grower health. The tasting room's industrial setting right off the highway leaves something to be desired, but the tasting bar inside is made from retired wine casks, and framed photographs of the valley throughout the seasons help set the right tone.

KNOW: *Watch for paranormal activity: the Victorian farmhouse where the winery's located is called The Spirithouse, after the ghost of an early 1900s pioneer woman who's said to roam these hills.*

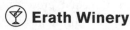 Erath Winery

9409 NE Worden Hill Rd, Dundee
MILE/EXIT: 26
503.538.3318
www.erath.com
OPEN: *Daily 11a–5p*

Dick Erath was one of Oregon's wine-making pioneers when he started Erath Winery in the late 1960s, and marked his place in history by releasing the first wine from the now-acclaimed Dundee Hills in 1974. Erath first started making pinot noir from California clones, but quickly looked to imported French vines to create a richer wine. The fruits of his labor can be enjoyed in the winery's cabinlike tasting room, set in a clearing of fir trees with views of the vineyard-covered Dundee Hills. Inside isn't anything special, but if the weather's fine, sit outside on the flagstone patio under a trellis of wisteria, surrounded by petunias and marigolds in wine barrel planters.

Sokol Blosser Winery

5000 NE Sokol Blosser Ln, Dayton
MILE/EXIT: 29
503.864.2282
www.sokolblosser.com
OPEN: *Daily 10a–4p*

College sweethearts Susan and Bill Blosser followed in the footsteps of generations of homesteaders when they purchased a prune orchard here in 1971 and, through their own sweat and labor, turned it into one of the region's most prominent and environmentally sustainable wineries. Run today by their children, Alex and Alison Sokol Blosser, the winery produces top-notch pinot noirs from 87 estate acres, under the help of Robert Mondavi veteran winemaker Russ Rosner. Don't overlook the winery's blends—try the soft red Medetrina or the crisp, citrusy Evolution. Sokol Blosser has shown incredible dedication to environmental preservation and has pretty much every certification under the sun: It was the first winery declared Salmon Safe, the first winery building to become LEED certified, and has been certified organic by the USDA and Oregon Department of Agriculture. The winery is also LIVE certified for its use of solar panels, biodiesel fuel, and recycled materials. Tours are available by appointment.

Red Ridge Farms

5510 NE Breyman Orchards Rd, Dayton
MILE/EXIT: 29
503.864.8502
www.redridgefarms.com
OPEN: *Wed–Sun 9a–5p*

What started as a lavender farm and specialty nursery has grown into a full-scale olive oil producer and winery in the heart of the Willamette Valley. More than 11,000 Arbequina olive trees (a Spanish variety strong enough to withstand Northwest winters) provide the fruit for the fresh, peppery oil released under the Oregon Olive Mill label. Taste your way through the vintages at Red Ridge Farms, which also has a gift shop that would do Martha Stewart proud, a small deli with local cheeses, and gorgeously landscaped garden grounds perfect for picnics. The Durant family, who owns the farm and state-of-the-art olive press, also cultivates 60 acres of vineyards producing pinot noir, pinot gris, and chardonnay. The farm's leafy setting is a great place to try the wines, and to escape into nature for an hour or an afternoon.

Vista Hills Vineyards & Winery

6475 Hilltop Ln, Dayton

MILE/EXIT: 29

503.864.3200

www.vistahillsvineyard.com

OPEN: *Daily noon–5p*

The bungalow-style Treehouse Tasting Room looks like something straight out of the pages of *Sunset* magazine, embodying the casual modern attitude of the West to a tee. The building is set at the top of a hill overlooking 42 acres of estate pinot noir and pinot gris, surrounded by a curtain of Douglas fir and white oak, all reflected in the calm pond next to the tasting room. Inside, high ceilings and plenty of windows give the room a spacious, airy feel. Sit on chairs made from old oak barrels, or take your glass outside to the deck and enjoy the view. Vista Hills's pinot noir is rich and round; the pinot gris is crisp and uncomplicated. All in all, this winery's a pleasant, casual spot to take a breather.

Domaine Drouhin

6750 Breyman Orchards Rd, Dayton

MILE/EXIT: 29

503.864.2700

www.domainedrouhin.com

OPEN: *Aug–Oct daily 11a–4p*

If you only visit one winery in the Willamette Valley, make it this one, the New World outpost of the celebrated Drouhin wine family of Burgundy. It's worth a visit for the chateau-style tasting room alone, set on acres of rolling farmland and vineyards that are the closest you'll come to replicating the European wine-tasting experience in the states. But the stunning setting isn't the only reason to visit—its pinot noirs and chardonnays the winery produces outclass most of its neighbors for their elegant structure, complex flavors, and clean finish. The Drouhin family came to America when Robert Drouhin, grandson of the winery's founder, traveled to the West Coast on a fact-finding mission in the late 1960s and became intrigued by Oregon's similarity to Burgundy and its potential for first-class wine-making. When an Oregon pinot nearly beat out a Drouhin pinot at the Judgment of Paris (see page 181), Drouhin purchased land in Oregon, intent on replicating the family's success 7,000 miles away. It worked. If you have time, do make a reservation for the Drouhin Experience tour ($25), which gives an overview of the winery and walks guests through a comparison of Burgundy and Oregon wine that's worth its educational weight in gold.

TOURS: *Wed–Sun 10a and 1p (reservations required)*

KNOW: *Interested in learning more about the story?* Check out Susan Sokol Blosser's 2006 memoir, At Home in the Vineyard: Cultivating a Winery, an Industry and a Life.

Stoller Vineyards

16161 NE McDougall Rd, Dayton

MILE/EXIT: 31

503.864.3404

www.stollervineyards.com

OPEN: *Daily 11a–5p*

The farm life has never been far from owner Bill Stoller's mind—he grew up on this property, back when it was the biggest turkey farm in Oregon. When the turkey industry flagged, he bought the 373-acre property with his wife, Cathy, on a hunch that the rocky terrain, low-yielding soils, and steep hillsides were a recipe for excellent pinot noir. The winery's pinot is top-notch—all blackberry jam and smoky finish—but it's the family's passion and dedication to the land that sets it apart. Stoller is solar powered and LEED, LIVE, Salmon Safe, and OCSW certified. More than that, the tasting room staff is friendly and ready to educate, and a visit to the winery can result in a crash course in Oregon wine-making. Stay for a round of Frisbee golf on a nine-hole course that winds its way through the vineyards—Frisbees are provided free of charge, and the staff will ensure that you always have a glass of wine in hand.

KNOW: *Spend a night in the estate vineyards at one of three vacation homes for rent on the property.*

Harvest Fresh Grocery & Deli

251 NE 3rd St, McMinnville

MILE/EXIT: 37

503.472.5740

www.harvestfresh.com

OPEN: *Mon–Fri 8a–8p, Sat 8a–7p, Sun 10a–7p*

McMinnville has come into its own in the past few decades as the heart of Oregon wine country, but it has always been the agricultural center of the Willamette Valley. This natural foods store is a great place to stop for grab-and-go items made from local, organic ingredients and hormone-free meats. It's conveniently located on a downtown corner, and offers local produce, microbrews and wines, a fresh juice and smoothie bar, a bakery and coffee stand, and a deli with hearty sandwiches, large salads, fresh bagels, roast chicken, and boxed lunches to go. Sit at the wrought-iron sidewalk tables and soak up the lively street scene on McMinnville's well-preserved, turn-of-the-century main drag.

 Red Fox Bakery & Café

328 NE Evans St, McMinnville

MILE/EXIT: 37

503.434.5098

www.redfoxbakery.com

OPEN: *Tue–Sat 7a–4p, Sun 7a–1p*

A small but mighty selection of pastries awaits customers at this cozy downtown cafe, including cinnamon rolls, incredibly moist macaroons, breads, croissants, and other baked goods made at the whim of the owner. Sandwiches to go are more inventive than the usual deli fare, like one made with turkey and Granny Smith apples, or the peanut butter and house-made strawberry jam. A bonus cookie is thrown in with every sandwich order. The cafe itself has warm yellow walls and a smattering of tables, serves good coffee, and provides board games for customers—it's a solid option to refuel or take a breather before plunging back into the rhythm of the road.

 Crescent Café

526 NE 3rd St, McMinnville

MILE/EXIT: 37

503.435.2655

OPEN: *Wed–Fri 7a–1p, Sat–Sun 8a–1p*

Get in line early for a breakfast at this popular local joint, where fresh ingredients and down-home cooking combine to produce one of the best meals in town. Blueberry pancakes come to the table bulging with fresh fruit, scrambles showcase the best local produce and meat, and the fresh blood-orange juice just needs to be ordered to be believed. Everything about this place is friendly and inviting: the warm welcome from co-owner Michael McKenney, the good vibrations from throngs of break-fasters happy with their meals, the low lighting that gives the room a pinkish glow. Walls are covered with playful tromp l'oiel windows and photographs of old McMinnville. I can't think of a better way to set your-self up for a day of wine tasting. This is definitely a breakfast to remember.

KNOW: *There's often a line, and the only way to bypass it is to get there early. If you are on your own, you might be seated at a table with other diners. Be prepared to get to know your neighbors.*

Brigittine Monks Gourmet Confections

2330 SW Walker Ln, Amity

MILE/EXIT: 41

503.835.8080

www.brigittine.org

OPEN: *Mon–Sat 9a–5:30p, Sun 1–5p*

I'm not gonna lie—a visit to this fudge-producing monastery is a pretty surreal experience. A short drive up a gravel road flanked by open fields ends at the big stone and wrought-iron fence that is the entrance to the monastery. The Brigittine order was founded in 1370 and dedicated themselves to a life of prayer and work—the monks' work here is to pro-duce great fudge made with real chocolate, fresh dairy, and local nuts. The tasting room is in the main building past a little garden. Knock, and a monk in a long gray habit answers the door, offers you a tray of samples, and talks about the monastery, his order, and its fudge production. The fudge itself is good and rich and tastes like the ingredients it's made from;

don't miss the hazelnut. A prominent sign reminds you that this is a place of prayer, and asks you to observe silence, but the monks can be surprisingly chatty in the tasting room.

KNOW: *This is the only Brigittine monastery in the world. If you're interested in learning more about the order, select services are open to the public.*

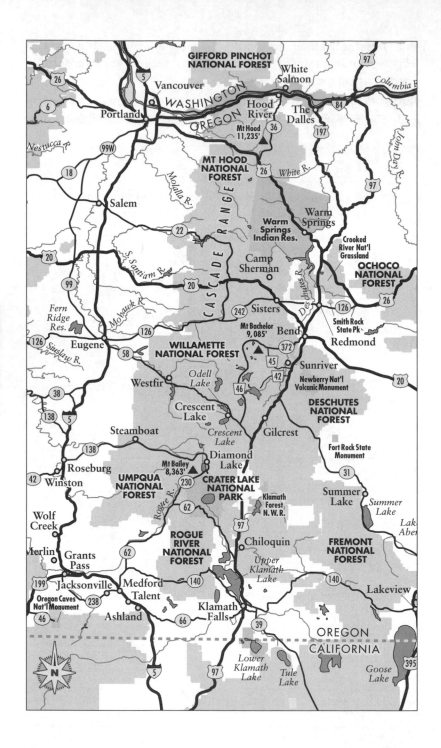

I-5: Oregon

START: Portland

END: Ashland

LENGTH: 286 miles

LOCAL FLAVOR: Artisinal cheesemakers, chocolatiers, coffee roasters, smokehouses, bakers, and more.

BEST TIME: Summer has the best local produce and the best opportunities for outdoor recreation.

WORD OF WARNING: Be careful driving in the winter on the hilly passes through the Siskiyous. Bring chains, stay out of the way of snowplows and sanding trucks, and check www.tripcheck.com for road status before you go.

MORE INFO: Southern Oregon Visitors Association (www.southern oregon.org)

OREGON

Southern Oregon seems stuck in the past—not because it's been left behind, but because it just hasn't seen a reason to change. Old-fashioned soda fountains still operate on small nineteenth-century main streets. A top local news story is about swear words written in permanent marker on school white boards. In many ways, this part of the state has been immune to the factory farm takeover—not because of its radicalism, but because of its indifference. Fascinating how progressives and isolationists can find common ground on which to fight the good fight.

The first part of the drive follows the lush Willamette Valley to Salem. I-5 is straight and boring, all fields and farmland; if you have time, I highly recommend taking old Highway 99 through Oregon wine country instead. Things get more interesting once you hit Eugene, the second-biggest city in the state, home to the University of Oregon, birthplace of writer Ken Kesey, and known for its natural beauty and range of outdoor opportunities, as well as for its history of radicalism and anarchism.

After Eugene the road begins climbing through the tree-covered Siskiyou foothills, and then opens into the Rogue River Valley.

I love the Rogue River Valley. It's sometimes called the "Italy of Oregon" for its Mediterranean climate and focus on local flavors, and its well-preserved small towns are home to bakeries, chocolatiers, smokehouses, microbreweries, and more culinary delights. It's a pleasant surprise to find so much good stuff in a relatively isolated region—though the growing influx of cultural tourists for Ashland's annual Oregon Shakespeare Festival is shaping the region's future.

Times might change, but change doesn't mean that the state will lose its hard-won independent character. To Oregon's immense credit, it's not a question of the new superceding the old; it's the old evolving into the new. This is the region to watch over the next decade.

ON THE ROAD

 Fifth Street Public Market

296 E 5th Ave, Eugene
MILE/EXIT: 194B
541.484.0383
www.5stmarket.com
OPEN: *Mon–Sat 8:30a–7p, Sun 9a–6p*

Support local business at this indoor/outdoor public market, which has been an anchor in Eugene's downtown business district since 1976. The original brick-and-wood building was once a poultry business, but has been revamped to hide most of its feathered roots. Three stories of local shops, restaurants, and patio cafes make it a good roadside stop with options to please everyone. Marche is an upscale restaurant serving French-inspired Northwest cooking, but its sister cafe in the main food court and nearby gourmet food store Marche Provisions are affordable alternatives. The market's best asset is its outdoor courtyard, with a brick fountain and picnic tables, and the balconies that overlook it from higher stories. Order something cheap and quick in the food court, which has everything from falafels to seafood, and then grab a table and soak up the freewheeling Eugene scene.

 Voodoo Doughnut

20 E Broadway, Eugene
MILE/EXIT: 194B
541.868.8666
www.voodoodoughnut.com
OPEN: *24/7*
Cash only (but ATM on the premises)

The Eugene outpost of Portland's famously quirky doughnut shop, known for unique flavors like bacon-maple, Cap'n Crunch cereal, bubble gum, mango, Butterfinger bar, and more. (For more details, see page 67.)

 King Estate Winery

80854 Territorial Rd, Eugene
MILE/EXIT: 182
DISTANCE FROM HWY: 15 miles
541.942.9874
www.kingestate.com
OPEN: *Daily 11a–9p*

Pass through Lane County's rolling hills, fields, and dairy and horse farms on the winding 15-mile road that leads to this hillside winery. The stunning tasting room is built in the style of an Italian villa, and serves up outstanding mountain and Lorane Valley views, especially from the huge outdoor patio. This isn't the type of winery you hit on the way to somewhere else; this is the type of winery you linger at all afternoon. Try the King Estate's signature pinot noir and pinot gris in the elegant tasting room, then hit the onsite restaurant for a fabulous lunch. Gourmet burgers and sandwiches are just on the affordable side of high-end, made with produce from the winery's 30 acres of organic orchards and gardens. Artisan cheese and charcuterie plates are good options during off-hours. King Estate sits on a thousand-acre parcel of land, including 470 acres of organically certified vineyards. A 45-minute walking tour gives newcomers an overview of the winery and company, and is worth doing if just to see more of the building and grounds. Whatever you do, build in some time to kick back and hang out here; I guarantee you won't be in a hurry to leave.

OREGON

K-R Drive Inn

201 Long John Rd, Oakland
MILE/EXIT: 148
541.849.2570
www.krdriveinn.com
OPEN: *Hours vary by season; call for details*

Known to Oregonians as "that ice cream place at the Rice Hill exit," this roadside shack has been serving ice cream cones to tired travelers for more than 40 years. Umpqua Dairy provides the drive-in with 38 sublime flavors of ice cream, made with fresh cream and local products from Northwest growers. The ordering system is a little Soup Nazi–esque—check out the handwritten "Rules" by the side of the window—but the massive cones are worth any inconvenience. The menu also offers shakes and ice cream sodas, along with a classic hamburger topped with lettuce, tomatoes, pickles, onions, and Thousand Island dressing. K-R's building has expanded over the years from one converted double-wide trailer to three, and because of its unique architecture there's no inside seating or bathrooms. A shady picnic area provides seating for the restaurant.

Tolly's Restaurant

115 Locust St, Oakland
MILE/EXIT: 148
541.459.3796
www.tollys-restaurant.com
OPEN: *Sun–Thu 11a–3p, Fri–Sat 11a–7p*

This old-fashioned pharmacy-turned-restaurant fits right in with the other brick storefronts on tiny Oakland's 1890s main street. A marble-topped soda fountain is the first thing you notice when you walk in—sit on a stool and sample phosphates, shakes, and other 1950s specialties. Bypass the curving staircase that leads to the second floor restaurant, which has a forgettable and expensive menu, and instead head into the adjoining bar for the "world's best burger." It's a half-pound beast made from natural grass-fed beef, and can be topped with ingredients ranging from mushrooms and cheddar to ham, pineapple, and house-made Reuben dressing. The nostalgic theme comes across as a bit forced (nothing like the delightfully unaffected soda fountain at the Grants Pass Pharmacy), but hey—a good burger is a good burger, and there's also an old-fashioned candy shop to pick up some treats for the road.

🍴 Wolf Creek Tavern

100 Front St, Wolf Creek

MILE/EXIT: 76

541.866.2474

www.historicwolfcreekinn.com

OPEN: *Hours vary by season; call for details*

Join centuries of weary travelers who have found respite at this historic inn and tavern, including President Rutherford B. Hayes, Jack London, and Clark Gable. The white Victorian hotel was built in 1883 by local entrepreneur Henry Smith as a "first-class traveler hotel" for passengers on the six-day stagecoach ride between Portland and Sacramento. The State of Oregon bought the property in 1976 and painstakingly restored it to its former historical glory, down to the original paint colors (check out the north room's fireplace, which still has boot marks from generations of men propping up their feet by the fire). It's still a functioning inn (with surprisingly reasonable rates), and also an old-fashioned tavern, with a short menu of breakfast classics and simple lunches. Mondays through Wednesdays, the tavern offers family-style dinners; Wednesday fried chicken night is a favorite.

KNOW: *Smith planted acres of orchards around the property, and the big pear and apple trees outside the dining room are his original trees from 1885.*

🍽 Grants Pass Pharmacy

414 SW 6th St, Grants Pass

MILE/EXIT: 58

541.476.4262

www.grantspasspharmacy.com

OPEN: *Mon–Fri 9a–7p, Sat 9a–6p*

My only experience with soda fountains is from Jimmy Stewart movies and Archie comics, and part of me has always been skeptical that they ever existed. So imagine my surprise to find a functional one still in existence, a time capsule back to a simpler time when hanging out in a pharmacy all day was the norm. This particular specimen has been

OREGON

unchanged since its heyday, with retro diner stools, a big mirror and wooden counter, and an old-timey, wholesome charm. Prices haven't changed either: Phosphates (flavors added to soda water, essentially) cost 25 cents, and there are shakes, malts, ice cream floats, sundaes, and banana splits. Retro touches like milk shakes in metal cups and vintage Coca-Cola napkin holders complete the picture, but they aren't there for show—they just haven't been changed since they were in vogue. The best news for road warriors? Coffee still costs only a dime.

Cary's of Oregon

413 Union Ave, Grants Pass
MILE/EXIT: 58
541.474.0030
www.carysoforegon.com
OPEN: *Mon–Fri 9a–5p, Sat 10a–2p*

"Soft-crunch" English toffee is the specialty and only offering at this Grants Pass sweet shop. Originally started as a holiday tradition for Cary Cound and his family from a recipe passed down from his wife's grandfather, it's now evolved into a full business, especially brisk during Christmastime. Unlike the crunchy Almond Roca style of toffee, Cary's has a softer, more pliable texture—it's not hard, but it's not chewy either, with a nice graininess that melts in your mouth. Toffee comes in milk and dark chocolate, with add-ins like Oregon hazelnuts, toasted almonds, and espresso, and it's all made with creamery butter and local ingredients whenever possible. Sample to your heart's content in the small retail shop. And come Christmas, there's always mail order.

Rogue Creamery

311 N Front St, Central Point
MILE/EXIT: 35
866.396.4704
www.roguecreamery.com
OPEN: *Mon–Fri 9a–5p, Sat 9a–6p, Sun 11a–5p*

In the 1950s, founder and owner Tom Vella (of Sonoma's Vella Cheese Company, see page 201) traveled to France and talked his way into the inner sanctum of the Roquefort Association of cheesemakers. When he returned to the states, Vella switched the focus of his 20-year-old creamery to blue, and re-created cheese caves in the French style. The resulting Oregon Blue vein cheese was an instant success, and the rest, as they say, is history. In 2002, Vella's son, Ignacio "Ig" Vella, decided to focus full-time on Vella Cheese Co. and sold Rogue to Cary Bryant and Dave Gremmels, who continue Vella's tradition while constantly pushing the company forward. Rogue River Blue is now the company's flagship cheese, ripened eight months wrapped in grape leaves soaked with Oregon pear brandy. Rogue also produces the complex Crater Lake Blue, Oregonzola, and Smokey Blue (smoked overnight in hazelnut shells). The staff is liberal with the samples in the tasting room as you taste your way through them, and you'll find a window into the production facility, photos of the cheese-making process, and awards on the wall.

KNOW: *The shop also has sausage, Gary West jerky, and bread if you want to make a picnic of it.*

🛍 Lillie Belle Farms

211 N Front St, Central Point
MILE/EXIT: 35
541.664.2815
www.lilliebellefarms.com
OPEN: *Mon–Fri 9a–5p, Sat 9a–6p, Sun 11a–5p*

Chocolatier Jeff Shepherd must have a lot of fun when he gets to work in the morning. This small artisan chocolatier consistently turns out some of the most inventive flavors to hit the chocolate world since M&Ms added peanuts. Sample them at this tiny shop next to the Rogue Creamery, whose Smokey Blue Cheese stars in its own truffle (it's divine). Also try the black pepper chocolate, sample marionberry and other berry flavors from the family's organic farm, and bite into the hippie crunch made with dark chocolate over caramelized chunks of rice. Edible art and sculptures, made by a local artist, are also available in the shop.

🍴 Roosters Restaurant

350 E Barnett Rd, Medford

MILE/EXIT: 27

541.779.3895

www.roostershomestylecooking.com

OPEN: *Mon–Tue, Sun 6:30a–3p; Wed–Sat 6:30a–8p*

Appropriately, the best time to visit Roosters Restaurant is at dawn. Join local early birds gorging on fresh-out-of-the-oven cinnamon rolls the size of your head, well-executed breakfast standards, and thick slices of pie made with whatever's in season in the Rogue Valley. The vibe in here is decidedly small town, with vinyl booths and the kind of waitresses who call you "hon" and make sure you always have enough coffee. Rooster paraphernalia is everywhere, but it comes across as homespun, not overly oppressive. This is comfort food at its very best: try the massive portions of steak and eggs and other breakfasts fit for a logger. I wouldn't kick a slice of pie out of bed, either.

Harry & David Country Village

1314 Center Dr, Medford

MILE/EXIT: 27

877.322.8000

www.harryanddavid.com

OPEN: *Mon 9:30a–7p; Tue–Thu, Sun 9a–7p; Fri–Sat 9a–8p*

The Rogue River Valley is famous for its pears—a fact company founder Sam Rosenburg banked on when he sold his prestigious Sorrento Hotel in Seattle in 1910 and moved to a 240-acre pear ranch in the Rogue River Valley. He died four years later, and his sons Harry and David took over the business. They rechristened their father's Cornice pears "Royal Riviera" to appeal to the fancy of a growing consumer class, and the pears were a success—that is, until the Depression hit and the market for luxury goods dried up. So the brothers got creative: they launched one of the country's oldest catalog mail-order services in 1934, pioneered a fruit-of-the-month club in 1938, and ensured their place in holiday traditions by introducing the something-for-everyone Tower of Treats in 1947. Today you can tour the factory and watch workers hand-pack each pear,

Ashland

Ashland is a haven of cultural activity and artistic energy, halfway between Portland and San Francisco. It's developed as such because of the annual **Oregon Shakespeare Festival**, which floods a town of 20,000 residents with 125,000 visitors annually. The festival was established in 1935 during the Depression on a restored Elizabethan stage and has been a hit ever since. The Tudor-themed and so-pretty downtown is pleasant to walk around, or you can enjoy a beer or glass of local wine on a deck overlooking the creek that runs through town.

then visit the bakery that turns out more than 130,000 fruitcakes a year. Don't miss the chocolate samples or the factory store when you're done.

TOURS: *Mon–Fri 9:15a, 10:30a, 12:30p, 1:45p ($5; reservations recommended)*

Standing Stone Brewing Company

101 Oak St, Ashland
MILE/EXIT: 19
541.482.2448
www.standingstonebrewery.com
OPEN: *Daily 11:30a–midnight*

Housed in a historic building with a casual vibe and good beer, Standing Stone is a solid option when you want dinner without a huge production. The nice back deck has panoramic mountain views; inside has views of the display kitchen. Beers include 350 Ale, a golden ale for a hot summer day; a Double IPA that gets serious; and intriguing specialty brews like Marionberry Wheat. Taste your way through them with a sample tray chased with a wood-fired pizza or burger topped with Rogue Creamery's Standing Stone Stout cheddar cheese. The restaurant is committed to local, organic ingredients and does its part for the environment by utilizing solar power, carbon offsets, plant-based to-go materials, and engaging in recycling and composting. The restaurant is located in the former Whitte Garage, built in 1925 and listed on the National Register of Historic Places. The building's original brick walls and open truss system remain.

Omar's Restaurant & Bar

1380 Siskiyou Blvd, Ashland
MILE/EXIT: 19
541.482.1281
www.omarsrestaurant.com
OPEN: *Hours vary; call for details*

Ashland's oldest restaurant hasn't changed much in the past 60 years. It's a throwback to the steakhouses of yore with its red vinyl banquettes and club chairs. The vintage neon sign should tip you off first, followed by the menus in the lobby that show the restaurant's history. Owner Omar Hill worked at the Brown Derby and Savoy Hotel in Los Angeles before opening this steakhouse with his wife, Hazel, in 1946, and it feels like a place where Hollywood power deals could have been brokered. But this is Ashland, and a mostly local crowd comes here. Despite an extensive menu, hand-cut, custom-aged steaks are still the things to order, and all meals come with salads prepared tableside.

Ashland Beanery

1602 Ashland St, Ashland
MILE/EXIT: 19
541.488.0700
www.allannbroscoffee.com
OPEN: *Mon–Sat 6a–7p, Sun 7a–7p*

An original coffeehouse in the great Oregon tradition, serving up organic, fair trade cups of joe in the same location since 1973. The Beanery is a local chain fueled by Allann Bros Coffee, and offers a selection of baked goods, a laid-back coffee shop vibe, and free Wi-Fi. True to the Oregonian spirit, the chain has deep entrepreneurial and ecological roots. Founder Allan Stewart opened the company in 1972 with a commitment to helping the farms he sourced beans from, and has spent much time traveling the globe and building relationships with his producers.

VARIOUS LOCATIONS *in Albany, Corvallis, Eugene, and Salem*

 Morning Glory Restaurant

1149 Siskiyou Blvd, Ashland
MILE/EXIT: 14
541.488.8636
www.morninggloryrestaurant.com
OPEN: *Daily 9a–1:30p*

A visit to this cheery, restored 1926 Craftsman bungalow, with its welcoming overflowing pots of flowers on the front stoop, is like going to brunch at a friend's house—if your friend happened to be a classically trained chef. Inside, old wooden floors continue the Craftsman style, sunlight streams in through the skylights, and the restaurants is surprisingly bigger than it looks from the outside. Owner/chef Patricia Garth is Culinary Institute of America (CIA)–trained and it shows in dishes like lemon-ricotta stuffed French toast with red raspberry syrup, scrambles with goat cheese and Swiss chard, and Moroccan oatmeal with currants, dried apricots, and enough turmeric and cinnamon to turn the milk a fragrant yellow. Wash it all down with the chipotle Bloody Mary, and it really is a glorious morning.

KNOW: *The line starts forming outside at 10 minutes to 8am—get there early or be prepared to wait.*

Dagoba Chocolate

1105 Benson Way, Ashland
MILE/EXIT: 14
541.482.2001
www.dagobachocolate.com
OPEN: *Mon–Fri 10a–4p*

This organic chocolate maker has done much to pave the way for the artisan chocolate movement since its opening in 2001. Inventive flavors like lavender blueberry, rosehips, chai, and xocolatl (Mexican spices) can distract from the fact that beans are sourced from fair trade farms and the chocolate factory does things like work with cocoa co-ops in Costa Rica on reforestation efforts. The 17 bars run the gamut from pure dark to milk, and they also make drinking chocolate and baking chocolate. The company was bought by Hershey in 2006, but the chocolate giant has pledged to continue Dagoba's commitment to sustainable business practices.

OREGON

DETOURS & DESTINATIONS

Jacksonville

MILE/EXIT: 33

DISTANCE FROM I-5: 6 miles

Everything's about 100 years old in Jacksonville, which has more than 80 preserved pioneer buildings that date back to its boom following a gold discovery in the 1850s. The prosperity soon went away, but the town still offers a very well-preserved look at what life was like back then, and is cashing in on it. Antique shops seem to be the main trade, and the town smells of money.

Gary West Smoked Meats

690 N 5th St, Jacksonville

MILE/EXIT: 33

DISTANCE FROM HWY: 6 miles

541.899.1829

www.garywest.com

OPEN: *Mon–Sat 11a–6p, Sun 11a–5p*

One of the Northwest's most well-known smokehouses turns out amazing beef jerky made from hand-cut whole top rounds (the fat is cut and taken to make sausage). At its worst, beef jerky tastes only of smoke and has the consistency of shoe leather—Gary West's jerky actually tastes like beef, and its subtle smokiness is jazzed up with a sweet glaze. The shop is like a country mercantile, updated in a newer building with concrete floors, with Gary's jerky and sausages along with local cheese, wine, and other gourmet items. A small on-site cafe has Gary's sausages on sourdough rolls or foot-long hot dogs, along with fried treats like deep-fried chicken curds or chicken wings with a side of Gary West's hot mustard. Try the corned beef—smoky, not too pickled, and on the lean side.

GoodBean Coffee

165 S Oregon St, Jacksonville

MILE/EXIT: 33

DISTANCE FROM HWY: 7 miles

541.899.8740

The motto of this artisan coffee producer says it all: "Be good. Not bitter." It's a reflection of the unique hot-air roasting process, which eliminates a lot of the bitter flavor that occurs when coffee is drum roasted per common practice, but also describes the laid-back vibe of the cafe. It offers 15 varieties of coffee, in every roast and from every origin imaginable, each with a very smooth cup, some certified by Oregon Tilth, and others certified organic and fair trade. The cafe is located in the circa 1852 Tablerock Billiards and Saloon Building, and the high ceilings, brick walls, and weathered wood speak to its place in history. It's a pretty democratic place, with locals playing board games, working on laptops, or hanging out. It's also been family owned and operated since its opening in 1990, making it one of the original roasteries in Southern Oregon.

OREGON

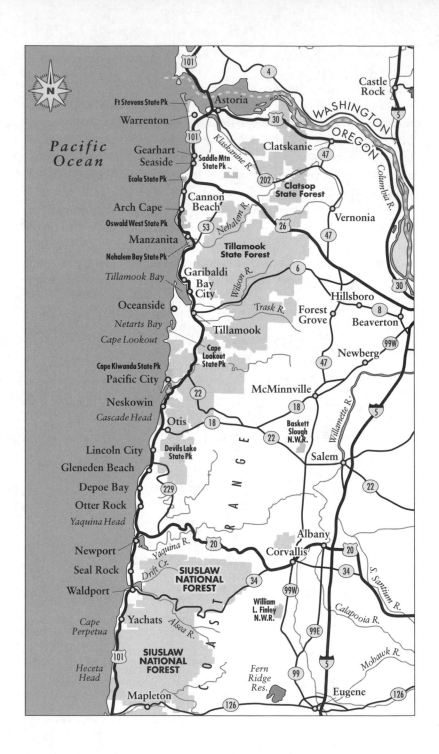

Highway 101: Oregon Coast

Trip Stats

START: Astoria

END: Brookings

LENGTH: 339 miles

LOCAL FLAVOR: Seafood—in every form imaginable, but namely clam chowder, fish-and-chips, and fresh crab.

BEST TIME: Summer, though there is no guarantee the weather will be good.

WORST TIME: Winter brings terrible storms to the coast, but there is a contingent of thrillseekers who come out just for the tumult.

LOCAL FOOD FESTIVALS:

- **Cranberry Festival:** Bandon (September). Cranberry-eating contests and live music set the scene at this cute festival celebrating the bright red berry.

WORD OF WARNING: Watch for cyclists on the narrow, winding highways. In the winter, wet pavement, fog, and standing water can make driving dangerous.

MORE INFO: Oregon Tourism (www.traveloregon.com), Oregon Coast Tourism (www.visittheoregoncoast.com)

OREGON

The Oregon Coast has always held a certain mystique for me. Summer vacations of my childhood were mostly spent on the sandy beaches of the Washington Coast—going on long walks, hauling wet sand for castles, writing messages with driftwood. The few summers we ventured down to the Oregon Coast, however, somehow felt more mysterious and exciting—finding new worlds in tidepools, admiring the violent collision of surf and rocks, staring up at the enigmatic and regal Haystack Rock, the third biggest monolith in the world. As an adult, I was happy to find that the place still provokes a childlike capacity for wonder.

Highway 101 begins in Astoria—a misty town at the mouth of the Columbia River where Lewis and Clark wintered—and ends in Brookings, the "Banana Belt of Oregon" where temperatures are often 70°F in the winter. The first part of the drive is foggy and cold unless you are blessed with good weather. After you pass Cannon Beach, the road begins to twist and turn its way through the mountains and stays curvaceous for the majority of the journey. Nature is unforgiving out here: fir trees bent sideways by the wind huddle against cliffsides pounded by the surf for centuries. After Yachats, sand dunes pushing 500 feet crowd the road before you hit the cliffs again. South of Bandon, it's all meadows and pastures and hay trucks, and the impossibly blue expanse of the Pacific.

The Oregon Coast was underwater as recently as two million years ago. The collision of the North American landmass and the Pacific plate formed the coastal mountain range, a jagged mess of basalt that's caused problems for sailors for centuries. Many of the towns on Oregon's north coast were formed because there was a shipwreck there, and the surviving crew had no other choice but to stay put. Natural attractions have names like Devil's Churn, Cook's Chasm, and Cape Foulweather.

For all of its rawness, there is a contradictory strain of East Coast civility about the coast. There have been "summer people" as long as there have been settlements—homesteaders seeking cooler climes on a coastal holiday. Early developers modeled resort towns like Seaside and Newport after their Eastern counterparts, and the tourist trade brought East Coast–style boardwalks, saltwater taffy, and resort hotels. When the Roosevelt Military Highway was built in the 1930s, it brought even more people to the coast.

The Oregon Coast is democratically known as the "People's Coast," and it's outdoorsy, accessible, and accepting. The entire coast is public land, and there are more state parks per square mile than anywhere else in the United States. It's dominated by ports, and populated by fishermen and loggers. The Oregon Coast might not a trendsetter for the future, but at least it doesn't hang its hat on the past.

Above all, the coast is a piscatorial culture, one that prides itself on fried fish and clam chowder. The question isn't whether meat is available—virtually every seafood shack has a burger on the menu—but why would you want it? This is some of the freshest fish in the country, and you'd do yourself a serious disservice to leave without sampling the coast's charms.

ON THE ROAD

 ## Josephson's Smokehouse

106 Marine Dr, Astoria
MILE/EXIT: 369
503.325.2190
www.josephsons.com
OPEN: *Daily 9a–5:30p*

Astoria was once known as the "Salmon Canning Capital of the World," thanks to the three dozen canneries that used to operate on the shoreline wharfs. Most shut down in the 1960s and '70s, depriving the town of its biggest industry, but a handful remain—including this highwayside smokehouse owned and operated by the Josephson family since 1920. The Smokehouse churns out hot- and cold-smoked, marinated, and cured seafood daily, from its operation in a century-old wooden structure originally built to house the Columbia River Fishermen's Protective Union. The no-frills shop is fragrant with alderwood smoke and dominated by a large deli case. Smoked or canned salmon comes in flavors like wine-maple, garlic, and pepper. Salmon jerky is a healthy, local version of the road trip classic. Purists will like the cold-smoked jerky, made with nothing but salmon and salt; I'm partial to the hot-smoked Original, which has a hint of caramelized sweetness from brown sugar.

KNOW: *Hungry for more history? Pay a visit to Astoria's Canning Museum on Pier 39, located in an 1875 building that once housed the Bumble Bee Tuna cannery. The museum offers an interpretive center and three preserved wooden gillnet boats on display. Afterward, head to the on-site Rogue Ales Public House for a beer and award-winning pub grub. (For more about Rogue Ales, see page 113.)*

 ## Ship Inn

1 2nd St, Astoria
MILE/EXIT: 369
503.325.0033
OPEN: *Daily 11:30a–9p*

Set nearly under the Astoria-Megler Bridge (the largest continuous truss bridge in the world), the Ship Inn offers unparalleled dining room views of the Columbia River—and some of the best deep-fried halibut on the

OREGON

Oregon Coast. It's golden-brown and fried to perfection: first there's a satisfying crackle, which yields to the pliable, creamy fish underneath. It's the only superlative thing on the menu—the chips are unremarkable, the chowder is fine, though too thick for my taste; we didn't stick around for a slice of the marionberry pie offered for dessert. The shiplike decor looks like it hasn't been updated in about 20 years—copper lamps, fading flowered carpet, paintings of ships on the walls, and bathrooms labeled "mermaids" and "seahorses." Avoid the dowdy interior and sit on the adjacent deck, a place made for drinking beer on a sunny day.

KNOW: *Astoria sits at the junction of the Columbia River and the Pacific Ocean, an area known to sailors as the "Graveyard of the Pacific" because of a treacherous, shifting sandbar that's claimed an estimated 1,500 lives. Food for thought . . . but don't let it spoil your appetite.*

Fort George Brewery

1483 Duane St, Astoria
MILE/EXIT: 369
503.325.7468
www.fortgeorgebrewery.com
OPEN: *Mon–Thu 11a–11p, Fri–Sat 11a–midnight, Sun noon–11p*

You can't help but wonder what John Jacob Astor would think, if he traveled 150 years into the future to discover a microbrewery on the site of his lonely trading outpost in the northern woods. Fort George Brewery *is* set on the original site of Fort Astoria (rechristened "Fort George" by the British during a brief occupation during the War of 1812) . . . but its current incarnation is a former car dealership and has the high ceilings, concrete floor, and garage-door windows that come along with it. The chalkboard menu lists what's on the 15 taps; beer is served in mason jars, which is downright charming. Fort George's brewing style is heartily Northwestern—big hops in the IPA, other suds made with local, seasonal ingredients (including cranberries!), and a special brew made with spruce tips that give a clean, piney finish to the pale ale. Nondrinkers can enjoy the spicy wasabi ginger ale. The innovation doesn't stop at the beer: the brewery also offers better-than-average pub grub (including housemade sausages).

KNOW: *Check the blog to see what's on tap: www.fortgeorgebrewery.blogspot.com*

Strange Brews

Word of warning: the usual beer tap suspects will seem boring and pedestrian after a sip of any one of these unusual suds.

Jasmine IPA: The perfumed aroma of jasmine follows with the subtle floral taste of this IPA, steeped with dried flowers in every batch. (Elysian Brewing Company, Seattle, WA, page 32)

Chipotle Ale: Based on an old Spanish recipe, Rogue's American Amber Ale is spiced with smoked chipotle chile peppers. (Rogue Brewery, various locations in OR and WA)

Spruce Tip Ale: "Fir trees" and "beer" don't sound like a winning combination, but the zesty freshness of spruce tips adds a crisp, outdoorsy element to this seasonal brew. (Fort George Brewery, Astoria, OR, page 102)

Marionberry Wheat: Fruit beers are a dime a dozen these days, but Oregon's signature berry brings a special fruity tang to this summery drink. (Standing Stone Brewing Company, Ashland, OR, page 93)

Cappuccino Stout: This dark, fully loaded stout is super-charged with Sebastopol's Hardcore Coffee, and only available in December. (Lagunitas Brewing Company, Petaluma, CA, page 159)

OREGON

🏠 Custard King

1597 Commercial St, Astoria
MILE/EXIT: 369
503.325.6372
OPEN: *Hours vary; call for details*

This highwayside stand is the color of a strawberry, the sign is a larger-than-life ice cream cone, and even if you're not craving a treat it's hard to resist the Custard King's siren song. Oddly, the Custard King doesn't sell custard. But it does serve a couple dozen flavors of Tillamook ice cream in all the standard flavors, including local faves like Oregon Black Cherry and Marionberry Pie. Under normal circumstances, this would just be another ice cream stand. But the Custard King has a certain homemade quality that makes it a worthy road food stop—like the handwritten, illustrated, and slightly lopsided cardboard sign indicating the available cone sizes.

KNOW: *The Custard King's burgers aren't bad, though my opinion might have been swayed by the charmingly inexplicable medieval-themed menu: burgers have names like Dragon, Palace, and Barbarian. They're all made with 80 percent lean beef from local producer Reed & Herting.*

Bowpicker Fish & Chips

Corner of 17th and Duane Sts, Astoria

MILE/EXIT: 369

503.791.2942

www.bowpicker.com

OPEN: *Hours vary by season and weather; call ahead for details*

It's surprisingly easy to miss this tiny fish-and-chips stand, considering it's housed in a reclaimed gillnet fishing boat permanently grounded in a grassy lot a block from the highway. It's a casual operation, like a backyard barbecue: Soft drinks are in self-service coolers, and the seating consists of communal picnic tables fore and aft. The boat itself serves as the kitchen and front desk. Stand on a sort of dock constructed next to the ship and order the only thing on the menu: albacore and chips, both fried in soy oil. Popular up and down the Oregon Coast, albacore is meatier and oilier than its commonly fried counterparts halibut and cod. The result is a firm fish-and-chips, lighter than chicken but with a similar heartiness. It's not my personal favorite— I prefer my fish-and-chips to have a crunchy skin and a giving, melting interior—but the family who owns Bowpicker chose it in a blind taste test, and if this stand's popularity is any indication, a lot of the population agrees with them.

KNOW: *Check out the Columbia River Maritime Museum across the street to learn more about the role gillnet boats played in the area's development.*

Pacific Way Bakery & Cafe

601 Pacific Way, Gearhart

MILE/EXIT: 380

503.738.0245

www.pacificwaybakery-cafe.com

OPEN: *Hours vary; call ahead for details*

Gearhart is a sleepy town directly north of the tourist madness of Seaside and Cannon Beach that offers two items of interest to foodies: it was the childhood summer residence of James Beard, and the beach offers some of the best razor clamming on the coast. This charming bakery is the perfect stop before a long day on the mudflats. The yellow storefront and bright red cafe tables are cheerful on the mistiest days, and inside, the old-fashioned tiled floor, the smell of cinnamon in the air, Belle & Sebastian playing softly on the stereo, and framed photos of the area's past can't help but bolster your spirits. Wake up with superlative baked goods and a cup of Caffe Umbria coffee (a roaster from Seattle) and do try the brown sugar maple roll—the flaky love child of a maple bar and a cinnamon roll. The cafe next door is a great stop after you've clammed and showered, offering a seasonally changing menu of thin-crust pizzas, pub favorites, and sophisticated seafood dishes like pan-seared scallops with a grapefruit, white wine, and butter reduction.

(🏠) Seaside Candyman

21 N Columbia St, Seaside
MILE/EXIT: 385
503.738.5280
www.seasidecandyman.com
OPEN: *Daily 10a–5p*

Seaside was the first resort community on the Oregon Coast, planned by railroad magnate Ben Holladay in 1873 as a lure to get Portlanders to take his train to the beach. At its heyday, it had a zoo, racetrack, luxe hotel, and concrete boardwalk known as "The Prom." Today, The Prom is all that's left, along with the usual beach-town slew of video arcades and saltwater taffy shops. But Seaside's fading carnival glory is best on display at the Candyman. Judging by the Uncle Sam logo and Americana displayed outside, you might wonder if the candy shop has been replaced by an army supply store. Then you get close enough to hear that creepy "Candy Man" song from the original Willy Wonka movie blasting from mounted speakers, and you know you're in the right place. Inside, the walls were once white but have settled into gray, and sugar-crazed children run up and down the aisles of rainbow taffy, their flip-flops pounding the primary-colored linoleum. A stooped, ancient man comes out of nowhere and hands you a photocopied key to the 170 flavors, a sort

OREGON

of Dewey decimal system of any given taffy's distinguishing character-istics and aisle location. ("GOLDEN PEAR—green jacket wht cntr ylow dot—M3.") Needless to say, the Candyman is not a place for people with discerning palates. But the kids seem to love it, and in the end I kind of did too, if only as an example of pleasure-seeking taken to its inevitable conclusion.

KNOW: *When your sugar high subsides, indulge in some high culture with a visit to the Lewis and Clark salt cairn, the so-called true end of the Lewis & Clark Trail. Here, the duo boiled seawater for seven weeks straight to get enough salt to preserve meat for the trip home.*

Ecola Seafoods

208 N Spruce St, Cannon Beach
MILE/EXIT: 394

503.436.9130

www.ecolaseafoods.com

OPEN: *Summer daily 9a–9p; winter daily 10a–7p; spring/fall daily 10a–8p*

This unpretentious fish shack is exactly what you want after a day of frol-icking on the beach. Families and locals chow down on fish-and-chips, clam chowder, and the shop's signature Dungeness crab melt sandwiches, which come open-faced and heaped with chunks of crab, melted cheese, and Thousand Island dressing, on just-garlicky-enough garlic bread. The maritime theme is everywhere, but it's subtle: the "order here" and "pick up order" signs are in the shape of sea creatures, the ceiling fan is made out of sailcloth, and a large mural of a fish market is painted on a wall above the counter. Another wall is papered with crayon drawings made by children. One features a smiling rainbow-hued fish underneath the words, "I come every year for Ecola fish." It's clearly printed by a child, and signed, "Gabby." The girl might only be in grade school, but she knows what she's talking about.

Bread and Ocean

154 Laneda Ave, Manzanita
MILE/EXIT: 406

503.368.5823

www.breadandocean.com
OPEN: *Wed–Thu 7:30a–2p; Fri–Sat 7:30a–2p, 5–9p; Sun 8a–2p, 5–8p*
Cash only

Spicy cardamom cinnamon rolls are the specialty at this cozy bakery, but they're certainly not all it has to offer. As the name suggests, bread plays a major role in the offerings, with a stable of standards like organic multigrain, sourdough, and baguettes along with a rotating collection of specialty breads that might include fig-walnut, brioche, stout beer–cheddar bread, or pain au chocolat with dried cherries. (Look to the chalkboard menu to see which bread's featured that day.) The loaves make a great foundation for the sandwiches, which go beyond the norm with organic ingredients and touches like Caesar mayo on the turkey, and quince paste on the hot smoked ham. Order one to go in a picnic lunch box—which also includes soup, salad or kettle-style chips, and a fresh baked cookie—or eat outside on the sunny patio decorated with flower-filled window boxes. On weekends, the bakery stays open for a weekly changing dinner menu, which showcases the best of the season and has influences ranging from Mediterranean to Thai, Middle Eastern, Mexican, and more.

 Pacific Oyster

150 Oyster Dr, Bay City
MILE/EXIT: 428
503.377.2323
www.pacseafood.com
OPEN: *Daily 9a–7p*

Watch oyster shuckers in action at the massive production facility for this West Coast seafood operation, then head into the marketplace/cafe to sample a dozen for yourself. It's nothing fancy—bare tables, fluorescent lighting, chalkboard menu—but the seafood's so good it stands on its own. Slurp your way through Kumamotos or Pacifics in any preparation you can think of: on the half-shell, in shot-glass shooters, deep-fried, in stew, on a burger bun. For non-oyster fans, there's also a simple menu of seafood specialties like shellfish steamers, crab Louie, fish-and-chips, clam chowder, and more. Pacific Seafood is the largest independently owned seafood company in North America, and has been committed to providing the best, freshest West Coast seafood to consumers since it opened as a small Portland retail shop in 1941.

KNOW: *The company is also an industry leader in sustainable business practices, which include environmentally responsible fishing and adopting eco-friendly, recyclable packaging.*

Tillamook Cheese Factory

4175 Hwy 101 N, Tillamook

MILE/EXIT: 434

503.815.1300

www.tillamookcheese.com/visitorcenter

OPEN: *Labor Day–mid-June, daily 8a–6p; mid-June–Labor Day, 8a–8p*

The sediment-rich Tillamook Valley is heaven for dairy farmers, thanks to its lush grasses and nearly 100 inches of rainfall a year. But instead of competing, dairy farmers here actually all do get along. In 1909, a group of 10 families pooled their resources to form the Tillamook County Creamery Association, a cooperative designed to work together to produce and market the best possible milk, cheese, cream, and butter from Tillamook cows. A century later, the co-op has expanded to 110 dairy families who run their farms based on a set of environmental and animal treatment best practices with the same goal as their forefathers. Check out the fruits of their labor in this visitor-friendly factory, which has been turning out Tillamook cheddar, ice cream, and other favorites since 1941. The self-guided tour lets you set your own pace to learn about the cheese-making process and history of the Tillamook Valley through videos, interactive presentations, and an observation window onto the factory floor. Afterward, head to the tasting bar to try all the cheeses the TCCA produces, along with cheddar "squeaky" cheese curds only available on the premises. There's also an ice cream shop with 25 flavors, including local varieties like Oregon Strawberry and Mountain Huckleberry. Stop in the Northwest Gourmet Foods Shop for picnic-friendly local products along with Tillamook yogurt, cheese, and sour cream. The on-site cafe serves an outstanding grilled cheese sandwich made from sharp Tillamook cheddar on sourdough bread, along with a standard diner breakfast and lunch menu.

KNOW: *Call ahead to find out what kind of cheese the factory's producing that day—it's made every day except major holidays.*

 Pelican Pub

33180 Cape Kiwanda Dr, Pacific City
MILE/EXIT: 458
503.965.7007
www.pelicanbrewery.com
OPEN: *Sun–Thu 8a–10p, Fri–Sat 8a–11p*

On a warm summer evening, there's possibly no better place to be than the patio of this bustling brewpub. Sit at a plastic table only a few feet from the sand, watch surfers take their last rides of the day, and enjoy the sunset behind Pacific City's massive Haystack Rock (not to be confused with the Cannon Beach monolith of the same name). Needless to say, you'll also be sharing a pitcher or two of the pub's tasty signature brews. IPA—India Pelican Ale, in this case—stays nicely balanced despite a big dose of Cascade hops, and MacPelican's Scottish Style Ale and the malty, floral Kiwanda Cream Ale are great alternatives to lighter brews. The menu continues the pelican theme: "Pelican Wings" are actually jumbo chicken wings in a spicy IPA sauce. The rest of the menu offers crowd-pleasers like clam chowder, thin-crust pizzas, mahi-mahi fish tacos, and Panko-crusted fish-and-chips marinated in Kiwanda Cream Ale. Most items have corresponding beer pairing suggestions. If you can't sit outside, the convivial pub isn't a bad alternative—it's full of travelers and locals broadcasting good vibrations. Pick up growlers, bottled beers, and Pelican Pub schwag, including fleece jackets and beach balls, at the gift shop.

TOURS: *Tours of the brewhouse are available upon request—call for details.*

Otis Café

1259 Salmon River Hwy, Otis
MILE/EXIT: 344
541.994.2813
www.otiscafe.com
OPEN: *Daily 7a–8p*

Blink and you'll miss this tiny one-room diner, next to an old post office in the small community of Otis. It's the kind of "two eggs, any style" greasy spoon you find in towns across America, where locals exchange gossip with waitresses, and foreigners are warmly greeted, then ignored. Except this particular greasy spoon has received write-ups in everything

OREGON

from the *New York Times* to *USA Today* and won a James Beard award, all for continuing the small-town diner tradition in the modern era. Order "The Original" German potatoes: hash browns topped with green onions and white cheddar, which taste fantastic and make a great hangover cure. Equally worthy are the sourdough pancakes, which cost $3 for the first and $1 thereafter (it's pretty much the same deal with waffles and French toast). It's a pricing scheme I personally appreciate because it takes the pressure off finishing an entire short stack of pancakes. Kids will love the teddy bear pancakes, and don't miss the legendary molasses brown bread.

Blackfish Cafe

2733 NW Hwy 101, Lincoln City
MILE/EXIT: 339
541.996.1007
www.blackfishcafe.com
OPEN: *Wed–Mon 11:30a–3p, 5–9p*

Lincoln City is an artist community and cultural center on the Oregon Coast, and this is the best restaurant in town. It's filled with locals enjoying date nights and celebratory dinners, and travelers bent on having a "nice" meal while they're on the road. The food here *is* consistently good, but doesn't quite hold up to the "nice" seafood restaurants in Portland or Seattle—which is maybe an unfair comparison, because Blackfish zooms past them when you consider its location. Much decorated chef/owner Rob Poundry goes out of his way to source seafood and veggies straight from the producer, and it shows in his thoughtful seasonal menus. You'd be perfectly content here with a glass of Oregon wine and a dinner of appetizers, especially succulent fried Yaquina Bay oysters, and a nearly perfect bowl of clam chowder that tastes equally of cream and the sea. Cioppino, one of the specialties, is more a pile of shellfish and fish in tomato sauce rather than a traditional soup, but the fish is fresh and generous, and the tomato base is well seasoned. Children are welcome (there's even a fleet of high chairs waiting for them), but make sure they're well behaved—this is the domain of grown-ups.

KNOW: *You should probably call ahead for reservations. When I showed up on a rainy Monday at 8pm, there was a 45-minute wait.*

 Gracie's Sea Hag

58 E Hwy 101, Depoe Bay
MILE/EXIT: 327
541.765.2734
www.theseahag.com
OPEN: *Daily 7a–9p*

"Seafood so fresh the ocean hasn't missed it yet" is the slogan of this adaptable cafe, which changes during the day to accommodate the shifting tides of tourism and local appetites. In the morning, it's a typical breakfast joint with strong coffee, rousing Bloody Marys, and incredible crab eggs Benedict, with hunks of fresh crab and a hollandaise so silky-rich I could have happily drunk a glass of it. Lunch and dinner bring in a touristy crowd for fish-and-chips and other seafood specialties, and after the sun goes down, the raucous party starts at the connected bar next door. The interior decor makes the place: stained glass between booths has a playful undersea motif, the wooden walls and ceiling make you feel like you're inside a ship, and large grainy prints of fishing photographs from the 1970s or '80s give the room a hip vintage vibe (though one wonders whether this is intentional).

KNOW: *On slow nights, proprietress Gracie Strom accompanies a live organist with her xylophone-like playing of the bar bottles. You kind of have to be there.*

Ainslee's

66 Hwy 101 SE, Depoe Bay
MILE/EXIT: 327
541.765.2431
www.ainslees.com
OPEN: *Daily 10a–5p*

Those who grew up watching *Sesame Street* and *Mister Rogers' Neighborhood* will appreciate the "how it's made" factory atmosphere of this family-run candy shop. The Ainslee family has used the same recipe for their famous taffy since 1947, and you can watch the whole process going down in the glassed-in kitchen, from cooking and cooling to pulling and wrapping. All flavors are available in bins along the wall, under murals of old-fashioned taffy pullers, and thoughtful touches like "allergy alert" signs on the peanut butter taffy show that the family is still engaged in the well-being of their customers, even after all these years. Along with taffy, the shop also offers caramel corn, fudge, and peanut brittle.

KNOW: *Sign up for the Taffy of the Month program on the website and get a new flavor sent by mail every month.*

Spouting Horn Restaurant

110 SE Hwy 101, Depoe Bay

MILE/EXIT: 327

541.765.2261

OPEN: *Wed–Sun 8a–8p*

This place serves "damn fine pies," to cop a line from Agent Cooper on *Twin Peaks*. He'd feel right at home in this salty institution—Betty Taunton's deep-dish creations have been pleasing crowds since 1951. She bakes a daily assortment of varieties based on whim and seasonality, often using local fruit, which means that favorites like marionberry are bursting with the flavors of the region. Sometimes Taunton gets inventive: peanut butter cream pie occasionally makes a cameo, mincemeat pie appears at Christmas, and in the height of summer, peach melba is the stuff of local legend. It's good to hunker down with a slice and a cuppa, gazing out at the Pacific Ocean through the wall of windows. If you're lucky, you'll see whale spouts (Depoe Bay is a famous whale-watching destination) or the sunset on a rare clear day. The food itself is pretty standard—hot crab and cheddar melts, crab Louie, fish-and-chips, grilled Yaquina Bay oysters—and a sizeable seafood buffet is offered on Saturday nights. Dinner is nothing worth going out of your way for. But trust me on the pies.

Sharks Seafood Bar & Steamer Co.

852 SW Bay Blvd, Newport

MILE/EXIT: 314

541.574.0590

www.sharksseafoodbar.com

OPEN: *Sun–Wed 4–8:30p, Fri–Sat 4–9p*

It's hard to know what's more famous at this casual seafood spot on Newport's historic bayfront: the cioppino, or the way the cioppino is made. We'll start with the soup, a deep red slurry of local seafood and shellfish that comes to the table in a bowl so full it's nearly overflowing. The broth hits all the high notes, built on a base of imported tomatoes and perfectly seasoned with fresh herbs. This is the dish that will restore you to life after a wet day on the beach, and it tastes even better when you know how it's prepared. Unlike most of its brethren, Sharks doesn't offer fish-and-chips or clam chowder; instead, it uses a patented system of steamer kettles imported from a submarine to steam and poach the daily catch. The result is a menu of delicate (and somewhat healthy) dishes, all infused with the flavors of the Northwest. No reservations are taken and the popular spot fills up fast; it's worth the wait for a table in back, where you can watch the steamer kettles in action.

KNOW: *If, like me, you fall in love with the cioppino, you'll be glad to know they sell vacuum packs in the store and online.*

Rogue

The growing Rogue Nation is a mighty force in the Oregon brewing scene, a cult of sorts led by Rogue's fearless leader and CEO Jack Joyce. Rogue Ales are known for their inventiveness and boldness, and Rogue Meeting Halls (the brewpubs themselves) are casual, homespun operations that invite lingering with board games and a large selection of brews on tap. Try classics like Dead Guy Ale and Shakespeare Stout, or go outside the box with Chipotle Ale, Chocolate Stout, or Hazelnut Brown Nectar. Rogue Ales are meant to be paired with food, and the menus at the brewpubs go above and beyond standard pub fare, sourcing local ingredients and working with seasoned chefs, restaurateurs, brewers, and even Iron Chef Masaharu Morimoto (who was rewarded for his help with his own line of ales). Burgers are uniformly tasty, made from Kobe beef from Snake River Farms in Idaho, and sauces for wings, calamari, and other dishes are made with Rogue Ales. All brewpubs are family- and dog-friendly, offering an extensive kids' menu and draught root beer, along with a unique menu of dog treats.

VARIOUS LOCATIONS *in Astoria, Portland, Eugene, Seattle, and San Francisco*

OREGON

Rogue Ales Public House

748 SW Bay Blvd, Newport

MILE/EXIT: 314

531.265.3811

www.rogue.com

OPEN: *Sun–Thu 11a–1a, Fri–Sat 11a–2a*

The first Rogue brewery, formerly called the Bayfront Brewery, was opened in 1989 at the encouragement of Mo Niemi, the owner of Mo's Chowder. She offered Rogue Brewery founder Jack Joyce a space in a garage she owned down the street on the stipulation that Joyce and partners "feed the fisherman" by giving back to the local community. Her likeness appears on the label of the brewery's Mom Hefeweizen, a Belgian-style blonde with hints of coriander and ginger. (There's also a snapshot of her naked in a bathtub on the wall to the left of the bar.) Spend a night upstairs in the brewery's "House of Rogue Bed & Beer," an affordable and comfortable lodging with views of the bay and complimentary bottles of Rogue Ale awaiting guests upon check-in.

The Original Mo's

622 SW Bay Blvd, Newport

MILE/EXIT: 314

541.265.2979

www.moschowder.com

OPEN: *Daily 11a–8p*

Stories abound about the original "Mo," Mohava Marie Niemi, quite the colorful character. The tough-as-nails proprietress opened her first chowder shack in 1946, and quickly became known for her generosity, hospitality, no-nonsense attitude, and secret clam chowder recipe. The combination earned her the acclaim of dignitaries, celebrities, and even Senator Robert Kennedy, but never distracted her from her mission of feeding hungry locals and travelers. Mo died in 1992, but her legacy is carried on in an expanded empire that now includes four locations and a brisk mail-order business, fueled by a chowder factory that churns out 500,000 pounds of the stuff a year. Mo's is a clean, well-lit place, decorated with copper salmon sculptures and framed stills of Newport maritime history on the walls, with efficient service and buckets of saltine crackers on the lacquered wooden tables. And the chowder? It's perfectly fine—above average, even—dominated by a smoky bacon flavor that's virtually unknown in these parts. It's probably not the best bowl of chowder you'll have in your life, but it's a consistent crowd-pleaser, and serves its purpose as a hot, reliable meal on the road. Order it in a sourdough bread bowl, called a "cannonball" in Oregon Coast lingo. The menu also offers fish-and-chips and other popular seafood dishes, and has a section called "flatlanders" with burgers and the like.

KNOW: *Hit up Mo's Annex, across the street, for Yaquina Bay views and cocktails.*

VARIOUS LOCATIONS *in Otter Rock, Lincoln City, Cannon Beach, and Florence*

Newport

Established in 1866 as a resort town, when former forty-niner Samuel Case built a grand hotel in the style of one he admired in Newport, Rhode Island. Despite a road that was passable only five months out of the year, "summer people" came from Portland in droves to partake in the pleasures of the beach. But Newport remained grounded with a thriving fishing community, built around the deep and fertile waters of Yaquina Bay. City boosters once claimed that it would become "The San Francisco of the Northwest," which never quite came to fruition. Today it's dominated by commercial and charter fishing operations, has the best aquarium on the Oregon Coast, and boasts a charming restored downtown with maritime murals. The town is cut in half by the bay, and the arched Yaquina Bay Bridge connecting the halves is one of its most distinguishable features.

OREGON

Oregon Oyster Farms

6878 Yaquina Bay Rd, Newport

MILE/EXIT: 314

DISTANCE FROM HWY: 6 miles

541.265.5078

www.oregonoyster.com

OPEN: *Daily 9a–5p*

A 10-minute drive along the curve of Yaquina Bay takes you to this oyster farm, which has been harvesting the local brand of Pacific oysters since 1907. The small retail shop and production facility is located on an old-school weathered jetty that extends from the oyster shell–strewn beach. You kind of feel like maybe you aren't supposed to be there, especially when you take a look into the back room and see a team of shuckers extracting oyster meat with incredible speed, efficiency, and a clatter like thundering hooves. However, everyone is super-friendly, and the bare-bones retail space sells oysters by the dozen with all the fixings. Bring your shucking skills if you want to enjoy them dockside.

KNOW: *During the summer months, waters in the bay get too warm for safe consumption of raw oysters. Signs in the store will alert you if this is the case.*

 South Beach Fish Market

3640 S Hwy 101, South Beach

MILE/EXIT: 312

541.867.6800

www.southbeachfishmarket.com

OPEN: *Daily 8a–8p*

Your introduction to this roadside shack is the large crab steamers out front, and if you're lucky (or unlucky, depending on how you feel about it), you'll get a front-seat view of the staff loading Dungeness crabs for their final bath. Inside the fluorescently lit shop, steamed crab is the item du jour, along with fine, but very salty, clam chowder and perfectly decent fish-and-chips. Make sure to try the salmon candy, a small cup of ruby-red smoked salmon with hints of smoke and maple that you eat with a toothpick. If the weather's cooperating, take your food to the cheery green picnic tables out front by the highway.

KNOW: *The seafood shop's attached to a convenience store, which is, well, pretty convenient if you need to stock up on road snacks.*

(ψ) Green Salmon Coffee & Tea House

220 Hwy 101 N, Yachats

MILE/EXIT: 290

541.547.3077

www.thegreensalmon.com

OPEN: *Tue–Sun 7a–2p*

Yachats (pronounced "ya-HOTS") is a hippie town in the glorious Oregon tradition, and its full bohemian culture is on display at this eco-conscious coffee shop. Only organic, fair trade espresso is used in the inventive coffee drinks like Mexican Coffee infused with cinnamon and chili powder, and the fragrant Kashmir Express with cinnamon, nutmeg, cardamom, and ginger. Non-coffee drinkers have plenty of options, too: Try Bolognese Chocolate, made with cocoa, fresh-squeezed orange juice, vanilla, and cinnamon (it sounds like a contradictory mess of ingredients, but it actually kind of works). The coffee shop's slogan, "Working upstream for a better world," is reflected in its environmentally friendly practices, which include composting pretty much everything, mopping floors with collected rainwater, employing solar power, and using only biodegradable packaging. Sit with locals at mismatched tables in the homey interior next to the vintage coffee roaster, or snag a table on the leafy patio. A small food menu has vegetarian- and vegan-friendly entrees. Don't miss the Berry Toast, a slice of toasted sourdough topped with mascarpone and fresh berries and finished with honey and powdered sugar.

KNOW: *Drinks are handmade, and can take a while. Give up, give in, pull up a chair, and people watch.*

(🐟) Luna Sea Fish House & Village Fishmonger

153 NW Hwy 101, Yachats

MILE/EXIT: 290

541.547.4794

www.lunaseafishhouse.com

OPEN: *Daily 8a–9p; winter 8a–8p*

Feel like part of the community at this small cafe on the highway, where locals gather for fish tacos, fish-and-chips, grilled fish sandwiches, and burgers made with grass-fed free-range beef. The tacos are outstanding—spices add heat to the marinated grilled fish, but the apple and

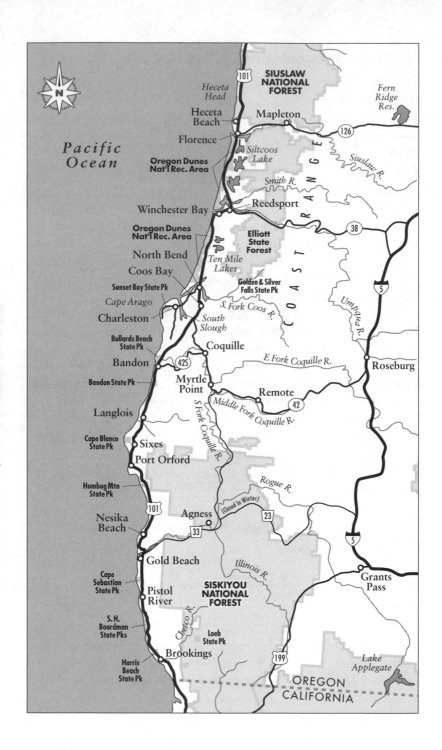

cabbage coleslaw and a cool dollop of guacamole temper the burn. One taco is enough for a small lunch, and pairs well with a Rogue beer. Five tables are available in the main dining room, dominated by a large nautical mural on the wall displaying a beach at sunset, and picnic tables out front have a view of a slice of the Yachats Bay through the trees. The main counter provides sustainably caught fish for the community, available fresh and smoked.

KNOW: *Put your name on the list at front if the tables are full; it's usually not a very long wait.*

BJ's Ice Cream Parlor

2930 Hwy 101, Florence

MILE/EXIT: 264

541.997.7286

OPEN: *Daily 11a–10p (open at 10a in summer)*

This retro ice cream parlor is exactly the kind of place you want on a beach holiday. It's super-local, for one: the cream comes from Umpqua Dairy, and natural ingredients provide the flavors, including five made entirely with Oregon products. Try the Oregon Trail, a rich chocolate blended with blackberry and hazelnut, or the seasonal pear ice cream with chunks of fresh fruit. At 14.5 percent butterfat, these ice creams are rich—and the staff isn't stingy with samples. BJ's has been a family-owned Florence fixture since opening in 1978, and the old-fashioned, pale pink interior hearkens back to the days before ice cream had additives and artificial flavorings. Vintage trays cover the walls around the BJ's sign framed with lightbulbs like a 1940s vanity mirror.

KNOW: *Saltwater taffy aficionados will appreciate the range of flavors, including local specialties like huckleberry, marionberry, and cranberry.*

Bliss Hot Rod Grill

1179 Hwy 101, Florence

MILE/EXIT: 264

541.997.6726

OPEN: *Sun 7:30a–8p, Mon–Sat 6a–8p*

A vintage car theme prevails at this burger joint, to the extent that two tables are built in well-preserved hot rods in the dining rooms. The walls are covered with the history of car culture—old road signs and photographs provide atmosphere as well as entertainment while you wait for your food. Kids love it, as evidenced by the number of families in attendance; luckily, the food has something to offer grown-ups as well. The burger is perfectly serviceable: get the Blue Velvet, a flavorful beef patty topped with blue cheese and grilled onions. Milk shakes come to the table in original metal containers. Along with the hot rod tables there are plenty of booths, plus a long lunch counter. As you leave, don't miss the "drive-through," an old car that's made to look like it's coming out of the side of the building.

KNOW: *To avoid the throngs of excited kids and tired parents, head into the dim back bar, which has an eclectic crowd of regulars.*

Cranberry Sweets

1005 Newmark Ave, Coos Bay

MILE/EXIT: 215

800.527.5748

www.cranberrysweets.com

OPEN: *Mon–Sat 9a–5p*

A candymaker with a local bent, this sweet shop offers more than 200 candy varieties but specializes in sugar-coated gummy gems known as *pâtes de fruits* in France. The shop's signature item is super-sweet cranberry jelly candies, made from a recipe purchased from a Bandon housewife in 1974. Unlike most jelly candies, these don't contain cornstarch and require a multi-week process to achieve the right consistency. The same principle is applied to iterations made with marionberries, citrus, and wine. Less successful is the fudge: the magenta, over-sweet cranberry loses much of the berry's tartness . . . and the less said about the neon cheddar cheese fudge the better. Regardless, there are always free samples, and the original Coos Bay location has large windows with a view into the production area.

KNOW: *The candymaker has a second location in Old Town Bandon (321 2nd St, Bandon; 541.347.9475).*

Bandon Baking Co.

160 2nd St, Bandon

MILE/EXIT: 190

541.347.9440

www.bandonbakingco.com

OPEN: *Daily 8a–4p*

Bandon is the center of Oregon's cranberry production, and this excellent refueling stop specializes in cranberry-studded bars, scones, quick bread, and cookies. The soft cranberry bar is nutty and buttery in all the right places, with a generous helping of sugar crumble on top. Cranberries replace raisins in one of the best oatmeal cookies I've ever had: nubbly, with the dried berry's tartness as a perfect foil for brown sugar sweetness and the crunch of California walnuts. The cafe also offers espresso, homemade soup, and sandwiches. Framed yellowing photos and newspaper stories in the adjacent dining room provide a lesson in town history while you eat.

KNOW: *Here's some backstory for the newspaper clippings: the Old Town of Bandon isn't actually all that old—though founded in the 1850s by Irish immigrants who named it after their hometown, the town burned to the ground in 1936.*

Bandon Fish Market

249 1st St SE, Bandon

MILE/EXIT: 190

541.347.4282

www.bandonfishmarket.com

OPEN: *Mon–Sat 11a–6p, Sun 11a–3p*

The best fish-and-chips in town, enjoyed on oilcloth-covered picnic tables overlooking Bandon's picturesque harbor. The flaky golden crust crunches when you bite into it and doesn't overwhelm the sweet flavor of the fish itself. Choose between cod, snapper, sole, and halibut (when in season), all fried in soybean oil and accompanied by deliciously crispy fries and a choice of coleslaw or garlic toast. The Little Matey, a small order of fish-and-chips paired with a cup of chowder, is enough for normal appetites. Corn dogs, chicken strips, and mac and cheese are also available for non-fish eaters. The building isn't very well-marked, but you'll know it from other kitschy tourist traps by the sign that says "Fish & Chips Chowder House" on the blue wooden exterior.

KNOW: *There are no bathrooms on the premises, but Bandon's public bathrooms are only a few yards away in the marina parking lot.*

 **Faber Farms**

54982 Morrison Rd, Bandon

MILE/EXIT: 190

DISTANCE FROM HWY: 2 miles

866.347.1166

www.faberfarms.com

OPEN: *Mon–Sat 10a–4p*

In 1885, a New Englander transplanted a cranberry plant from his native Cape Cod and Bandon had a new cash crop. Though production has dwindled since its heyday, you can still get an up-close-and-personal look at the cranberry bogs that once dominated the region at this small family-owned farm. Seasonal tours of the bogs are available (call for hours), or just take a gander at them on your own, especially in the fall when the berries rise to the surface in a vermillion bloom just before harvest. Most will be satisfied with just a cursory glance before hitting the Cranberry Scoop gift shop, which has a dazzling array of all things cranberry, from chocolate-covered berries to the children's book *Clarence the Cranberry Who Couldn't Bounce.*

 Crazy Norwegian's Fish & Chips

259 6th St, Port Orford

MILE/EXIT: 164

541.332.8601

OPEN: *Wed–Sun 11:30a–7p*

Named by *Sunset* magazine as one of the top ten fish-and-chips joints on the West Coast, the Crazy Norwegian definitely doesn't disappoint. Big chunks of fresh fish are fried in a light batter and accompanied by a tasty house-made tarter sauce heavy on the dill. For my money, it's the best fried fish on the coast. Locals sit at tables inside the knotty pine-paneled interior and take advantage of the free Wi-Fi or browse the lending library. Also on the menu are burgers, seafood sandwiches, crab cakes, and local beer on tap.

KNOW: *Get your order to go and take it down to the picturesque Port Orford harbor, where it's so windy that commercial fishermen have to raise and lower their boats into the harbor by crane.*

🍴 Oceanside Diner

16403 Lower Harbor Rd, Brookings

MILE/EXIT: 109

541.469.7971

OPEN: *Daily 4a–1:30p*

Get to this NASCAR-themed diner early enough to have breakfast with local fishermen loading up on calories before heading out for the day. (The restaurant opens at 4am catering to them, and the eavesdropping is the best, bar none.) The food is surprisingly tasty—the chef is a CIA graduate, and his training is put to good use in homemade biscuits and omelets like the seafood-rich "Oceanside," stuffed with shrimp, scallops, and calamari. Breakfasts come in lite, medium, or large portions—lite or medium is plenty unless you're going to spend the rest of the day hauling pounds of fishing nets out of the water. Sack lunches are also available; a wholesome package that includes a sandwich, chips, fruit, granola bar, potato salad, and soda.

KNOW: *The diner also sells daily fishing licenses for Oregon and California.*

Larger Than Life

The biggest food on the West Coast:

Frying pan: Long Beach, WA

Artichoke: Castroville, CA

Clam: Pismo Beach, CA

Doughnut: Los Angeles, CA

OREGON

California is a queer place—in a way, it has turned its back on the world, and looks into the void Pacific . . . It's sort of crazy-sensible. Just the moment: hardly as far ahead as carpe diem.

—D. H. LAWRENCE

NORTHERN CALIFORNIA

Wine tasting in Napa Valley, the wild expanse of the North Coast, the pristine wilderness of Mount Shasta, and more eco-friendly food than you thought was possible.

Region Stats

LOCAL FLAVOR:

- **Wine:** Almost every varietal is well represented in this prolific wine region, from the big reds of Napa to the subtle pinot noirs of the Russian River Valley.

- **Beer:** The dozens of microbreweries were leaders in the craft-brewing movement, and are known for their hop-charged IPAs and experimental Belgian ales.

- **Cheese:** Once you try cheese from Sonoma and Marin County cows, you'll never go back. Something about the salty air from the coast makes it taste that much better.

- **Bread:** European-style bakeries crop up in almost every town, turning out artisan loaves made with old-world methods.

- **Oysters:** Tomales Bay oysters are some of the best you'll ever have, either self-shucked or barbecued.

The first thing that strikes you about Northern California is how empty it is. The land up here is still largely uninhabited, and it's astonishing that a state with nearly 40 million residents could still have these vast, virgin swaths of nature just sitting there.

The region was first explored by scrappy mountain men like Jebediah Smith, then fed by a steady stream of settlers who veered south from the Oregon Trail in Idaho on what became known as the California Trail. Exploration became settlement, settlement became ownership, and many families have owned farms and businesses here for generations.

They intend on owning them for generations to come. Northern Californians have a special relationship with the land they farm, and a deeply ingrained dedication toward environmental stewardship. Their

CALIFORNIA

eco-conscious ethos isn't about the past or present—it's about preservation for the future.

It's easy to understand when you're driving through it—this land is worth preserving. It's so beautiful you almost can't believe it exists: the celestial calm of Mount Shasta, the quiet mystery of the redwoods, the misty and inhospitable coastline, the tawny vineyard-dotted hills of Napa Valley. It's a land well worth the effort.

Sustainable farming and local sources mean that the food up here is some of the simplest and best. Northern Californians have been unconsciously practicing the 100-mile diet before it was a twinkle in Michael Pollan's eye. Here you'll find great sandwiches made with artisan bread, cheese, and charcuterie; some of the best beer and wine on the West Coast; elegantly composed salads made with vegetables from a garden you can see from your table. The food is simple, but it's the epitome of fresh, in season, and local.

Trips in Northern California

I-5: Northern California
Mount Shasta's mystical pull and messy, delicious burgers. (Page 129)

Highway 101: Northern California
Pass through ancient redwood forest and fertile valleys, home to some of the best wine, beer, and cheese in the country. (Page 143)

Highway 1: North Coast
Rocky, lonely, and breathtakingly beautiful, this is a drive to remember. (Page 169)

Napa and Sonoma Valleys
There's nothing intimidating about this famous wine region. (Page 185)

San Francisco
Eat your way through the City by the Bay. (Page 213)

I-5: Northern California

Trip Stats

START: Oregon border

END: Sacramento

LENGTH: 280 miles

DETOUR TO SAN FRANCISCO: 334 miles

LOCAL FLAVOR: For all its beauty, the land isn't very productive. Shasta County's main agricultural focus is livestock, hay, and pastureland. Expect burgers, steaks, and olives.

BEST TIME: The weather's pleasant most of the year. Wildflowers abound in early summer, after the mountain snows melt.

WORST TIME: Driving through Mount Shasta in winter is not something you want to do without snow chains, an emergency preparedness kit, and winter-driving know-how.

LOCAL FOOD FESTIVALS: Corning Olive Festival, Corning (August). Quirky three-day parade and beauty pageant in the "Olive Capital of the World."

WORD OF WARNING: Watch road conditions carefully from late fall through spring. The road is often icy, and sometimes impassable.

MORE INFO: Shasta Cascade Wonderland Association (www.shasta cascade.com)

It's my favorite moment of all 1,380 miles of I-5—that long, downward slope as you enter California. It seems like it's always sunny in the Golden State, even if it was overcast in Oregon moments before, and as you descend into the forested valley it feels as though you've made it to the promised land.

I like to imagine this joy was shared by the first American settlers coming down the California Trail (which I-5 closely parallels). It's not a huge stretch to picture how the land looked to them—the country up here is wild and empty, and for about two hours the scenery is about as gorgeous as it gets. I-5 skirts the Klamath National Forest and then opens

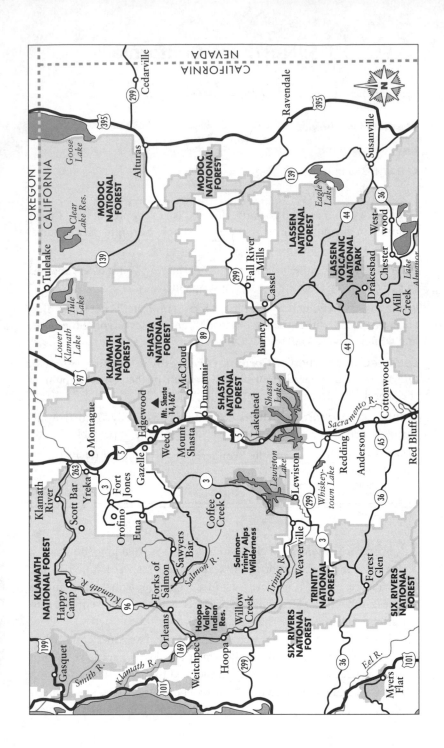

onto a long, storybook valley. The 14,000-foot volcanic cone of Mount Shasta rises from the south like a mirage. The air is so clear, the sky is so blue, and the mountain takes on an ethereal, otherworldly quality. It's almost too beautiful to look at.

Which might be a good thing, because you've got some tricky driving ahead. The road demands all your attention as you close in on the mountain and starts climbing dramatically as it winds its way past Black Butte Summit. You pass over the bridges of massive Lake Shasta, dotted with houseboats and sparkling in the sun.

The landscape changes dramatically after Redding as you enter the northern end of the long, dry Sacramento Valley. It's still ineffably California, but it's a different California—low hills in the distance, more golden grass than trees, and such a straight expanse of dull emptiness that even the roads stop having names. Occasionally the monotony is broken by fields of rice or olive groves, but mostly it's just you and the highway stretching ahead.

Towns don't offer much salvation. They are mostly ghosts of their former selves, formed and abandoned thanks to the booms and busts that characterized so much of the West. Men came here first looking for gold and silver, then to build a railroad, then to construct the hydroelectric Shasta Dam. Most restaurants are relics of those days. The region's found a nice stride today with outdoorsy tourism, but the food scene has some catching up to do.

ON THE ROAD

Mt. Shasta Brewing Company

360 College Ave, Weed
MILE/EXIT: 747
530.938.2394
www.weedales.com
OPEN: *Daily noon–9p*

The cheeky slogan of this brewing company is "Try legal weed," which gives you an idea of the kind of place it is. Not to imply that it's full of stoners; it's just got a certain irreverence about it, seen in the old-timey bikes and other knickknacks hanging from the ceiling, and the youthful crowd thanks to its proximity to the College of the Siskiyous. The "weed" in question is actually Abner Weed, the man who opened the lumber mill that later became the town of Weed. His namesake golden ale is the company's flagship, a refreshing Pilsner-style brew great for the patio on a sunny day. It, and the other locally named brews this small 15-barreled brewhouse produces (Lemurian Lager, Shastafarian Porter), are made with 100 percent pure Shasta spring water, which is said to have healing properties. The food is nothing to write home about, a simple assortment of hot dogs, nachos, and the like.

KNOW: *There's a good story behind the name "Lemurian Lager." Mount Shasta's serene energy has drawn a unique sect of oddballs and crystal-seekers to the region, including a cult called the Lemurians, who believe—and I swear I am not making this up—that there is a lost race of men living in a jewel-bedecked city deep within the mountain.*

Vivify

531 Chestnut St, Mount Shasta
MILE/EXIT: 740
530.926.1345
www.vivifyshasta.com
OPEN: *Wed–Mon 5:30p–close*

Owners Sachio and Ayako Kojima were deep in the San Francisco rat race as owners of the popular Japanese restaurant Kabuto, but that all changed when Ayako was diagnosed with cancer. The couple moved to Mount Shasta to slow things down and take advantage of the mountain's rumored healing powers. The pair's serene, organic Japanese restaurant reflects their new outlook on life, offering sushi made from whole unpeeled veggies and organic rice (gummier than most), along with the usual list of Japanese standards with gorgeous presentations. The large portion of the menu dedicated to vegan and raw food sets Vivify apart. This is sushi pushed to its limit: one roll has tempeh, avocado, green beans, and potato, and the Vivify Roll contains polenta, shiitake, spinach, avocado, and a tempura carrot. Only the truly die-hard will brave the raw Walnut Pumpkin Loaf—a mash of walnuts, pumpkin seeds, almonds, carrot, onion, yam, celery, parsley, and soy sauce that tastes better than it sounds. Dessert offers organic sake ice cream, along with a simple menu of house desserts and a vegan/raw selection.

🍴 Seven Suns Coffee & Café

1011 S Mount Shasta Blvd, Mount Shasta
MILE/EXIT: 740
530.926.9700
www.mtshastacoffee.com
OPEN: *Daily 6a–4p*

Wake up with a "white" espresso shot at this cozy coffeehouse. The shot is actually pale yellow, made from beans that have been roasted for a shorter time than the usual dark brews, and have a less bitter, slightly nutty taste, and more caffeine than regular coffee. All of the beans come from Has Beans Coffee in Chico, a local roaster that specializes in free trade and organic. As far as locations go, Seven Suns has pretty much the best one in town. It's in a historic stone house that looks like something out of a Grimm's fairy tale. Inside, worn wood floors covered with rag rugs complete the homey feel. Order coffee and pick a table in the cafe's warren of rooms. Or head outside to the flagstone patio and feel the mystic pull of Mount Shasta in the distance. The cafe's menu has breakfast burritos and sandwiches, along with lunchtime fare including a signature burger with pepper jack, grilled jalapenos, bacon, avocado, lettuce, tomato, and onion, and a very good "Super BLT" with thick-cut bacon and avocado on grilled sourdough.

🍔 The Goat Tavern

107 Chestnut St, Mount Shasta
MILE/EXIT: 738
530.926.0209
www.thegoatmountshasta.com
OPEN: *Daily 11:30a–9p*

Every mountain town should have a pub like this. Set in a ramshackle building, offering rickety patio dining and beer-tap decor, populated with locals, outdoorsmen, bohemians, and everyone in between, this is exactly the kind of place you want after a day of hard recreation in the great outdoors. Replenish your calorie count with the Wino Burger, an astonishingly delicious meld of high-quality beef, thick bacon, peppered goat cheese, spicy salad greens, and red onions cooked in a cabernet-rosemary reduction sauce, all atop a nice bun. If you want to go big, go

CALIFORNIA

Most Memorable Burgers

I love the simple burger-stand hamburger as much as the next gal, but these five heavyweights are in a class of their own.

Communication Breakdown Burger: A gloriously messy handful—topped with Tillamook cheddar and grilled mushrooms, onion, and bell peppers—is an excellent complement to a cold brew. (McMenamin's, various locations in WA and OR)

Wino Burger: Finish off a day in the Shasta National Forest with this delicious meld of high-quality beef, thick bacon, peppered goat cheese, spicy salad greens, and red onions cooked in a cabernet-rosemary reduction sauce. (The Goat Tavern, Mount Shasta, CA, page 133)

Squeeze with Cheese: This legendarily addictive burger comes adorned with a glorious "cheese skirt," something akin to a Parmesan wafer, made with a third-pound of cheddar and kitchen alchemy. (Squeeze Inn, Sacramento, CA, page 229)

Grilled Top Sirloin Burger: Sober up after a day of wine tasting with this decadent burger topped with caramelized onions and your choice of white cheddar or cambozola cheese, served on a toasted brioche bun. (Fig Café, Glen Ellen, CA, page 207)

Ambrosiaburger: This sublime burger—made with specially ground beef from Carmel Meats and Specialty Foods, served medium rare, and complemented with secret "ambrosia sauce"—is worth every penny of $14. (Nepenthe, Big Sur, CA, page 277)

with "Possibly the Best Burger in the World." It might well be: a mess of smoked cheddar, fried onion rings, bacon, basil mayo, and barbecue sauce. Choose from 12 local beers on tap, which are rotated frequently from a house selection of 60 microbrews.

 Jack's Grill

1743 California St, Redding
MILE/EXIT: 681B
530.241.9705
www.jacksgrillredding.com
OPEN: *Mon–Sat 4–11:30p*

Locals don't mind waiting their turn for steak at this Redding institution, where nothing much has changed since its opening in 1938. Not the façade or neon signage, not the cash register, not the dimness of the interior, and certainly not the portions or quality of the steaks. The place was opened by local rogue Jack Young, who saw an opportunity to sell one-pound steaks to the large population of working-class men working on the Central Pacific Railroad and Shasta Dam in town. Jack's favorite, claims the menu, is the still 16-ounce New York Strip, which is probably the thing to get unless you want to try Jack's Stack—bits of filet, New York steak, and sirloin steak sautéed with onion and peppers, doused in a light gravy, and served on hot garlic bread. Dinners come with garlic bread, baked potato or fries, and a throwback iceberg-and-green-bean salad with homemade dressing (get the blue cheese).

KNOW: *There's almost always a wait unless you get there before the kitchen opens at 5pm. Don't worry—come at 4, sit at the bar, order a classic cocktail, and soak up the atmosphere as you wait.*

Bartel's Giant Burger

18509 Lake Blvd E, Redding
MILE/EXIT: 680
530.243.7313
OPEN: *Mon–Sat 10a–9p, Sun 11:30a–9p*

Confession: I've never stopped in Redding without getting in a fight with a traveling companion. It's the first major town after a whole lot of nothing, and in my memories, at least, the weather is always inhumanly hot (Redding is the second-sunniest city in the United States, beat only by Yuma, Arizona, and temperatures peak at around 110 in the summer). These squabbles usually take place in the soulless parking lot of a Starbucks or fast-food chain, but maybe some of the crankiness and tension would be relieved at a place with history and personality— a place like this basic roadside burger joint, which has been peddling

CALIFORNIA

"old-fashioned quality" to locals and travelers since 1975. One gets the sense, looking over the linoleum floors, worn bar stools, and uncomfortably hard-looking booths, that the owners haven't invested a lot in the interior since. The burger itself is just fine, as burgers go—which is to say, it's delicious—cooked to order and topped with crisp lettuce, onions, tomato, and secret sauce. A burger like this might not be the secret to world peace, but it will certainly lighten your mood.

KNOW: *Buoy your spirits even more with a quick hike in Redding's 300-acre Turtle Bay Exploration Park, just a few minutes down the Highway 299. Don't miss the park's über-modern, $23 million Sundial Bridge across the Sacramento River, designed by Spanish architect Santiago Calatrava.*

 Buz's Crab

2159 East St, Redding
MILE/EXIT: 678B
530.243.2120
www.buzscrab.com
OPEN: *Daily 11a–9p*

A crab shack is the last thing you'd expect in a landlocked mountain town, but Buz's high-quality fish has earned the loyalty of locals. The menu offers seafood in all manner and preparation, but naturally, the thing to get here is crab. And there are plenty of options: creamy crab chowder, crab burrito, crab Louie with house-made sauce, crab sandwich, crab burger, crab cakes. All are loaded with generous portions of Dungeness crab—you can actually taste the clean flavor of the ocean—and served with sourdough bread baked daily. Buz's bills itself as "Redding's own Fisherman's Wharf," and it certainly has the seafaring theme down to a tee. The decor can only be described as "nautical-kitsch," a potpourri of porthole covers, boats (both large-scale and miniature), crab traps, buoys, nets draped from the ceiling, and undersea wall murals that look distinctly handmade. Still, something about it all works, and you'd almost swear you heard the faint cry of seagulls and felt a distant ocean breeze.

KNOW: *The adjacent seafood market sells house-made tartar and cocktail sauces, sourdough bread, fresh fish, and a whole mess of marinades, batters, spices, and cookbooks. (Market open daily 9a–9p.)*

In-N-Out's Secret Menu

It's not much of a secret these days, but there's a whole language to master at In-N-Out Burger. I promise the staff won't look at you like a crazy person if you order from this cheat sheet of tried-and-true modifications:

- **2x4:** Two patties with four slices of cheese, and any variation of it up to 4x4.

- **Animal Style:** My personal favorite. A beef patty is cooked with mustard, then pickles, cheese, dressing, and grilled onions are mixed together in a cheesy mess on the grill. Delicious. Try getting your fries Animal Style too.

- **Flying Dutchman:** Two burger patties held together with two slices of melted cheese. It's Atkins to the extreme.

- **Protein Style:** Lettuce instead of a bun.

- **Grilled Cheese:** A cheeseburger without the burger patty. Order Animal Style to spice it up.

- **Cheese Fries:** Fries with cheese melted on top. (Obvs.)

- **Fries light or well-done:** Specify how long you want your spuds to sit in the oil.

In-N-Out

1275 Dana Dr, Redding
MILE/EXIT: 678A
800.786.1000
www.in-n-out.com
OPEN: *Sun–Thu 10:30a–1a, Fri–Sat 10:30a–1:30a*

There are people who will tell you that In-N-Out is overrated. These are probably the same people who told you there was no Santa Claus— spoilsports all too eager to ruin the fun for everyone else. The truth is, In-N-Out is neither overrated nor underrated but simply rated: rightfully known as the best fast-food burger west (or east) of the Mississippi. The secret is its simplicity. You won't find egg rolls, breakfast sandwiches, or even chicken strips on the menu, which has remained essentially unchanged for the past sixty years. What you will find is a short list of perfectly executed hamburgers, cheeseburgers, French fries, and milk shakes, all made to order from fresh ingredients (there are no microwaves or freezers on the premises). There's an ostensibly secret sub-menu; but the cat's out of the bag for anyone who knows how to use Google. (See sidebar for tested methods.) In-N-Out has been a pioneer in the fast-food industry since the beginning—it was the first fast food drive-through when Harry and Esther Snyder opened it in Baldwin Park in 1948.

KNOW: *This was the northernmost location of the chain at press time, which has more than 200 locations up and down California highways. Want to know if there's one in the vicinity? There's an app for that. (Free at the iTunes store.) There's also a downloadable location guide on the website with handy check boxes.*

VARIOUS LOCATIONS *throughout California*

 The Olive Pit

2156 Solano St, Corning
MILE/EXIT: 631
530.824.4667
www.olivepit.com
OPEN: *Daily 7a–8p*

Corning is known as the "Olive Capital of the World." Production-wise, it's not even the olive capital of California—Tulare County claims that honor—but the nickname speaks to the marketing genius of 1890s real estate developer Warren Woodson, who created an entire land-buying campaign around the crop because it was the only thing that would grow in the climate. The olive legacy still lives on in places like this friendly roadside pit stop, where visitors can sample what seems like every variety of olive on earth at the tasting bar, or browse the store's selection of local nuts, rice, dates, figs, and other edibles. The shop also has a deli with sandwiches, including pitch-perfect, extremely filling muffuletta. The Olive Pit started life in the mid-1960s as a burger stand, and when owners Pete and Ann Craig put some olives from their trees on sale, the public responded in a major way. Their son now runs the family business.

 Granzellas

451 6th St, Williams
MILE/EXIT: 577
530.473.2545
www.granzellas.com
OPEN: *Mon–Fri 6a–9p, Sat–Sun 6a–10p*

The muffuletta sandwich doesn't get much play on the West Coast, which is a surprise not only because California produces most of the country's olives, but also because West Coasters love a good sandwich. And pretty much nothing beats a good muffuletta, piled high with cold cuts, tangy from the olive salad, all the juices soaking into the crusty bread. Granzella's offers an excellent rendition, generous with the meat and cheese, perfect on house-baked bread. This roadside deli has been around since 1969 and used to be housed in a historic Wells Fargo building, but suffered catastrophic losses in a 2007 fire and had to be rebuilt. Efforts have been made to restore it to its former glory, but forced authenticity is never the same. Still, the food more than makes up for any lack of ambience: along with the first-rate deli, there's a huge variety of olives at a tasting bar similar to the Olive Pit's, and many jars of house-made pickled items like capers, marinated garlic, and more that make excellent pantry supplies for dinner parties.

KNOW: *Granzella's is attached to an inn, if you're looking for a place to stop for the day.*

DETOURS & DESTINATIONS

Detour: I-80 to San Francisco

It's kind of incredible. This freeway is flat, dull, and dead, and then BAM! Around Vacaville you hit the suburbs, and you're back in civilization and in the tractor beam of San Francisco. Watch for traffic nearing Berkeley and onto the Bay Bridge (heads up: it's a toll bridge).

 Nut Tree

1681 E Monte Vista Ave, Vacaville

MILE/EXIT: 55

707.447.6000

www.nuttreeusa.com

OPEN: *Mon–Thu 11a–6p, Fri–Sun 11a–7p*

Back when Interstate 80 was State Route 40, Nut Tree was a roadside attraction *par excellence*—a simple farm stand that eventually grew into a quirky gift shop, bakery, and restaurant with an indoor aviary that was an early pioneer of California cuisine. It had its own zip code, railroad, and airport, and was visited by luminaries like Presidents Reagan and Nixon, Queen Elizabeth II, and Bing Crosby. Then it was bulldozed in 2003 and replaced with a shopping mall with the same name and location. One has to admire the endless American capacity for reinvention. These days, there's not much of a reason to stop here unless you need a break. Potential pick-me-ups include a Peet's Coffee, old-fashioned ice cream parlor Fentons Creamery, and Winters Fruit Tree, still selling California almonds and other dried local fruit and nuts. Tucked away in a corner is a wall of historic photos showing the place's former glory, but I don't recommend swinging by unless you're in the mood to get depressed and crank up "Big Yellow Taxi" when you're back on the road.

KNOW: *There's a very pleasant, if slightly ersatz, plaza with a kid-sized train, life-size chess and checker sets, carousel, and picnic area.*

Jelly Belly Visitor Center & Factory

One Jelly Belly Ln, Fairfield

MILE/EXIT: 44

800.522.3267

www.jellybelly.com

OPEN: *Daily 9a–5p*

Unless you're traveling with children or have a disproportionate love for jelly beans, there are only two reasons to visit this splendiferous factory: to stock up on cheap bags of factory-imperfect "Belly Flops," and to glory in the kitschy spectacle of U.S. presidential portraits rendered in Jelly Bellys. The fact that these seem entirely normal in the moment is a testament to the mind-boggling amount of Jelly Belly branding inside the factory's four walls. The assault actually starts outside the front entrance, with the outsize blow-up of mascot "Mr. Jelly Belly" slightly bobbing a greeting in the wind. Inside, prepare yourself. Jelly Bellys are literally everywhere you look: printed in the carpet, covering the walls as decals, hanging from the ceiling in fiberglass models. Even the pizzas and burgers in the cafe are kidney shaped. That said, the free 45-minute tour is pretty interesting, in a Mr. Rogers sort of way. Put on a silly white paper hat and learn why it can take up to three weeks to make a Jelly Belly, and how they make that one taste so much like buttered popcorn. Afterward, head to the candy store tasting bar to try all the flavors in the rainbow, or confirm your suspicions that orange, tangerine, and orange sherbet all taste pretty much the same. (Spoiler alert: Impressively, they don't.)

TOURS: *Offered daily 9a–4p, depart every 15 minutes or so, and are 45 minutes long and free. It's usually pretty painless to join a tour, though the wait can creep up to an hour on certain holidays and popular weekends (spring break, summer, etc.).*

CALIFORNIA

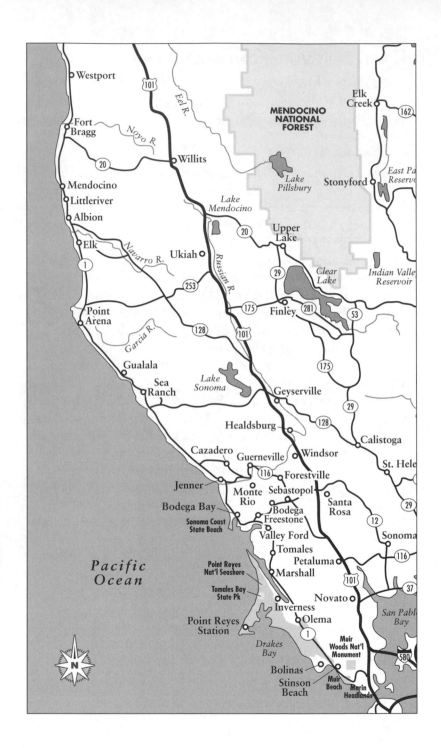

Highway 101: Northern California

𝒯𝓇𝒾𝓅 𝒮𝓉𝒶𝓉𝓈

START: Crescent City

END: San Francisco

LENGTH: 377 miles

LOCAL FLAVOR: Locavore cuisine, beer (especially extra-hoppy IPAs), wine, fruits and vegetables (especially apples and pears), cheese.

LOCAL FOOD FESTIVALS:

- **Hops in Humboldt:** Fortuna (August). Dozens of local breweries come to this festival, located deep in the Redwood forest.

- **Gravenstein Apple Fair:** Sebastopol (August). "The sweetest fair in the Sonoma County" offers apple-tasting contests, local food vendors, and plenty of apple pie to go around.

WORD OF WARNING: Heavy, soupy fog is common in the Redwoods, especially north of Arcata. Watch for Roosevelt elk grazing near the road.

MORE INFO: California Travel and Tourism Commission (www.visit california.com)

I fell hard for Northern California, a love I didn't see coming and won't likely get over soon. I've never been to a place where the food and land are so deeply intertwined. The majestic redwood groves and lush river valleys that make up this region are host to farms, vineyards, dairies, and breweries that work with the land and with each other to create a robust culinary ecology all their own.

It rises out of a firm belief that man should give back as much as he takes from the land; he should leave the earth a better place than he found it. Organic and biodynamic farming, environmental sustainability, solar power, and carbon offsets—these aren't catchphrases or passing trends here, but ways of life. This is a place where owls and hawks do the work of herbicides, and restaurants without vegetarian menus and local ingredients are the exception, not the rule. This is the place where the first

CALIFORNIA

organic beer in the country was brewed, and the first winery was declared carbon-neutral. It's a place that makes make you believe in the dream of Ecotopia.

The consideration paid to the environment might have to do with the way the region was settled. America never had to conquer this land outright, just farm it. Technically everything south of the Oregon border was owned by Spain, then Mexico, but neither empire had the resources to maintain their northern frontier. The land north of Healdsburg just sat there as enterprising Americans trickled in, establishing homesteads and farms and communities.

Or maybe the environmental dedication is because Northern Californians live life in the shadow of the oldest trees on earth. "The redwoods, once seen, leave a mark or create a vision that stays with you always," wrote John Steinbeck, describing the intangible, sublime calm that these giants seem to elicit in all. There is something magnificent about them, something untouchable. Their lives began before humans existed on this land, and that solemnity must provide those who live under them perspective, meaning, hope.

Over the past half century, another type of battle has been fought for the land—not for the right to farm it, but for the right to preserve it. Radicals might not chain themselves to redwoods anymore in a fight against big logging, but there's a smaller fight against big agriculture—a fight Northern Calfornians are taking on only for themselves.

It all adds up to a region of family-owned farms, cafes, wineries, and breweries. Some have been around since the Spanish ruled the area; some have been opened in the past decade by urban transplants seeking a simpler life. All share a passion for food and life; that passion in turn shines in their dishes, made from honest ingredients, lovingly coaxed to full flavor.

ON THE ROAD

 Beacon Burger

160 Anchor Way, Crescent City
MILE/EXIT: 790
707.464.6565
OPEN: *Hours vary; call ahead for details*

True to its name, this bright yellow burger shack beacons hungry travelers from the northern tip of the curved beach that gives Crescent City its title. Beacon Burger provides reliably, if not extraordinarily, good roadside hamburgers and cheeseburgers, fried mushrooms, potato gems (addictive tater-tot-like fried missiles), a varied milk shake selection made with local cream, and a simple menu of other burger-stand classics. Salt air makes everything taste better. With that spirit in mind, take your food outside to the picnic tables next to the parking lot, or pay a visit to the harbor's resident sea lions. You'll hear them before you see them, at their local hangout on the floating docks by the main promontory.

North Coast Co-Op

811 I St, Arcata
MILE/EXIT: 713
707.822.5947
www.northcoastco-op.com
OPEN: *Daily 6a–9p*

Arcata (pronounced ar-KAY-ta) was founded as a mining supply town, but has since become a favorite hangout of hippies and activists, due to Humboldt State University and the not-quite-legal cash crop growing in the nearby hills. All the elements of a good hippie co-op are firmly in place at this one: the grind-your-own peanut butter stand; the endless aisles of bulk grains, flours, and nuts (more than 400 in all); the fill-your-own-bottle shampoos and lotions; and a whole new generation of flower children with dreadlocks and unshaved armpits. After taking in the local character, forage for supplies—co-ops are excellent places to find regional foods consolidated in one place. Here, browse the organic produce, extensive microbrew selection, and in-house bakery and deli that

CALIFORNIA

focus on organic and natural ingredients whenever possible. Of course, there are plenty of options for vegetarians and vegans.

KNOW: *The co-op has another location in nearby Eureka (25 4th St; 707.443.6027).*

Golden Harvest Cafe

1062 G St, Arcata

MILE/EXIT: 713

707.822.8962

www.goldenharvestcafe.com

OPEN: *Mon–Fri 6:30a–3p, Sat–Sun 7:30a–3p*

"Herbivore, carnivore, we have what you're looking for!" The cheerful greeting on the top of the menu announces this family-owned cafe's non-discriminatory policy toward the most important meal of the day. The menu caters to all breakfast proclivities by offering diners the freedom of choice: you decide whether your California Benedict comes on a biscuit or English muffin; with bacon or tofu bacon; includes tomato, avocado, or a poached egg; and is smothered in hollandaise or cream sauce. Other house favorites include potato cakes—country potatoes grilled with cheese, veggies, and/or meat and formed into a cakelike shape—and pancakes made with white or whole wheat flour. No matter what you order, everything is fresh, unprocessed, and organic whenever possible, including coffee and orange juice. The lunch menu offers sandwiches and burgers, with patty options including beef, New York steak, chicken, veggie burgers, tofu, and seitan.

Samoa Cookhouse

908 Vance Ave, Samoa

MILE/EXIT: 713

DISTANCE FROM HWY: 7.4 miles

707.442.1659

www.samoacookhouse.net

OPEN: *Mon–Sat 7a–3:30p, 5–9p; Sun 7a–10p*

The cookhouse was the center of life for turn-of-the-century loggers—a place for brawny men to enjoy a little communal living, hearty victuals, and good conversation. Meals were served family-style from metal carts; it's said a lumberman could judge the day of week based on the menu. This particular cookhouse, first started by the Hammond Lumber Company, has been continually serving hugely caloric meals since 1890, though it now caters mainly to people who have never done a day of hard labor in their lives. Three meals are offered daily, but breakfast is the best. One Wednesday morning featured bottomless fluffy biscuits, a tureen of country gravy, platefuls of scrambled eggs, potatoes, and spicy breakfast sausage, along with toast, a mini-pitcher of orange juice, and a thermos of coffee. It's all still served from metal carts, pushed around by a highly efficient team of career waitresses. The tables are long and communal, covered with aging checked oilcloth, and the yellowing photos of lumberjacks on the white wooden walls and the old-timey banjo music in the background make you feel a kinship with the long line of loggers who once dined there, even if walking to your car is the most physical activity you'll get that day.

KNOW: *Before you eat, take a peek into the museum in an adjacent room. More than rusting logging implements and old photographs, the museum gives a great overview of the region's lumbering past and the cookhouse's role in it.*

Lost Coast Brewery

617 4th St, Eureka
MILE/EXIT: On Hwy 101 at 4th St
707.445.4480
www.lostcoast.com
OPEN: *Sun–Thu 11a–10p, Fri–Sat 11a–11p*

I was stoked to visit this brewery for a couple reasons. It's one of the only female-owned and -operated breweries in the United States, a notable feat in itself. It's also home to a few of my all-time favorite beers: Down Town Brown, a nutty, full-bodied brown ale, and Great White, a refreshing and citrusy white beer that's got a kick from a secret combo of Humboldt herbs (no, not *those* Humboldt herbs). The experience didn't let me down. The beers at the brewery are more varied than I imagined, and I was pleasantly surprised to find a number of interesting fruit beers like Tangerine Wheat, Raspberry Brown, and Apricot Wheat. Food is standard pub grub like burgers, sandwiches, and nachos—necessary if you work your way through the 10-beer tasting flight (a steal at $10). For dessert, you can't go wrong with a float made with stout or house-made root beer. Overseeing your every move is a large black-and-white photograph of the Fraternal Order of the Knights of Pythias, a secret society that built and owned the brick building for a century until owners Barbara Groom and Wendy Pound took it over in 1990.

Old Town Coffee & Chocolates

211 F St, Eureka
MILE/EXIT: F Street
707.445.8600
www.oldtowncoffeeeureka.com
OPEN: *Sun–Wed 7a–9p, Thu–Sat 7a–10p*

Perfect stop for a quick pick-me-up in Eureka's elegantly restored Victorian downtown. The air in this brick-walled cafe smells like baking sugar, thanks to the hot-off-the-iron waffles from a short menu that also includes pastries, bagel sandwiches, and soup. These are no ordinary waffles. They're shaped like boats, and can be filled with maple or boysenberry syrup, strawberries and whipped cream, bananas and pecans, or ice cream. The coffee selection is larger than you'd expect, offering organic and regular beans from around the world, plus the cafe's own blends with names like Foggy Dog and Redwood Roast. Locals linger in the adjacent room and take advantage of the free Wi-Fi; there's also a computer hooked up to the Internet available for a small fee. It's an excellent spot to take a breather while you plan your next move.

Eel River Brewing Company

1777 Alamar Way, Fortuna
MILE/EXIT: 688
707.725.2739
www.eelriverbrewing.com
OPEN: *Daily 11a–11p*

"Be natural, drink naked" is the motto of the country's first USDA-certified organic brewery, but it's thankfully not an ethos currently practiced in the pub and sizeable beer garden. The brewery turns out locally acclaimed beers like the crisp California Blonde Ale, sweet certified organic Amber Ale, and inky-black Ravens Eye Stout, along with more unusual brews like Hazelnut Porter and Apricot Wheat. The menu has pub grub favorites, but the standout is the stout-smoked meats, from local cows that feed on grass and leftover grains from the brewing process. In 2007, the brewery moved its main operation to the former old-growth redwood mill in nearby Scotia, a 20,000-square-foot facility newly vacated by the Pacific Lumber Company. Recycling and eco-friendly practices come naturally to owner Ted Vivatson, a former land surveyor turned brewmaster who opened the brewery with his wife, Margaret, in 1994.

 Woodrose Café

911 Redwood Dr, Garberville
MILE/EXIT: 639B
707.923.3191
www.woodrosecafe.com
OPEN: *Mon–Fri 8a–2p, Sat–Sun 8a–1p*

Garberville is the nearest town to the towering Avenue of the Giants in Redwood National Park, and it's been ground zero for the fight for the preservation of the ancient trees since the 1970s. All those activists and radicals have gotta eat somewhere. They head to this small-town cafe, which has offered organic, healthy breakfasts and lunches since 1977. Slide into a booth, or take a seat at a swivel chair at the well-worn breakfast counter and strike up a conversation with the locals. The cafe sources the freshest ingredients possible, and the difference shows in dishes like huevos rancheros, where farm-fresh eggs elevate a classic to new heights. (Vegans can sub in tofu.) Prices are a couple dollars higher than the average diner, but you're paying for the quality of the ingredients, and in my mind that's always an investment worth making.

Ardella's Downtown Diner

77 S Main St, Willits
MILE/EXIT: 674
707.459.6577
OPEN: *Wed–Sat 7a–2:45p, Sun 8a–2p*
Cash only

Organic, fresh ingredients are great and all—but sometimes a girl wants a gloriously greasy breakfast. Enter Ardella's, where locals go to grub and gab. This friendly diner serves lunch, but it's known for its breakfasts: near-legendary omelets, scrambles, pancakes, French toast, and corned beef hash, each of which could put you in a food coma for the rest of the morning. The welcoming interior has checked floors and red vinyl chairs, and is usually filled to capacity with the residents of Willits, a town in the center of Mendocino County that was the original home of Seabiscuit. Eavesdrop on local conversations over a scramble made with fresh produce, and leave sated and satisfied with your taste of the local community.

 ## Mendocino Wine Co.

501 Parducci Rd, Ukiah
MILE/EXIT: 552
707.463.5350
www.mendocinowineco.com
OPEN: *Daily 10a–5p*

How many conservationists does it take to open a carbon-neutral winery? Only two, as it turns out—if the conservationists in question have the credentials of Paul Dolan and Tim Thornhill. In 2004, the duo teamed up and bought Parducci Wine Cellars, the oldest winery in Mendocino County, with the dream to turn it into the new face of sustainable wine-making. Drawing on their backgrounds and shared passion (Dolan's an expert in organic farming and sustainable business, Thornhill's a horticulturist dedicated to preserving heritage trees), the pair has done an impressive job of achieving their goal. The winery only sources grapes from family-owned farms, runs its organic farm on 100 percent green power and recycled water, uses biodiesel to fuel its equipment, makes packaging and labels from eco-friendly products, and became the first winery in the country to be certified carbon-neutral. Their pride, confidence, and responsibility to the land is reflected in the award-winning wines: very good pinot noirs, sauvignon blancs, and chardonnays, many made from organic grapes. Sipping earth-sensitive wine under the brick arches of the classic cellarlike tasting room is enough to make you believe in the future.

TOURS: *Call for an appointment.*

 ## Ukiah Brewing Co. & Restaurant

102 S State St, Ukiah
MILE/EXIT: 551
707.468.5898
www.ukiahbrewingco.com
OPEN: *Mon–Thu 11a–11p, Fri–Sun 11a–1a*

It's not just the beer that's organic—it's everything from the hops to the ketchup at this downtown Ukiah brewery. It became the first brewpub (and second restaurant) to be certified organic by the California Certified Organic Farmers (CCOF) in only its second year of business, and shows no signs of slowing down. Longtime craft brewer Bret Cooperrider started the brewery with his parents, both biologists involved in Mendocino County ecological issues. The menu features pub standards like fish-and-chips and burgers (made with produce, meat, and seafood from independent local producers), which coexist peacefully with vegetarian, vegan, and raw selections. The beers are also organic, of course, and include the basic Pilsner Ukiah, the heady Comptche Logger in the California "steam beer" style, and the rich Coops Stout, which is served on nitrogen taps to velvety perfection. German-style beers like Liberator bock, Emancipator doppelbock, and Renegade barleywine are also on the menu. The whole operation is housed in a stately historic brick building with wood floors, a dark wood bar, and booths by large windows that are perfect for scoping the scene in downtown Ukiah.

KNOW: *Most nights feature live music, which brings in the community; it can make for a noisy dinner if you're eating late.*

Brutocao Cellars

13500 S Hwy 101, Hopland
MILE/EXIT: 14 miles south of Ukiah on Hwy 101
800.433.3689
www.brutocaocellars.com
OPEN: *Daily 10a–5p*

No one has mastered the art of hanging out and enjoying life quite like the Italians, but this charming winery comes close to channeling the spirit of *la dolce vita*. Taste your way through the chardonnays, sauvignon blancs, and Italian varietals the winery is known for, in the light-filled tasting room with a prominent mural of Venice behind the bar. After a quick sample of the family's estate-grown, Tuscan-style olive oils, head outside to the regulation bocce ball courts. There are six of them in all, and visitors are encouraged to stay and make an afternoon of it. The on-site restaurant, the Crushed Grape, has classic Italian food executed with a light touch, including wood-fired pizzas and house-made pastas, and also has a fully stocked bar if you're not in a wine mood. As expected of Mendocino wineries, Brutocao is committed to sustainable wine practices on its 400 acres spread over four vineyards. The Anderson Valley offshoot specializes in pinot noir and has a tasting room of its own, set in a peaceful valley with

CALIFORNIA

a rustic barn and a wisteria-covered arbor with rough-hewn picnic tables perfect for an afternoon. (7000 Hwy 128, Philo; 800.661.2103)

KNOW: *The winery's logo is the winged Lion of St. Mark's, the logo of the Venetian Republic.*

Mendocino Brewing Company

13351 S Hwy 101, Hopland

MILE/EXIT: 14 miles south of Ukiah on Hwy 101

707.744.1361

www.mendobrew.com

OPEN: *July–mid-Sept Sun–Thu noon–8p, Fri–Sat 11a–10p; mid-Sept–June Mon–Thu 1–7p, Fri–Sat noon–8p*

Birds of prey are the mascots for this brewery's aggressive ales, from the distinctive red-tailed hawk that graces the label of the signature Red Tail IPA, to the fierce-looking hawk that signifies the intensity of the Eye of the Hawk select ale. This was the first brewpub in California to open after Prohibition, and its setting in a former saloon echoes the glory of alehouses gone by. Many of the bar's original elements have been lovingly preserved, including a tin-embossed wall (which can be seen in the hanging historical black-and-white photos), and though the blonde oak and brass bar is new, it was built to replicate the style of old San Francisco saloons. The brewery's specialty is traditional English ales with a hoppy California twist; the outlier is the delicate Blue Heron Pale Ale, the only brew not represented by a raptor. There's currently no food at the brewery, but the staff has plenty of delivery menus on hand. The hop-vine- shaded beer garden in back is a nice place to while away an afternoon.

KNOW: *The brewery also makes barbecue sauces and marinades with Red Tail Ales, which can be sampled and purchased in the adjacent gift shop.*

Dry Creek General Store

3945 Dry Creek Rd, Healdsburg

MILE/EXIT: 512

DISTANCE FROM HWY: 5.7 miles

707.433.4171

www.drycreekgeneralstore1881.com

OPEN: *Mon–Sat 6a–6:30p, Sun 7a–6:30p*

Artisanal sandwiches, local wines, picnic items, and kitchen wares are what's for sale these days at this former general store. A gourmet makeover hasn't changed the look and feel of the place, which has the faded signage, rickety front porch, and creaky screen door appropriate for a building from 1881. A sign painted on a rusting saw above the deli counter boasts that these are "the best sandwiches you ever 'saw'"—not only that, they're some of the best you'll eat too. The sandwich menu has an Italian slant, but also has American favorites like a Reuben with apple sauerkraut, and a curried egg salad sandwich with prosciutto, fresh mozzarella, and tomatoes. Eat inside at the dining tables surrounded by the store's eclectic inventory, or take your food to the porch's Adirondack chairs and nearby picnic tables and feast on a view of the vineyards and rolling wooded hills. Small touches like geraniums in an old Coca-Cola dispenser help tie the old to the new, and the old-fashioned wooden bar in back is a good spot for a beer.

KNOW: *The staff is very knowledgeable about the area's wineries—hit them up for recommendations if it's not too busy.*

Lambert Bridge Winery

4085 West Dry Creek Rd, Healdsburg
MILE/EXIT: 512
DISTANCE FROM HWY: 7.2 miles
707.431.9600
www.lambertbridge.com/winery
OPEN: *Daily 10:30a–4:30p*

How does one make a Bordeaux blend? What is a Bordeaux blend, anyway? These questions and more are answered during the 45-minute blending seminar offered at this peaceful Dry Creek winery, which teaches visitors about major Bordeaux grapes like cabernet sauvignon, merlot, cabernet franc, and petit verdot, and then turns them loose to create their own masterpieces ($45, call for an appointment). Unsurprisingly, Lambert Bridge is known for Bordeaux blends and varietals aged entirely in French oak, as part of a wine program headed up by 30-year veteran Jill Davis, who earned her chops at venerable California institutions like Beringer and Buena Vista. The tasting room and grounds embody the character of the valley, from the 1947 Ford flatbed truck that greets visitors to the handsome redwood bar and

CALIFORNIA

ℋealdsburg

Nestled at the northern end of Sonoma County at the convergence of the Dry Creek, Russian River, and Alexander Valleys, Healdsburg is a laid-back commercial and culinary center for the prolific wine and produce regions that surround it. The town is centered around the nineteenth-century Healdsburg Plaza, framed by tasting rooms and lively cafes, and the lazy, winding Russian River sets a pace far removed from urban life. Healdsburg is where the highway starts to leave redwoods and enter farm country, a productive and diverse region settled in the years following the gold rush. It also serves as the jumping-off point for bicycle trips though the valleys, and has an excellent Saturday morning farmers market.

---

massive stone fireplace in the tasting room. The landscaped grounds are worth a ramble for the wisteria-cloaked patio, pretty gazebo, shady picnic tables, and extensive culinary garden that supplies ingredients for a food, wine, and cheese tasting flight.

TOURS: *Available upon request and staff availability.*

Medlock Ames & Alexander Valley Wine Bar

3487 Alexander Valley Rd, Healdsburg
MILE/EXIT: 507
707.431.8845
www.medlockames.com/visit-us
OPEN: *Tasting room daily 10a–5p; wine bar daily from 5p*

This super-hip tasting room and bar opened in a renovated general store in 2010, and has since emerged as a front-runner in the new guard of Alexander Valley wineries. Taste your way through the cabernet sauvignon, merlot, and chardonnay that the valley is known for, or try flights paired with seasonal produce from the on-site organic garden. That same produce makes an appearance in jars of homemade preserves and pickles that line the walls, and in seasonal cocktails in the speakeasy-like Alexander Valley Bar just beyond the tasting room. Owners Chris Medlock James and Ames Morison stayed true to the building's turn-of-the-century roots, and elements like the tin ceiling, big oak bar, and Victorian banquettes conjure up visions of Old West saloons. If the night is warm, snag a seat on the outdoor patio and soak up the views of Alexander Valley spread in front of you. Medlock Ames is more green than most: only 56 of its 335 acres are dedicated to vineyards, with the rest left in their natural state of oaks and wildflowers. The winery also employs organic farming methods and runs on solar power.

 Jimtown Store

6706 Hwy 128, Healdsburg

MILE/EXIT: 507

DISTANCE FROM HWY: 5 miles

707.433.1212

www.jimtown.com

OPEN: *Mon–Fri 7a–5p, Sat–Sun 7:30a–5p*

Celebrate Americana in all its Technicolor glory at this roadside deli and shop in Alexander Valley. A retro sign in front promises "Good Coffee & Real Food," and that's basically what you get: seasonal soups, salads, entrees, and sandwiches, in a location that pays homage to the past while remaining hip and forward-facing. The Jimtown Store started life in 1895 as a general store, post office, and meeting place for the valley's farming community. A century later, it was bought by a former Silver Palate partner and his wife, given a facelift by a team of San Francisco architects, and reopened as a destination for locals and tourists alike. The food spotlights the best of the season: An August afternoon offered watermelon gazpacho; vegetarian enchiladas with chickpeas, zucchini, and corn; and buttermilk coleslaw. Sandwiches are inventive and come with the store's signature spreads, like a tasty one made with prosciutto, Point Reyes blue cheese, and Jimtown's fig and olive spread. Eat on a glossy red picnic table in the vineyard-shaded back patio, and when you're done, browse the candy, housewares, and unique gift items in the adjacent store. Wash it down with a local wine or the store's own Jimtown blend, made in a partnership with nearby Hawkes vineyards. Box lunches are available with 24 hours' notice for Wine Country picnics.

KNOW: *Like what you taste? Pick up a copy of the shop's cookbook on your way out.*

 Oakville Grocery

124 Matheson St, Healdsburg
MILE/EXIT: 504
707.433.3200
www.oakvillegrocery.com
OPEN: *Daily 8a–6p*

The second location of Napa Valley's famous picnic-stocking spot, in a sunny location on Healdsburg's nineteenth-century main plaza. (See page 154 for more details.)

Bear Republic Brewery

345 Healdsburg Ave, Healdsburg
MILE/EXIT: 504
707.433.2337
www.bearrepublic.com
OPEN: *Sun–Thu 11a–9p, Fri–Sat 11a–10p (stays open later in summer)*

This brewery just off Healdsburg Plaza makes Racer 5, a bright, hoppy ale that's the go-to IPA for many Californians. It's widely available, but many of the brewery's other beers are not, and a visit to the tasting room gives you a chance to appreciate the full extent of brewer Richard Norgrove's genius when it comes to blending hop aromas and flavors. It turns out that Racer 5 is only the tip of the IPA iceberg: try the Hop Rod Rye, a rye IPA with an earthier character than its floral cousins, or tackle the super-strong Apex IPA, a supercharged ale that explodes on your palate. I was also surprised by the number of Belgian-style ales made by the brewery, which nicely straddle the balanced nuance of Belgian brews with the assertiveness of Northern California ales. Try them all with a tasting sampler that includes information on how different hops and brewing styles influence the final product. The beer's all the better at a table on the creekside patio.

KNOW: *Norgrove drives a stock car competitively in his free time, which explains the brewery's car-racing theme.*

Kendall-Jackson Wine Center

5007 Fulton Rd, Fulton
MILE/EXIT: 495A
707.571.8100
www.kj.com/visit
OPEN: *Daily 10a–5p*

Visit the culinary gardens before you do anything else at this large, family-owned winery—they provide a sensory wine-and-food education that sticks with you far longer than any lecture on the theme would. Taste and smell your way through the wine sensory gardens, a showcase of the common flavors and flavor-affinities of wine varietals. (For example, the chardonnay garden features apples, pears, gardenias, peaches, and melons, while the zinfandel-syrah corner spotlights blackberries, pomegranates, black currants, and lavender.) Home cooks will want to linger in the international gardens, which feature the produce and herbs used in various world cuisines. The gardens are interesting in themselves, but are really meant to educate visitors on how to pair wine with food. (You might notice that the French garden is heavy on herbs, which also appear in the chardonnay and pinot noir sections, two of France's most popular wines; or that the Italian section overlaps heavily with the sangiovese section.) After a quick glance through the herb, heirloom tomato, and edible flower

---

Sonoma County Farm Trails

Sonoma County was famous for its orchards and produce fields way before it was famous for its vineyards. There are literally dozens of family-owned farms in Sonoma County, and Sonoma County Farm Trails has done an excellent job of compiling them into user-friendly driving maps. Download the guide from their website or order one for mail delivery; you can also pick one up at visitor centers throughout the region. Spend a day getting lost in the back roads and see the agrarian side of this rural county. Download a guide from the official website (www.sonoma countyfarmtrails.org).

CALIFORNIA

gardens, head into the pretty chateau-style building for a tasting of the large-scale winery's Vintner's Reserve and Highland Estate wines, which aren't usually found in supermarkets. For a splurge, try the wine and food tasting, which pairs wines with food made from produce in the gardens.

KNOW: *Every September the winery hosts the Heirloom Tomato Festival, a tasting of the 170-some varieties of heirlooms grown on the estate.*

TOURS: *Guided garden tours conducted daily 11a, 1p, and 3p (weather permitting).*

Korbel Champagne Cellars

13250 River Rd, Guerneville

MILE/EXIT: 504

DISTANCE FROM HWY: 15 miles

707.824.7000

www.korbel.com

OPEN: *Daily 10a–5p*

Marie Antoinette would feel right at home at the grand, ivy-bedecked brick tasting room of this celebrated sparkling wine producer. Strolling around the landscaped grounds that surround the 1882 Korbel family home, including a 250-variety heritage rose garden, it's easy to forget that the family started out as humble farmers. In the 1870s, Czechoslovakian immigrants Francis, Anton, and Joseph Korbel shared a ranch in the lush Russian River Valley, growing prunes, beets, wheat, corn, and alfalfa. One day they started experimenting with pinot noir, the principal grape in France's Champagne region and relatively unusual in California at the time. A decade later, they'd settled on sparkling wine and sent for a Czech winemaker to come to the states and help them with champagne-making using traditional French methods. As a result, the Korbels virtually invented California-style sparkling wine, which has more fruit and less yeast than its French counterparts. Today Korbel practices sustainable farming and produces a range of sparkling wines made from different grapes and with different methods. Stop in the deli and then take a sandwich and wine out to the patio, to breathe in the redwoods and the winery's unique place in history.

KNOW: *The 50-minute winery tour is worth the time investment. It takes you through the historic champagne cellars and a museum that shows the history of the winery and its production methods. You'll never look at a bottle of bubbly the same again.*

TOURS: *Winery tour daily 11a–3p (50 min), garden tour daily 1p and 3p (mid-April through mid-October).*

Russian River Brewing Co.

725 4th St, Santa Rosa

MILE/EXIT: 490

707.545.2337

www.russianriverbrewing.com

OPEN: *Sun–Thu 11a–midnight, Fri–Sat 11a–1a*

One of the state's most interesting breweries has a colorful backstory to go with it. Once upon a time, Korbel Champagne Cellars decided to flirt with beer-making and opened this innovative brewery in the heart of Wine Country in 1997. Their honeymoon was over by 2002, and Korbel sold the works to brewmaster Vinne Cilurzo and his wife—but not without imparting its emphasis on quality wine-making on its successor. Cilurzo makes strange brews that have as much depth and nuance as wine—take Supplication, a Belgian-style brown ale aged in French oak pinot noir barrels with yeasts and sour cherries. It's a sour, complex beer with as many aromas and flavors as a good glass of pinot. Sour beer is a heady, acquired taste. Ease into things with Temptation, aged in French oak chardonnay barrels to produce a mild Belgian blonde ale. Complicated European ales aren't the only trick up Cilurzo's sleeve, however. He produced the first double IPA in the country at his original Blind Pig brewpub, which has since evolved into the über-hoppy Pliny the Elder, a double IPA that will knock your socks off. Beer this big has a high alcohol content, and the menu delivers good food that will tame the tipsiness. Snack on pizza bites, bread covered with cheese and dipped in marinara, or one of the delicious wood-fired pizzas.

Lagunitas Brewing Company

1280 N McDowell Blvd, Petaluma

MILE/EXIT: 476

707.778.8776

www.lagunitas.com

OPEN: *Wed–Fri 3–9p, Sat–Sun 1–7p*

Equally famous for its IPA, one of the best-selling in the state, as it is for founder Tony Magee's lucid rants on the labels. Magee is what they used to call a "creative spirit," and his energy comes through in his brewing. Lagunitas consistently experiments with new brewing styles done with irreverent attitude—take, for instance, the line of limited-edition beers Magee released to commemorate each of hero Frank Zappa's albums. Hopheads will be happy here, too: Hop Stoopid is a seriously big ale, but not as big as Lagunitas Maximus, which as the name suggests, is about as big as IPAs get. The recognizable dog label echoes the canine theme in the rest of the brewery, and the company regularly donates beer to fund-raisers for PETA and the Animal Rescue Foundation in Mill Creek.

Adobe Pumpkin Farm

2478 E Washington St, Petaluma
MILE/EXIT: 474
707.763.6416
www.adobepumpkinfarm.com
OPEN: *Daily 10a–6p, late Sept–Oct 31*

Set on 30 acres, this family-friendly farm is open during the harvest season and offers U-pick pumpkins, flowers, gourds, Indian corn, and everything else to make any harvest festival a success. Kids will love the corn maze, haunted barn, hay rides, and "Pumpkin Fairy Godmother," who rises from the pumpkin patch on weekends to tell stories and sprinkle "fairy dust" on pumpkins. The farm was started in 1998 by lifetime flower grower Robert Neve, who wanted to put his green thumb to use by bringing the joys of farm life to a younger generation. The farm also plays host to "Green Halloween," a local initiative to promote a healthier holiday.

Petaluma Creamery

621 Western Ave, Petaluma
MILE/EXIT: 474
707.762.3446
www.springhillcheese.com
OPEN: *Daily 9a–6p*

The creamery building has been a downtown Petaluma institution for nearly a century, and now turns out 25 varieties of cheese made from a herd of 400 Jersey cows on the nearby Spring Hill Jersey Cheese farm.

Jersey cows produce milk much higher in butterfat than the far more common Holsteins, but the breed's relatively low yield has pushed it to the provenance of small-production dairies like this one. Taste the difference a cow makes at the sampling bar, which showcases the creamery's diverse offerings, including cheddars, Jack cheeses, cultured butter, and fresh cheeses like quark, a German-style cream cheese that comes plain or flavored with lemon, garlic, or herbs. Fresh cheese curds are also available, along with Jersey ice cream, in standard flavors with a few outliers like lemon and white chocolate apricot.

Della Fattoria

141 Petaluma Blvd N, Petaluma
MILE/EXIT: 474
707.763.0161
www.dellafattoria.com
OPEN: *Tue–Thu, Sat 7a–3p, Fri 7a–9p, Sun 9a–3p*

This bakery deserves its reputation as one of the best breadmakers in the region, consistently showing up on the shelves of all the gourmet markets in Wine Country. The quality is due to owner Kathleen Weber, former bread baker for the French Laundry who takes bread-baking seriously. She adheres to traditional European methods and uses local, organic ingredients—*della fattoria* means "from the farm" in Italian. Her dozen or so breads come from a natural starter, and she only uses organic flours, California olive oils, and Brittany sea salt to form loaves like campagne, ciabatta, and baguettes. Also good are specialty loaves like Meyer Lemon Rosemary, Pumpkin Seed and Walnut (made with Lake County walnuts), and a small selection of pastries. The deep red walls of the bakery echo her passion for food, which also shines in the cafe menu of light breakfast and lunch items, all of them outstanding and fresh, organic, and local. If you only order one thing, get the sublime lunchtime BLT, made with thick-cut bacon and heirloom tomatoes on fresh sourdough.

KNOW: *The bathrooms are located on the third floor of the building, and to get to them you need to walk through the kitchen. Even if nature isn't calling, it's worth a trip to see the large-scale ovens in action and behind-the-scenes workings of the bakery.*

 Marin French Cheese Co.

7500 Red Hill Rd, Petaluma
MILE/EXIT: 474
DISTANCE FROM HWY: 11 miles
800.292.6001
www.marinfrenchcheese.com
OPEN: *Daily 8:30a–4p*

The company's soft flagship cheese, Rouge et Noir, was a favorite of San Francisco dockworkers in the late 1800s. In those days, it had to be transported by horse and wagon to the Petaluma River, then taken to San Francisco by paddle boat. Times have changed, but the cheese remains the same at the oldest continually operating cheese company in the United States. The creamery now produces more than 30 different types of soft-ripening cheeses, including brie, camembert, and blue-veined goat, all made from milk sourced from neighboring dairies. Take the tour to learn about the cheese-making process and the company's unique place in Northern California history, then hit the deli for a sandwich and some local wine and head outside for a picnic by the scenic duck pond.

TOURS: *Daily 10a, 11a, noon, and 3p (most cheese-making occurs Mon–Thu 10a–noon).*

DETOURS & DESTINATIONS

Side Trip: Lake County Farm Trails

MILE/EXIT: 555

ADDED LENGTH: 52 miles

Take an extra hour or two to meander through Lake County, an understated agricultural region just east of Highway 101 north of Ukiah. The area has dozens of family farms, wineries, artisan producers, and more, offering a glimpse into rural life and a chance to cut out the middleman and interact directly with the producer. Depending on the season, expect to find a local cornucopia of strawberries, corn, peaches, tomatoes, peppers, beans, walnuts, and the county's famous mountain pears, along with eggs, honey, dried fruit, nuts, and preserves. Highway 20 will take you to Clear Lake; from there you can take the afternoon to circle the lake, or cut back over to Highway 101 on Highway 175. Download a map from the Lake County Tourism website (www.lakecounty.com).

Side Trip: Highway 128 and Anderson Valley

MILE/EXIT: Head west on Highway 128 at Cloverdale

DISTANCE: 50 miles

There's culinary gold in them hills, if you're willing to drive into the valleys of the coastal range to find it. This scenic hour-long road winds its way through vineyards, apple orchards, and coastal redwood forests before dead-ending at the Pacific Ocean. The lush Anderson Valley has been farm country since the mid-1800s, and what was once primarily an apple and hops region now relies mostly on wine-making. The area is known for its excellent pinot noirs, sparkling wines, and, to a lesser extent, Alsatian wines like riesling and gewürztraminer. Farm stands abound along the highway, selling apple cider and local produce.

Do not pass Boonville, the valley's biggest community, without stopping in the **Anderson Valley Brewing Company**. Taste the award-winning Boont Amber, Barney Flats Oatmeal Stout, and other brews in the solar-powered, Bavarian-style pub and beer garden, or grab a six-pack and sign up for a round of Frisbee golf on the brewery grounds. **The Boonville Hotel** is locally renowned for its meals sourced mostly from its own garden, and is a fancier lunch option. Keep your ears

CALIFORNIA

pricked for Boontling, a secret language developed by isolated farmers to pass the time. Many of AVBC's beers are named for Boontling slang.

Meandering along the highway, you'll start passing wine-tasting rooms. One of the best is **Goldeneye Winery**, whose single-minded focus on pinot noir results in some of the best bottles in the country. (The winery's 2005 pinot was served at President Obama's inaugural luncheon, to give you an idea of its pedigree.) A little farther along, pick up a jug of fresh apple cider, jars of chutney, or other apple-based goodies at **Philo Apple Farm**. The unpretentious **Navarro Vineyards** offers daily tours of their environmentally friendly wine estate, followed by a free tasting of their gewürztraminer, chardonnay, pinot noir, and nonalcoholic grape juice. For a grand finale, hit up the **Roederer Estate**, an extension of the revered French champagne house that created Cristal. A flight of sparkling wine while overlooking dramatic valley views will make anyone feel like French aristocracy.

Anderson Valley Brewing Company

17700 Hwy 253, Boonville
707.895.2337
www.avbc.com

The Boonville Hotel

14050 Hwy 128, Boonville
707.895.2210
www.boonvillehotel.com

Goldeneye Winery

900 Hwy 128, Philo
800.208.0438
www.goldeneyewinery.com

Philo Apple Farm

18501 Greenwood Rd, Philo
707.895.2333
www.philoapplefarm.com

Navarro Vineyards & Winery

5601 Hwy 128, Philo
707.895.3686
www.navarrowine.com

Roederer Estate

4501 Hwy 128, Philo
707.895.2288
www.roedererestate.com

Side Trip: Sebastopol

MILE/EXIT: 488B
DISTANCE FROM HWY: 7 miles

To know a town, look to the nickname it gives its highway. Hwy 116 runs straight through Sebastopol, but it's known locally as the "Gravenstein Highway" after the orchards that line its path. The city revolves around the apple, especially during harvest season from August to November, and it pops up in everything from pies and ice cream to hard cider. You've got to understand, the Gravenstein is not just any apple: it's the pinot noir of apples, picky about its region and requiring a certain finesse to grow, but eminently rewarding with its creamy, sweet-tart flesh and superlative pie texture. The Gravenstein is the lasting legacy of the Russians at Fort Ross, who brought the fruit to California in the 1820s and later realized it grew best a little farther inland. However, times are changing, and Sebastopol is no longer a one-fruit town: vineyards now compete with apple orchards for space along the highway.

🍎 Screamin' Mimi's Ice Cream

6902 Sebastopol Ave, Sebastopol
MILE/EXIT: 488B
DISTANCE FROM HWY: 7 miles
707.823.5902
www.screaminmimisicecream.com
OPEN: *Daily 11a–11p*

A visit to this pale-pink ice cream shop on the corner of Highways 12 and 116 brings back memories of childhood trips to a long-since closed local ice cream shop, magic times when all seemed right in the world. I'm guessing owner Maraline Olson had a similar image in mind when she opened her shop in 1995, following a personal quest to find the home-made ice cream of her youth. She now has more than 300 flavors in her repertoire, made fresh daily depending on the season and whim, often utilizing products from Sonoma County. Stretch your horizons with unusual flavors like lavender, olive oil, ginger, apricot, and fig, or go tra-ditional with Mimi's Mud, a slurry of chocolate and brownie. No matter what, don't leave without at least a taste of Gravenstein apple sorbet if it's in season. You'll know the shop by the large ice cream cone hanging outside the door.

KNOW: *The ice cream is priced by weight, not scoop—it can add up, so take care to only order what you know you'll eat.*

 ## Hopmonk Tavern

230 Petaluma Ave, Sebastopol
MILE/EXIT: 488B
DISTANCE FROM HWY: 7 miles
707.829.7300
www.hopmonk.com
OPEN: *Sun–Thu 11a–9:30p, Fri–Sat 11:30a–9p; bar generally open until 1:30a*

The old and the new blend seamlessly at this hip brewpub and bistro, opened by Gordon Biersch co-founder Dean Biersch in 2008 as a way to get back to his beer-loving roots. The low, picturesque stone building is on the National Register of Historic Places, but inside it's pure mid-century modern, outfitted with 100-year-old Douglas fir floors and plush red booths. Hang out all afternoon in the back beer garden, which fea-tures long, rustic wooden tables and benches, and a trellis of hop vines. Hopmonk is primarily a beer bar with 16 taps that encompass a curated list of local microbrews, European imports, and a handful of Biersch's own brews, including a very drinkable pilsner, lightly floral California pale ale, and Bavarian-style dark wheat beer. There's also a well-appointed wine list heavy on Sonoma wines, and no corkage fee if you want to bring your own. The beer-friendly menu focuses on pub classics with a global slant—samosas and tandoori chicken skewers share space with burgers, brats, and seasonal entrees.

KNOW: *A second Hopmonk Tavern location has opened in Sonoma (691 Broadway; 707.935.9100).*

🥧 Mom's Apple Pie

4550 Gravenstein Hwy N, Sebastopol
MILE/EXIT: 488B
DISTANCE FROM HWY: 20 miles
707.823.8330
momsapplepieusa.com
OPEN: *Daily 10a–6p*

Betty "Mom" Carr started selling apple pies in the late 1970s to supplement the income from her and her late husband's eight-acre Gravenstein apple orchard, and demand has only increased ever since. "Mom" herself is usually behind the counter in this delightful roadside pie stand, wearing a red-and-white checkered apron, dishing up her all-American double-crust pies made from an old family recipe. Her reach has expanded to include 12 double-crust fruit pies made with local ingredients, including apricot, peach, rhubarb, wild blueberry, and raspberry, along with cream and meringue pies. The stand also offers a small lunch menu of salads, sandwiches, and chili, all to be enjoyed with views of vineyards and apple orchards.

KNOW: *Carr also bakes up sugar-free apple and blackberry pies daily, sweetened with apple juice concentrate.*

CALIFORNIA

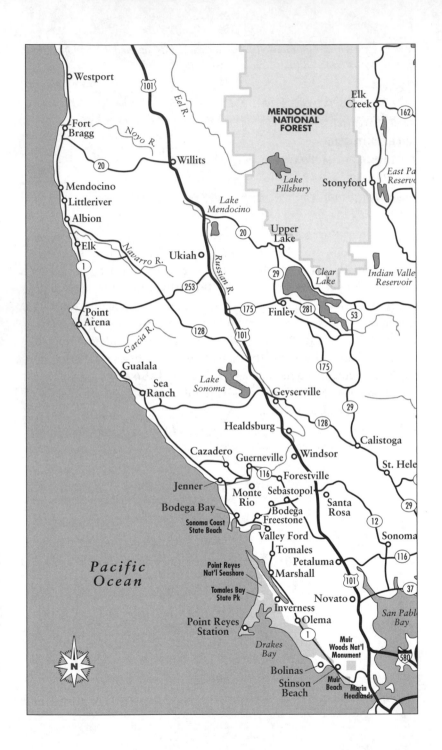

Highway 1: North Coast

Trip Stats

START: Leggett

END: Point Reyes Station

LENGTH: 180 miles

LOCAL FLAVOR: BBQ oysters, bakeries, cheese.

BEST TIME: Fall is when the fog lifts.

WORST TIME: Depends. Summer, if you're looking for sun. Winter, the rain can be unpleasant and make for dangerous driving.

WORD OF WARNING: You'll lose cell service for the majority of the drive. This eventually ceases to matter.

MORE INFO: North Coast Tourism Council (www.northcoastca.com)

It was a typical August day on the North Coast: foggy, gray, and so cold I was wearing two pairs of socks and several layers of T-shirts for insulation. A heavy cloud had settled over the road at Fort Bragg and stubbornly hung in the air over the next 45 miles of winding highway, creating a colorless, veiled environment, the landscape of mystery novels. By 4pm, the sun had given up trying to penetrate the fog, and as the light dwindled, we decided it was time to stop for the day.

Later that evening, warming up over whiskey at Point Arena's only bar, my friend and I struck up a conversation with a local abalone diver and fisherman. He told us that the weather was typical for that time of year—warm air inland actually pulls a blanket of fog over the land. The nicer it is in the valleys across the mountains of the Coastal Range, the colder and more damp it is on the coast. I mentioned that it must be lonely to live there. "You have to have a lot of country in you," he replied, and I realized how much pride North Coast residents take in their isolation.

The region is physically cut off from the rest of California by the mountains and treacherous rocky coastline. For a long time, this was land no one else wanted. Sir Francis Drake cruised up the coast for a while in the 1500s looking for a good harbor, but eventually gave up. The Russians came in the 1800s and established Fort Ross as a supply outpost, but sold and moved out 30 years later because it was too isolated to maintain. Mendocino sprung up when a group of New Englanders bound for San Francisco shipwrecked more than 100 miles north instead. (Hence the Cape Cod–style architecture, all the weathered shingles and picket fences.) So the North Coast has, and probably always will, drawn a particular sect of outsiders who have banded together and formed a community unto themselves. It's sometimes referred to as the "Lost Coast," but if it's lost or forgotten, it's only because the residents chose it to be that way.

Highway 1 is rightfully known as one of the most scenic in the country. It's a serpentine, sinuous route that takes you past thousand-foot cliffs, tiny weather-beaten towns, headlands matted with grass. Bull kelp floats in the water, volcanic rocks protrude from the pounding surf. At times the road becomes a tunnel of eucalyptus and moss-draped coastal redwoods; at others it skirts the cliff's edge so closely it's not advisable to look down. There are no guardrails. God help you if the fog rolls in.

The highway is so ruggedly beautiful that you lose perspective as you wind your way south. Beauty becomes ordinary. When the sun comes back and the hills start to even out, you know you're reaching the end. Southern Sonoma and Marin Counties are all baked yellow hills overlooking the sea. It's still wild, but it's a tamed wilderness—an established farm and dairy region, with a tangible connection to San Francisco. For a minute you miss the foggy dream of the wild north, and wonder if you have more country in you than you thought.

ON THE ROAD

Jenny's Giant Burger

960 N Main St, Fort Bragg
MILE/EXIT: MEN-64
707.969.2235
OPEN: *Daily 10:30a–9p*

"Giant burger" is a bit of a misnomer—it's a throwback to a time before double quarter-pounders, when a third-pound burger was considered indecent, or at least unladylike. In fact, everything about this parking lot burger joint is a throwback, from the red Formica booths to the simple burger/fries/milk shake menu. The burger itself is a glorious rendition of that dying art, the burger-stand burger. Cooked crisp on a flat grill, with plenty of nooks and crannies oozing with American cheese, Jenny's "giant burger" is then garnished with tomatoes, red onions, and iceberg lettuce and presented with little fanfare on a Wonder Bread bun. The large-cut fries are nothing special, but they do the trick. The meal wouldn't be complete without dessert: shakes, malts, floats, and sundaes all hit the spot.

North Coast Brewing Co.

455 N Main St, Fort Bragg

MILE/EXIT: MEN-64

707.964.3400

www.northcoastbrewing.com

OPEN: *Sun–Thu 11:30a–9:30p, Fri–Sat 11:30a–10p*

Recover from the nail-biting highway drive at this bustling brewpub, which has won the hearts of locals and critics alike for its strong, unusual brews that cop from several beer-making styles. North Coast Brewing is best known for Old Rasputin, a velvety signature imperial stout that's as thick as motor oil and, at 7 percent alcohol by volume, is strictly limited to two per customer. Even more intense is the Old Stock Belgian-style ale, a port-like concoction at 12.5 percent ABV, and inadvisable if you plan to tackle more of Highway 1's winding roadway after lunch. Better stick to the lighter beers, like the refreshing Scrimshaw Pilsner and copper-colored Red Seal pale ale. North Coast revived the historic San Francisco Acme Brewing label in 2000, and the California-style pale ale and IPA under that brand are also worth drinking. The comfortable dining room and bar are equally suited to families and couples, and decorated with moose heads, logging implements, vintage beer signs, and other relics from Fort Bragg's lumbering past. Fish-and-chips, clam chowder, and a long list of salads, sandwiches, and burgers are all solid options. This is the kind of place where you'll want to hang out (or sober up) all afternoon.

KNOW: *The main brewery across the street was in expanded in 2010, with brewery tours resumed late in the year.*

CALIFORNIA

Fort Bragg Bakery

360 N Franklin St, Fort Bragg

MILE/EXIT: MEN-64

707.964.9647

www.fortbraggbrewery.com

OPEN: *Wed–Sat 7:30a–4p*

When in doubt, do it yourself. That's the MO of owner Chris Kump, former chef at Mendocino's critically acclaimed Café Beaujolais, where he started to bake his own bread to complement dinner service. In 2009 he and his wife bought the old Fort Bragg Bakery, which had been in operation for nearly a century. One of his first moves was to track down the original bricks from the historic wood-burning oven, which had been destroyed in a fire and dumped unceremoniously in a nearby backyard. The reconstructed oven, proudly displaying vintage bricks stamped with forge dates and names of California brick factories, is the centerpiece of the small European-style bakery. This is a great place to pick up a loaf of bread for a picnic—try the crusty sourdough or North Coast rye—or a sweet treat like a flaky croissant, chocolate fudge cookie, or slice of decadent chocolate torte. Lunch, served daily from 11am–2pm, offers soups, salads, sandwiches, and pizzas fired in the brick oven.

Eggheads Restaurant

326 N Main St, Fort Bragg

MILE/EXIT: MEN-64

707.964.5005

www.eggheadsrestaurant.com

OPEN: *Daily 7a–2p*

Like *The Wizard of Oz*? Then you'll love this tiny theme restaurant on Highway 1. Menu items have names like Flying Monkey Potatoes and Glinda's Garlic and Crab Omelet, and one wall is covered by a mural depicting Dorothy and the gang following the yellow brick road to a distant Emerald City. Lucky for you, paradise is significantly closer. Every step down the restaurant's own yellow brick road, painted on the floor, gets you closer to the best eggs Benedict this side of Oz. Select from indulgent ingredients like sausage and crab and then pick your poison, hollandaise-wise. The sauce comes in three flavors (original, champagne, and tequila) and all are rich, creamy, and buttery in all the right ways. A clean plate might necessitate an afternoon nap—but remember that even Dorothy had to succumb to a little shut-eye before she reached salvation.

(🍴) Cowlick's Ice Cream Co.

250B N Main St, Fort Bragg

MILE/EXIT: MEN-64

707.962.9271

www.cowlicksicecream.com

OPEN: *Daily 11a–9p*

Best known for its seasonal mushroom ice cream, this quirky ice cream shop has been hitting Fort Bragg's sweet spot since 2000. The infamous funghi flavor isn't as disgusting as one might imagine; the mushrooms in question are candy caps, and you'd be hard-pressed to distinguish it from maple ice cream in a blind taste test. The shop's other unique flavors include root beer float, chai, huckleberry, ginger, and pear sorbet, but picky eaters don't need to worry—the usual favorites also make the cut. Dairy is sourced from Sonoma County cows, and local ingredients are used whenever possible. There's plenty of seating at the retro chairs and tables, or take your cone, cup, or sundae to go and window shop along Fort Bragg's main drag.

(🛍️) Harvest at Mendosa's Market

10501 Lansing St, Mendocino

MILE/EXIT: MEN-51

707.937.5879

www.harvestmarket.com

OPEN: *Daily 7:30a–10p*

Isolation has its perks—and one of those is a refreshing lack of supermarkets on the North Coast, leaving the opportunity open for local chains like the Harvest Market. The original Fort Bragg location opened in 1985, and two decades later this Mendocino outpost opened in the 100-year-old Mendosa's Market & Hardware building. Stop here before heading out to the Highlands for the best picnic supplies in town, including a whole aisle of premade sandwiches, salads, finger foods, and desserts. Try

CALIFORNIA

the Harvest Club, a twist on the classic sandwich with turkey, brie, avo-cado, bacon, lettuce, and tomato on rustic bread. Supplement the meal with gourmet sides like barbecue potato salad and orzo feta pasta salad, and top everything off with a local cheese or tub of house-made chocolate mousse, and a bottle of Mendocino County wine. If you're shopping for groceries, Harvest has the largest seafood selection on the North Coast, the meat counter sells organic, grass-fed beef, and many of the store's products are local.

Moodys Organic Coffee Bar

20450 Lansing St, Mendocino

MILE/EXIT: MEN-51

707.937.4843

www.moodyscoffeebar.com

OPEN: *Daily 6a–8p*

Mendocino's yuppie revitalization over the past decade has earned it the nickname "Spendocino," but the town's original roots as an artist com-munity are still present and accounted for in quirky pockets like this busy coffee shop and cafe. Local art graces the walls of the small work room across the hall from the espresso bar, where the laptop-to-customer ratio is almost 1:1. They're here for the atmosphere, but also for the coffee: Moodys' own organic espresso blend is rich and dark, a great pick-me-up for flagging afternoon energy. Lighter options include a long list of inter-esting teas, yerba mate lattes, and the Mocha Moody Frappe, a richer take on the Starbucks Frappuccino.

Mendocino Café

10451 Lansing St, Mendocino

MILE/EXIT: MEN-51

www.mendocinocafe.com

OPEN: *Mon–Fri 11:30a–4p, 5–9p; Sat–Sun 11:30a–4p, 5–10p*

Every restaurant's menu is at the whims of its chef, but the menu at this upscale casual spot is definitely a narrative of the places owner Meredith Smith has traveled. The cuisine can only be described as "global," with influences from Asia, Europe, and Africa, and the menu offers a Thai burrito, Italian pasta dishes, and Brazilian seafood stew, alongside a great burger and sandwich selection. A small wine list focuses on local wines at reasonable prices. The restaurant is also a showcase of Smith's life philosophy: produce, beans, and rice are certified organic, the chickens are free-range, and no antibiotics or growth hormones are used in the local beef. And it's just a fabulous space—a little white house with a wisteria-laden garden patio offering up sweeping views of the town, and thoughtful interior touches like fresh flowers at every table. If Mendocino puts you in the mood for a fancy restaurant meal, this is the place to have it.

(☺) Mendocino Chocolate Company

10483 Lansing St, Mendocino

MILE/EXIT: MEN-51

707.937.1107

www.mendocino-chocolate.com

OPEN: *Daily 11a–5:30p*

Sweeten a ramble on the Mendocino Highlands with a truffle from this wee fudge shop, in its original location in a tiny house in town. (There's a second location in Fort Bragg at 232 N Main St; 707.964.8800). Truffles come in nearly 30 flavors, many with local names. Don't miss the "Angela," orange with dark chocolate that was Angela Lansbury's fave while she was filming *Murder She Wrote* (Mendocino's Cape Cod–style architecture made it the perfect stand-in for the fictional Maine coastal town of Cabot Cove). Equally worth your time is the "Buena Vista," an Irish cream and coffee truffle topped with white chocolate, named for the San Francisco cafe where the bracing drink was invented. Dark chocolate lovers must try the "Mendocino Macho," dark ganache dipped in a dark shell and finished with a dark chocolate leaf. If you're not a truffle fan (my deepest sympathies), the shop also offers fudge, toffee, chocolate-covered cherries, nut clusters, and more.

KNOW: *Attractive gift boxes are made from local redwood.*

CALIFORNIA

🍴 Queenie's Roadhouse Café

6061 S Hwy 1, Elk

MILE/EXIT: MEN-34

707.877.3285

OPEN: *Daily 8a–2p*

This is where locals go for what might be the best breakfast on the North Coast. The eggs Benedict is a big hit, with a slightly lemony hollandaise, thick Canadian bacon, and herbed biscuits; corned beef hash made from scratch and waffles are also favorites. Good strong coffee, too. It's nothing special, but just shows that local, organic ingredients really make all the difference. The simple cafe has a homespun vibe, with wood floors, large windows that give a view of the sea over the bluffs, and lots of locals. The fact that the 250-resident hamlet of Elk could have such a great breakfast spot is a testament to the truly food-centric culture of Northern California.

KNOW: *Don't stop here if you're in a hurry. It's a one-woman show, and service can be slow.*

🍰 Franny's Cup & Saucer

213 Main St, Point Arena

MILE/EXIT: MEN-15

707.882.2500

www.frannyscupandsaucer.com

OPEN: *Wed–Sat 8a–4p*

Franny's Cup & Saucer has the sophistication and deft execution very few bakeries ever attain in cities, and is practically unheard of in the fifth-smallest city incorporated in America. Unheard of, that is, until you learn that owner Barbara Burkey used to be the pastry chef at Chez Panisse and original owner of the Tomales Bakery. Her daughter, Frances (Franny), grew up in bakery kitchens and eagerly stepped in to help her mother run this girly bakery. There's no sign, but you'll know it from the robin's-egg blue façade and block lettering that simply says "Bakery." The magenta interior is sweet, feminine, and totally homemade. Shabby-chic vintage display cases present the daily rotating cast of French pastries, which range from the simple (butter croissants, danishes) to the complicated (chocolate cinnamon rolls, tortes). Savory lunch pastries are also available, along with Uncommon Grounds espresso and Mexican hot chocolate. Behind the counter, the entire baking operation is on display (including a huge stack of baking cookbooks, which I found comforting). In fact, the whole scene is totally charming, because you can see the passion the women put into their work. One morning, Edith Piaf murmured quietly in the background as Barbara greeted local customers by name and exchanged tidbits of gossip. One man mentioned that he'd just returned from San Francisco's legendary Stella Pastries, and thought that Franny's was superior. Barbara's excited smile lit up the room. "I'll have to tell Franny. That's one of our favorites."

KNOW: *The bakery doubles as a gift shop, with a fun little selection of notebooks, cards, change purses, and novelties.*

⊛ The Pier Chowder House & Tap Room

790 Port Rd, Point Arena

MILE/EXIT: MEN-15

707.882.3400

www.thepierchowderhouse.com

OPEN: *Daily 11:30a–9p*

Turn off Highway 1 and drive down the road that leads to Point Arena Pier, and you'll come to this weather-beaten chowderhouse. Nestled in the hillside overlooking the tiny, rock-walled bay, this is a superb spot to try local microbrews and soak up the small-town culture. The 24 beer taps read like a who's who of Northern California craft brewers, including North Coast, Lost Coast, Eel River, Anderson Valley, Mendocino, Firestone-Walker, Bear Republic, and Lagunitas. Overwhelmed? The beer list is divided by type, not brewer (e.g., IPA, amber, dark, etc.), and the bartenders are happy to guide your selections with plenty of samples. The wine list is heavy on local wines, many unavailable outside the North Coast. The food here is fine—I recommend sticking with standards like fish-and-chips or clam chowder—and the ocean view out the wall of windows is unbeatable. Sit at the bar and chat with the locals, or commandeer a table in the dining room and watch the sunset.

KNOW: *The Point Arena pier is open to public fishing, no license or fee required.*

🍴 Dinucci's Italian Dinners

14485 Valley Ford Rd, Valley Ford
MILE/EXIT: SON-2
707.876.3260
www.dinuccisrestaurant.com
OPEN: *Mon–Fri 4–9p, Sat 11:30a–9p, Sun 11:30a–8p*

For all its advertising, let's be honest, a meal at Olive Garden never really feels like family. It's too bright, too clean, too corporate—the antithesis of a place like Dinucci's, where you actually do feel like a temporary member of the Dinucci clan. It's partially the dim, slightly dingy interior, which takes the pressure off. It's partially the family photos and Little Italy kitsch decor, which make you feel like part of a tradition. But it's mostly the food and the family-style service that have kept local families and travelers coming back since the restaurant opened more than 100 years ago as a resting stop for the Pacific Narrow Gauge Railway. Word of advice: Bring an appetite. The meal starts with an antipasto platter, followed by a bowl of locally famous minestrone soup, a salad, and a side of ravioli or spaghetti—and that's all before the entrees. Choose from decent Italian standards like chicken marsala, spaghetti and meatballs, and veal Parmigiana, or hedge your bets with "Half & Half," a divided plate with your choice of lasagna, spaghetti, or ravioli. Wash it all down with house red or white served in jugs for the table.

KNOW: *Monday and Thursday nights offer dining specials at the bar, which is the best place to get friendly with the locals.*

🍰 Tomales Bakery

27000 Hwy 1, Tomales
MILE/EXIT: MRN-45
707.878.2429
OPEN: *Thu–Sun 7:30a. Sign on door says, "Close: Until we run out . . . ," which is mid- to late afternoon, depending.*

The best bakeries bring me back, Proust-style, to my mother's kitchen on weekend mornings—me stumbling downstairs in pajama pants, hair all askew, to find her pulling a blueberry coffee cake, tray of cinnamon rolls, or loaf of fresh bread out of the oven. This friendly bakery in the tiny town of Tomales effortlessly summons up those same feel-good vibes—the bright yellow walls are sunshine even on a cloudy day, and the vintage flowered aprons and cake tins decorating the walls give the place a feminine, though not overtly girly, feel. It's just a quiet reminder that baking has traditionally been a womanly art. The women behind the counter are kind and welcoming; the pastries have that imperfect look that proves they're homemade. Offerings change every day, with standards like nutty shortbread, perfectly tart lemon squares, and hearty slices of seasonal fruit pie. Bread and savory snacks like mini-pizzas and pesto-and-gorgonzola bread twists are also sold.

Hog Island Oyster Co.

20215 Hwy 1, Marshall
MILE/EXIT: MRN-38
415.663.9218
www.hogislandoysters.com
OPEN: *Mon–Sat 9a–5p*

You might not have to harvest your oysters but you still have to work for them at this Tomales Bay oyster farm. Choose your oysters from the short menu of local varieties, and pay a fiver more for a tray filled with ice, a lemon, a bottle of hot sauce (pick between Crystal and Tapatio), an oyster knife, a sturdy rubber glove, and a short but comprehensive shucking lesson from one of the ruddy-cheeked oystermen. Then you're on your own, walking over to the bayside picnic tables and praying like hell you'll remember the lesson. Turns out oyster shucking is a snap, once you get the hang of it, but these oysters would be worth any amount of inconvenience. Hog Islands are more meaty than Kumamotos but just as sweet, with a slight hint of the sea. They are among the best on the West Coast, made all the better for the setting and experience. Once you've got shucking down, you can graduate to barbecuing 'em: there's a grill for every picnic table, and Hog Island provides chimney lighters, mesquite charcoal, and a quick tutorial before turning you loose. Keep in mind that if you want anything more than oysters, you need to pack it in yourself (though plans for an on-site bar were in the works at press time).

KNOW: *Entry to the picnic area costs $8 on weekends, $5 weekdays per person—that includes the shucking materials, lesson, and oyster fixings, but not the oysters themselves. Weekends fill up fast, and reservations (available online) are recommended—up to one month in advance during the summer.*

VARIOUS LOCATIONS *in Oxbow Market (page 198) and San Francisco's Ferry Building (page 216)*

 **Marshall Store**

19225 Hwy 1, Marshall

MILE/EXIT: MRN-38

415.663.1339

www.themarshallstore.com

OPEN: *Fri–Mon 10a–6p, Wed–Thu 10a–5p*

Happiness is a dozen barbecued oysters at this highwayside seafood shack, the best place around to try the regional specialty. A bakers dozen Tomales Bay oysters are grilled in-shell with an indecent amount of garlic butter and parsley, then finished with a dollop of mild horseradish chipotle sauce. They come to the table smoky and warm and totally delicious, a complex bite of garlic and spices that's not chewy or rubbery in the least. Perfectly charred garlic bread is a great way to soak up the sauce. The oysters are so good they'd be a transportive experience in a garbage dump, but to enjoy them in the sun mere feet from the lapping shore is an experience almost too sublime to bear. Round out your meal with an excellent cup of clam chowder or sandwich from the inside deli. There's a well-rounded selection of local wine and beer, too.

KNOW: *Consumption of alcohol isn't permitted on the premises . . . luckily the long, reclaimed wood table supported by weathered wine barrels isn't technically on the premises.*

 Point Reyes Vineyards

12700 Hwy 1 N, Point Reyes Station

MILE/EXIT: MRN-29

415.663.1011

www.ptreyesvineyardinn.com/winery

OPEN: *Summer (May 31–Nov 14) Fri–Mon 11a–5p; winter (Nov 15–May 31) Sat–Sun 11a–5p (or call for appointment)*

As the first tasting room in Marin County since Prohibition, this homey winery already has certain local cache, but it's backed up with a surprisingly large range of big reds (cabernet sauvignon, syrah, zinfandel) and whites, including a sparkling blanc de blancs that pairs very well with oysters. Buy a bottle to take to Hog Island Oyster Co., or BYOP (bring your own picnic) and head out to the patio—a peaceful place adorned with a gurgling fountain, koi pond, and sweeping views of the

---

The Judgment of Paris

It was the cork-pop heard 'round the world. On May 24, 1976, France's best and brightest culinary experts assembled at Paris's ritzy Intercontinental Hotel and conducted a blind taste test of French and American wines—and gave top marks to Napa bottles in both the white and red categories (a 1973 Chateau Montelena chardonnay and 1973 Stag's Leap cabernet, respectively). The event had been designed as a publicity stunt to definitively prove French wine-making superiority; ironically enough, it served as American wine's coming-out party. Naturally, the embarrassed French were keen to sweep the whole incident under the carpet, and it might have become a historical footnote if American journalist George Taber hadn't been on the scene. His subsequent blurb in *Time* magazine—appropriately titled "The Judgment of Paris"—caused an instant uproar in the United States and finally put California wines in the spotlight.

65,000-acre preserved wilderness of the Point Reyes National Seashore. If you're lucky, you might even get a visit from the winery dog and cat.

KNOW: *This is also a bed-and-breakfast, and the family brings that B and B hospitality to the tasting room. The staff is knowledgeable and happy to educate. Tasting price ($5 for 5 tastings) is waived with purchase.*

🏠 Cowgirl Creamery & Cantina

80 4th St, Point Reyes Station
MILE/EXIT: MRN-29
415.663.9335
www.cowgirlcreamery.com
OPEN: *Wed–Sun 10a–6p*

Well deserving of its reputation as one of the state's best creameries. Cowgirl Creamery takes up most of the space inside Tomales Bay Foods, an old barn restored to a gourmet's boutique, with its cheese-making facility; counter for tasting and purchases; shop with cheese books, knives, and condiments; and the Cowgirl Cantina deli. Watch cheese-making happen before your very eyes every day, or sign up for "Cheese

101," a 60-minute cheese-making class and guided tasting offered Fridays at 11:30am ($5 per person, reservations recommended, not suitable for children under 7). Or just head to the tasting counter and sample your way through the inventory, made with milk sourced from Marin and Sonoma County cows. Mild Mount Tam is a buttery soft triple-cream, Red Hawk is more pungent, Wagon Wheel is a harder cheese with a slightly nutty flavor, and the earthy Pierce Point is washed in red wine and local herbs. The Cowgirl Cantina offers out-of-this-world sandwiches, salads, and rotisserie chicken, all made with local ingredients and all very good, along with locally produced picnic fare, wine, and charcuterie.

KNOW: *Can't get enough? Sign up for an in-depth cheese-making class at the newer Petaluma creamery (not a retail location): $30 per person, at 11:30a on Wednesdays, reservations necessary (419 1st St, Petaluma).*

🍰 Bovine Bakery

11315 Hwy 1, Point Reyes Station

MILE/EXIT: MRN-29

415.663.9420

OPEN: *Mon–Fri 6:30a–5p, Sat–Sun 7a–5p*

"This is an espresso-free establishment," reads a sign above the coffeemaker, a bold statement for any coffee shop. But the rich, organic brew from Mendocino's Thanksgiving Coffee Company subs in for an Americano nicely, and pairs excellently with the superb baked goods. Bear claws, fruit slippers, bittersweet chocolate cookies, morning buns . . . it's all delicious, so pick what looks good to you. If there's a picnic in your future, wood-fired Brickmaiden bread would be great with Cowgirl Creamery cheese. It's not unusual to see a gaggle of cyclists in bike shorts outside, carb-loading before hitting Point Reyes National Seashore, but the bakery's primarily a local hangout—the staff greets customers by name, and a shelf near the counter holds a line of "private mugs" reserved for Point Reyes residents. A simple lunch menu of soups, wood-fired pizzas, and sandwiches is also available.

🍴 Station House Café

11180 Hwy 1, Point Reyes Station

MILE/EXIT: MRN-29

415.663.1515

www.stationhousecafe.com
OPEN: *Daily 8a–9p*

The busiest breakfast and lunch spot on the town's well-preserved nineteenth-century main drag, the Station House Café has been turning out fresh, local, and sustainable meals for locals and hungry outdoor enthusiasts since 1974. The menu is a primer on the region's bounty: oysters from Drake's and Hog Island come barbecued, deep-fried, or served on the half-shell; beef for burgers comes from Niman Ranch; and the milk shakes and root beer floats flaunt dairy from Straus. Breakfast favorites include waffles, buckwheat pancakes, and Hangtown fry made with Drake's oysters. Eat in the breezy dining room, or sit outside on the redbrick garden patio, a slice of shady heaven with flowering bushes, vine-covered trellises, a gazebo, and a small garden that provides produce for the cafe's kitchen. If there's a wait for a table, sip a specialty cocktail at the large, bustling bar.

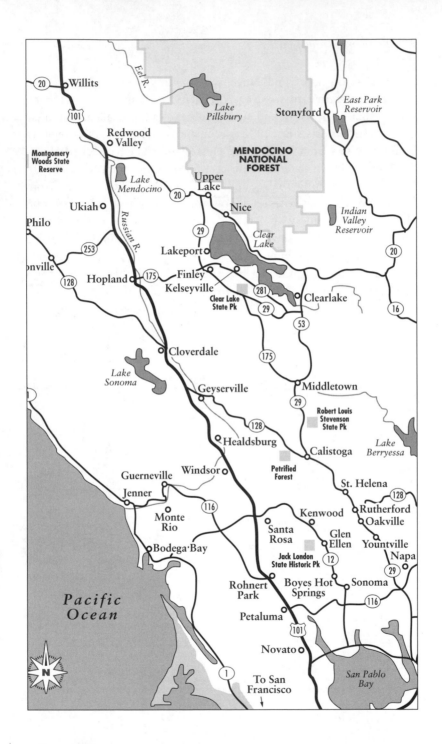

Napa and Sonoma Valleys

Trip Stats

BEGIN: Calistoga

END: Santa Rosa

LOCAL FLAVOR: Wine (obviously), artisan sandwiches and charcuterie, olive oil, farm-fresh produce.

BEST TIME: Pick your season. Early spring is particularly scenic, with fields of yellow mustard in bloom along the highways. Summer brings an explosion of flavor and long, sun-filled days. Fall harvest has a celebratory feel.

WORST TIME: Strictly speaking, there's no bad time to visit. In January, the grapes are pruned back and temperatures are cool; on the other hand, you have the valleys practically to yourself.

LOCAL FOOD FESTIVALS:

- **Napa Valley Mustard Festival** (February/March). Events and specials to commemorate the beginning of spring.

- **Sonoma County Harvest Fair** (October). A weekend of wine tasting and festival atmosphere.

WORD OF WARNING: Napa Valley can be overrun with tourists on popular travel weekends, and traffic on Highway 29 can back up for miles.

MORE INFO: Napa Valley Destination Council (www.legendary napavalley.com), Napa Valley Vintners (www.napavintners.com), Sonoma County Tourism (www.sonomacounty.com), Sonoma County Vintners (www.sonomawine.com)

I know enough about wine to know that I don't know very much, and a visit to Napa and Sonoma, quite frankly, intimidated the hell out of me. The Napa of my imagination was populated with snobby tasting room pourers snickering to each other behind my back. ("Can you believe it? She said she tasted blackberries in the merlot." "What a rube. Let's openly mock her inferior palate.")

But it turns out that Napa's not like that, and Sonoma's even less so. Don't get me wrong—there's definitely an elitist element to the valleys, where it's possible to spend upwards of a thousand dollars on a bottle of wine, let alone dinner—but that part's the exception, not the rule. People here embrace a casual lifestyle unique to California, and simply want to share their love of wine and food with you, without pretension. The only wine jerks I encountered were other guests in the tasting rooms.

The valleys are so famous for a couple of reasons. This is the birthplace of California wine, a few times over. Sonoma is widely believed to be the site of the first grapevines in California, planted by a Spanish missionary intending to use them for sacramental wine. It's also the site of the state's first winery, thanks to a maverick Hungarian nobleman who imported thousands of vines from France, Spain, and Italy (see page 202). And more than a century later, Napa chardonnays and cabernets beat out French wines in a blind taste test conducted in Paris, a game-changer for the formerly scoffed-at California wine industry. (See "The Judgment of Paris" on page 181.)

Napa and Sonoma also happen to be blessed with the perfect combination of climate, geography, and soil necessary to grow wine grapes. Like the great wine-making regions of France, the weather is warm during the day, but cooled off by ocean breezes at night. The valleys, too, have a unique *terroir*. They are separated by the volcanic ridge of the Mayacamas mountains, and millions of years acting as the depository for loose sand, gravel, and volcanic runoff have paid off. Both have well-drained, mineral-rich soil—Napa Valley alone has more than three dozen different types—and uneven floors with plenty of ridges and dells to create microclimates. The by-product is a stunning countryside of rolling hills dotted with vineyards, mimosa trees, oaks, and small farms.

All of this has attracted a set of visionary, entrepreneurial winemakers dedicated to producing great wines. Napa winemakers put old-fashioned American innovation to work in their wine-making, displaying a willingness to experiment with new styles, methods, and grape combinations without the limitations of regulation and tradition. It's entirely possible for two wineries side by side, with the exact same grapes, to produce completely different wines. If nothing else, it makes for interesting wine tasting.

For all they have in common physically, the two valleys could not be more different in terms of personality. Napa is the cosmopolitan one, with its Michelin-starred restaurants (including Thomas Keller's French Laundry, arguably the best restaurant in the United States); celebrity winemakers like Francis Ford Coppola, Mumm, and Robert Mondavi; and ostentatious estates like the Castello di Amarosa, a painstaking reproduction of a medieval castle. Napa has big-city energy, too—driving down the 28-mile stretch of Highway 29, the vineyard-lined, two-lane highway from Calistoga to the town of Napa, you pass names of wineries you've heard of, bottles you see in the store every week.

Sonoma, on the other hand, is much more easygoing, small town, and agrarian. It's a valley of multigenerational family farms, and vineyards here share space with apple orchards and vegetable crops. Instead of lining up neatly along the highway, wineries tend to be hidden down country lanes, and the tasting experience is often more personal and laid-back.

The culinary ethos of the region was summed up nicely by a tasting room pourer I talked to: "It's all about salumi, cheese, and bread." And it's true—I strongly believe that Napa and Sonoma have more incredible sandwiches per square mile than anywhere else in the country. The cuisine in general keeps things simple, focusing on high-quality, local ingredients designed to complement the wine. Don't be surprised to find a strong Mexican influence from the migrant workers who pick the grapes—Napa in particular has some of the best taco trucks in California.

One more note: The two valleys combined have hundreds of wineries, and choosing what to include was a Herculean task in itself. I tried to pick a range of commercial operations and smaller family-owned wineries that gave a sense of the region as a whole, but know that for every winery I included, there were three more that I loved and had to leave out. Pick up a guide in any tasting room and go where sounds good. Above all else, don't be intimidated. The tasting room pourers are on your side; they're there to educate, not to scold. You'll walk away with a better sense of what you like and why you like it, and the more you learn, the more you realize there is to know.

CALIFORNIA

ON THE ROAD

Buster's Southern BBQ & Bakery

1207 Foothill Blvd, Calistoga
MILE/EXIT: NAP-36
707.942.5605
www.busterssouthernbbq.com
OPEN: *Open Mon–Sat 9a–8p, Sun 11a–6:30p*

Pretension is left at the door of this down-home joint, where locals enjoy solid barbecue dinners at long, weathered wooden communal tables on a partially covered outdoor patio. I can't vouch for the 'cue's authenticity—I've been schooled by enough Southerners to know to keep my mouth shut—but I can certainly vouch for its deliciousness. The tri-tip is tender and served with a hunk of garlic bread that holds up impressively to the dark red sauce—which is a feat in itself. This sauce is a force to be reckoned with, packing such serious heat that the sides are built to tame it. The corn bread is superb: sugary, sticky, appropriately coarse. Coleslaw is unusually sweet and fruity—almost like fruit ambrosia—and would be a deal-breaker under any other circumstances. Here, it's an excellent antidote to the sauce's slow burn. The best part of all? Buster's also stocks a good selection of wine and beer, including Berkeley-based Trumer Pils. All the more reason to pull up a plastic patio chair and get friendly with the neighbors.

KNOW: *Be sure to specify "mild" if you can't take the sauce's full onslaught. Or, ask for "half and half," a blend of both that only results in a mild taste bud singeing.*

Vallarta Market

1009 Foothill Blvd, Calistoga
MILE/EXIT: NAP-36
707.942.8664
OPEN: *Open daily 9a–8p*

Stop and line your stomach before a full day of wine tasting—or after one, when you have that light-headed, half-drunk flightiness and no patience for a restaurant. Vallarta is a ramshackle roadside hotel that houses a tiny *tienda* on its ground floor. The deli at the back of this market is known locally as some of the best Mexican food in the valley. Insid[e] crowded aisles and order the al pastor burrito at the deli coun[ter] not a burrito to take lightly. Tender pork marinated in a dark re[d] spicy sauce, hunks of avocado, rice, beans, sour cream, Monterey cheese, and salsa, all well distributed and melded together in the de[li]cious slurry that makes up a perfect burrito. It's also massive—easily able to feed two people—and a steal at six bucks. I didn't try the tacos, but I have it on very good authority that they are similarly worthy.

Castello di Amarosa

4045 N Saint Helena Hwy, Calistoga

MILE/EXIT: On Hwy 29, 2.6 miles south of Calistoga

707.967.6272

www.castellodiamorosa.com

OPEN: *Open Mar–Oct 9:30a–6p, Nov–Feb 9:30a–5p*

Dreams can come true—just ask Dario Sattui, the winemaker who spent decades researching medieval castles before building this replica twelfth-century Tuscan castle on the hillside overlooking Napa Valley. It's worth a visit for the 121,000-square-foot building alone—107 rooms spread over eight levels (half of which are underground), including such medieval standbys as a moat, drawbridge, five towers, courtyards, ramparts, and a mural-covered great hall. To give it the proper authenticity, Sattui even imported nearly one million antique bricks from Europe. The rest of the 30-acre property features a chapel, stables, and wandering goats, alongside vineyards clinging to the steep hills. Castello di Amarosa ("castle of love") isn't just a modern-day Xanadu, however. Sattui knows his way around wine (he also owns V. Sattui down the road), and especially excels at estate-grown Italian-style blends. The catacomblike tasting room sets an appropriately reverential mood, all the better to appreciate full-bodied reds like Il Brigante and La Castellana, a Super-Tuscan blend. In the summer, don't miss Gioia, a well-balanced Sangiovese rosé made for a hot afternoon.

KNOW: *The $16 entry fee includes five tastings. It's a splurge, but an extra $10 gets you a trip to the reserve tasting room, where you can sample the reserve wines while sitting in medieval splendor.*

TOURS: *Daily 90-minute tours give an extensive overview of the castle and grounds, and conclude with a private wine tasting. ($31 per person, includes entry fee.) Wear walking shoes and call ahead for reservations—they fill up fast.*

CALIFORNIA

ry & Italian Market

.4 miles south of Calistoga or 1.6 miles north

...ur–Oct daily 9a–6p, Nov–Feb daily 9a–5p

It might share an owner and many of the grandiose architectural flourishes as Castello di Amarosa up the street, but these two wineries couldn't be more different. The castle is intimate, with an air of reserved nobility; V. Sattui is boisterous, designed for the people. Picnicking families pack the winery's grassy, oak-shaded picnic area on sunny Saturday afternoons, enjoying food from the extensive deli and wine cellar. Don't get distracted just yet; you have some foraging to do. Follow the signs past the picnic area to the handsome stone building that houses the marketplace and tasting room. The market passes old world muster with its worn wood floors, salami hanging from rafters, and more than 200 varieties of cheese and Mediterranean-style snacks from the deli case. Taste whatever samples the winery's offering that day, and then head through the arched doorway into the main tasting room. It's built for scale more than personalization, but the tasting is affordable, and so are V. Sattui's 35 wines. Pick the one you like the best (the winery is known for its sweet whites), get whatever looks good from the deli, and snag a picnic table to ride out your wine buzz. After a meal, and maybe a nap, head to the other stone building to take the self-guided tour of the production facilities, underground aging cellars, and small exhibit of Sattui family history in the region, which dates back to 1885.

KNOW: *V. Sattui sets up a barbecue on the picnic grounds on weekends during the summer, spring, and fall. Along with tri-tip, salmon, and Italian sausage sandwiches, there are also wood-fired pizzas, fresh or barbecued oysters, and fresh mozzarella pulled twice daily.*

Gott's Roadside

933 Main St, St. Helena
MILE/EXIT: NAP-29
707.963.3486

www.gottsroadside.com

OPEN: *Summer 10:30a–10p, winter 10:30a–9p*

Owners Joel and Duncan Gott ruffled a lot of local feathers when they changed the name of this roadside institution in March 2010. The drive-in formerly known as Taylor's Refresher has been a Wine Country mainstay since 1949, and many regulars, including my dining companions, considered the switch a harbinger of things to come. As it turns out, nothing much else has changed. The grass-fed beef burgers are still thick and juicy, the fries are still crisp and salty, and the shakes are still made with local Double Rainbow ice cream and taste like the local fruit that's thrown in. The menu isn't limited to burgers, either—Gott's offers an extensive list of hot dogs, sandwiches, dinner salads, and interesting seafood and chicken options like an ahi burger with ginger wasabi mayo. Order at the front counter (there's usually a line, but it moves fairly quickly), sit at a picnic table on the back lawn, and wait for your number to be called. Service is speedy, but it hardly matters. It's so pleasant to sit in lingering midsummer twilight, watching families enjoying hamburgers and playing on the grass in a kind of Norman Rockwell perfection, that even my begrudging companions had to admit that Gott's still has it, name change or not.

KNOW: *In true Wine Country style, Gott's offers $1 corkage and a well-curated list of California wines and microbrews.*

VARIOUS LOCATIONS *in Oxbow Market (page 198) and San Francisco's Ferry Building (page 216)*

Pizzeria Tra Vigne

1016 Main St, St. Helena

MILE/EXIT: NAP-29

707.967.9999

www.travignerestaurant.com

OPEN: *Sun–Thu 11:30a–9p, Fri–Sat 11:30a–9:30p*

Margherita. Prosciutto e Funghi. Quattro Stagioni. When it comes to Neapolitan-style pizza toppings, it often seems like there's nothing new under the sun. This family-friendly pizzeria has managed to go way outside the box with its wood-fired pizzas, while still staying true to classic Italian flavors. The standard Margherita is represented, but then the menu quickly breaks new ground with pies like the Positano, a surprisingly

CALIFORNIA

perfect combination of salty crescenza cheese, sautéed shrimp, chopped scallions, and a slight tang from thin slices of fried lemon. Other pizzas come topped with outliers like chicken apple sausage, broccoli, and cauliflower. Another lesser-seen menu item is the Piandine: oven-baked flatbread topped with a luscious salad that's folded and eaten like a taco. Despite its connection to the ritzy Tra Vigne trattoria next door, the atmosphere here is decidedly low-key. The hip interior has black vinyl booths, a pool table, and vintage Italian posters of sci-fi movies, and the adjacent patio is framed with climbing wisteria and a bobbing string of lights.

KNOW: *Top off the meal with house-made gelato, in traditional flavors like Valrhona chocolate, strawberry, and hazelnut. Or try sorbet flavored with white peaches and champagne.*

🍶 St. Helena Olive Oil Company

1351 Main St, St. Helena
MILE/EXIT: NAP-29
707.968.9260
www.sholiveoil.com
OPEN: *Daily 10:30a–5p*

Sample your way through estate vintages of Napa's other crop—its burgeoning boutique olive oil industry—at this friendly emporium. Started by a former San Francisco CPA who moved to Napa with her children in 1994 in search of a slower life, the olive oil company offers nearly a dozen extra-virgin olive oils from different Napa Valley estates. Sampling them in rapid-fire succession affords the rare opportunity to understand the difference *terroir* makes for artisan olive oil. Contrast the mellow Napa flavors with a line of extra-virgin oils from Spanish and Italian olives grown in warmer Central Coast conditions, or sample flavored oils, including orange, basil, lemon, lime, and rosemary. Get back to the grapes with red, white, and sparkling Napa Valley wine vinegars, along with a line of balsamics in unusual flavors like cranberry, raspberry, fig, and blueberry that will spice up any salad. Both locations have friendly, knowledgeable staff, and are located in reclaimed historic buildings. The smaller St. Helena outpost is located in a former Bank of Italy. The Rutherford flagship store was once Wilcox Tractor Manufacturing, the first tractor manufacturer in the valley, and still has original tracks on the ceiling that were once used to haul engines. (8576 St. Helena Hwy; 707.967.1003, ext. 14)

KNOW: *The St. Helena location carries the shop's line of organic lavender bath and body oils, with lavender essential oil sourced from Kahn's ranch in south Napa.*

🏠 Oakville Grocery

7856 Hwy 29, Oakville

MILE/EXIT: NAP-22

707.944.8802

www.oakvillegrocery.com

OPEN: *Mon–Thu 7a–5p, Fri–Sat 7a–6p, Sun 8a–5p*

With its 1881 façade and worn wooden floors, this Wine Country institution looks like an old-fashioned general store from the history books—until you take a look at the inventory and realize that the simple folks of the olden days wouldn't recognize anything on the shelves. It's now a general store for gourmands, and has been *the* Napa Valley picnic stop for more than a century. Despite a 2007 acquisition by New York gourmet giant Dean & Deluca (who also opened their only West Coast branch down the street), the market has managed to retain its independent spirit. The narrow aisles can be chaos on busy weekends, but it's manageable if you know how to play the game. Take a number and then decide what to order: the alluring deli cases offer finger foods and salads, ranging from a stellar house green salad with roasted chicken, blue cheese, currants, walnuts, and apples, to cold pasta, Asian noodles, and asparagus salads. Sandwiches are something of local legend, available grilled or cold. Turkey and pesto mayo is a basic favorite—moist turkey roasted that morning, grilled on foccacia with a tang from the pesto mayo, it's the turkey sandwich dreams are made of. If you can successfully resist the jars of cookies on the counter, you're made of stronger stuff than me. The rest of the store has foodie-friendly items like jars of dried fig compote, wild sage honey, and a cheese counter and DIY olive bar; there's also a wine cellar with the best Napa vintages. The coffee bar up front stays busy throughout the day. Box lunches and cheese platters are available with 24 hours' notice.

KNOW: *Skip the lines and head to the cold case in front for drinks and premade sandwiches and salads.*

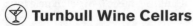 Turnbull Wine Cellars

8210 Hwy 29, Oakville

MILE/EXIT: NAP-22

800.887.6215

www.turnbullwines.com

OPEN: *Daily 10a–4:30p, reserve tasting room closes at 4p*

It's conveniently located right off the main highway. Its relatively small size ensures one-on-one attention from tasting room staff. It's in the heart of Oakville, which makes it a great place to try the appellation's powerful reds without the pretension and crowds of a bigger winery. Honestly, what's not to love about Turnbull? The brown wooden winery building actually offers two tasting rooms facing each other across a sunny courtyard, which also affords views of the estate vineyards beyond. The light-filled main room offers a basic flight of the winery's cabernet sauvignon, merlot, sauvignon blanc, and the signature Old Bull Red blend. As you sip, wander around the small store and taste gourmet sauces made with wine, including mustard and a dark chocolate ganache. Across the courtyard, the high-ceilinged barrel aging room doubles as the reserve tasting room, with black-and-white historic photographs of old California on the walls and a very helpful staff that pairs "black label" vintages with cheese, chocolate, and salt to tease out the flavors. Tasting fee is $10 in the main room, $20 for reserve.

KNOW: *The label has been the family's crest since the 1300s, when a family member saved Robert the Bruce from a bull that was about to gore him. The grateful Scottish king gave his subject the name "Turnbull" and the bull crest.*

Bouchon Bakery

6528 Washington St, Yountville

MILE/EXIT: NAP-19

707.944.2253

www.bouchonbakery.com

OPEN: *Daily 7a–7p*

You know a place is special when even the dollop of whipped cream on the lemon tart is something to rhapsodize over. The cheapest and most accessible of all of the Keller restaurants, Bouchon Bakery has expanded to a thriving chain with outposts in Las Vegas and New York. It oozes the class of an upscale Paris boulangerie, with its pale green walls, black-and-white tiled floor, and light jazz soundtrack. Windows into the kitchen and the scent of fresh bread add to the anticipation as you wait in line. After everything one has heard about the place, it's easy to let expectations run wild—but Keller's food is actually as good as its reputation suggests. The bittersweet chocolate Bouchon bites are a dark chocolate fantasy, and the TKO Oreo is a fun take on Keller's favorite guilty pleasure snack, made gourmet with chocolate sable dough and sweet white chocolate ganache. Brioche is light, sweet, bready, and breakfasty. Sandwiches are also available, including a stellar horseradish-kissed roast beef on pretzel bread, best grilled. The bakery has no inside seating, but does offer tables in the sun-dappled courtyard next to a rustic brick wall. Snag a seat, take a deep breath, and take it all in. You're officially in Wine Country.

KNOW: *Bathrooms are available at the back of the courtyard across from the coffee stand; they're shared with Keller's bistro Red, but you don't need to go into the restaurant to access them.*

Yountville

Yountville is the Manhattan of Wine Country, center of everything glitzy and glamorous about the Napa Valley lifestyle. The 1.2-mile town boasts more Michelin stars within four blocks than you can count on one hand, half of which belong to culinary god Thomas Keller. The town is also said to be the site of the first vineyards in Napa Valley, planted by town founder George C. Yount in the nineteenth century. Despite its finery, it's possible to get a taste of Yountville without forking over your life savings. Do a drive-by of the quaint stone building that houses the French Laundry (in the morning, you can see the chefs picking the night's dinner at the garden across the street), then head to Bouchon Bakery, a place for mere mortals to taste Keller's culinary magic without a significant investment.

CALIFORNIA

NapaStyle Paninoteca & Wine Bar

6525 Washington St, Yountville

MILE/EXIT: NAP-19

707.945.1229

www.napastyleottimocafe.com

OPEN: *Store open daily 10a–6p, deli open daily 11a–4p*

NapaStyle is the domain of Food Network personality and cookbook author Michael Chiarello, who has made a career out of the easy lifestyle of Napa Valley. The chain has grown across California, but the flagship Yountville store is still the best place to try Chiarello's food, in the form of panini, salads, and antipasto platters that showcase the best of the season and region. The sandwiches are so good they make you forgive the man for calling his deli a "paninoteca." The Forever Roasted Pork sandwich is an oozing handful of slow-roasted heritage pork, Fontina cheese, and *mustarda di frutta* (an Italian condiment blending candied fruit and mustard-flavored syrup), all contained in a crispy baguette. The decadent PLT substitutes pancetta lardons for bacon. Salads range from a garlicky Caesar to a cold rice salad with veggies and a citrus vinaigrette. The shop also offers wine and olive oil tastings, and a deli case stocked with tiny jars of deliciousness like Parmesan dip, bruschetta, and prosciutto pâté will enhance any picnic. Box lunches are available with 24 hours' advance notice.

KNOW: *NapaStyle is hidden from the road in the V Marketplace, a collection of upscale shops in a handsome brick building that started life in 1870 as the Groezinger Winery.*

VARIOUS LOCATIONS *in Costa Mesa and Los Gatos.*

Goosecross Cellars

1119 State Ln, Yountville

MILE/EXIT: NAP-19

707.944.1986

www.goosecross.com

OPEN: *Daily 10a–4p*

A short drive through the neighborhoods of Yountville takes you to the agricultural fields beyond, and the quiet, vineyard-lined lane that leads to this off-the-beaten-path winery. Goosecross is a small-production facility, and the experience is more intimate than you find in most Napa tasting rooms: all tasting is done within feet of the aging barrels, and led by a team of approachable pourers who are there to educate as well as sell. The winery actually has a full-time director of education on staff, Nancy Hawks Miller, who also leads the 90-minute Estate Winegrowing Tour into the vineyards every Saturday afternoon from August through November. No matter how up close and personal you decide to get with the vines, expect a warm welcome in an oh-so-Napa atmosphere, and a chance to try the winery's crisp Estate Chardonnay and bold reds, including a cabernet from the prestigious Howell Mountain appellation, the first distinct AVA within Napa Valley.

KNOW: *Looking for the perfect anniversary gift? Look no further than the chocolate-dipped wine bottles, made in conjunction with a Yountville chocolatier.*

TOURS: *Sat 2p, May–Oct—$40 per person, includes tasting fee and bottle of wine to take home. Reservations necessary.*

Domaine Chandon

1 California Dr, Yountville

MILE/EXIT: NAP-19

888.242.6366

www.chandon.com

OPEN: *Daily 10a–6p*

The year: 1968. The company: Venerable French champagne house Moet & Chandon. Their mission: To find the world's next big sparkling wine region. After five years of searching, they'd found it in Carneros, and partnered with cognac producer Hennessy to open Domaine Chandon, the first French-owned sparkling wine venture in the states. More than 30 years later, the Yountville tasting room has morphed into a full-scale visitor center, complete with a Michelin-starred restaurant and scenic landscaped grounds dotted with local art. The tastings don't come cheap, but there's something decadent about a flight of sparkling wines in the afternoon, and it's always nice to feel fancy once in a while. If you're getting a pair of flights, sharing a pricier varietal or reserve tasting along with the classic lineup is the way to go—it's fun to compare, and really helps you understand the difference that quality grapes and production methods make in the final product. Domaine Chandon was a pioneer

CALIFORNIA

in sustainable viniculture, and continues to employ environmentally friendly practices to all of its vineyards.

KNOW: *If you really feel like a splurge, try the food pairings from on-site restaurant Etoile. The specially selected tasting room menu includes snacks like Valhrona chocolate–dipped strawberries, smoked mushrooms, and oysters with ginger mignonette designed to complement the flavors in the wines.*

TOURS: *Learn more about Domaine Chandon's history and wines, and take a peek into the winery production room—11:30a and 3:40p; 35 min; $12 per person.*

Oxbow Public Market

610 1st St, Napa

MILE/EXIT: NAP-11

707.226.6529

www.oxbowpublicmarket.com

OPEN: *Mon–Sat 9a–7p, Sun 9a–6p, but individual stalls' hours vary*

This airy, industrial-chic indoor market is basically a Cliffs Notes of the best of the Bay Area. Designed by the same architects as San Francisco's Ferry Building, and with the same mission of promoting local food and sustainable business practices, Oxbow is different from its big-city sibling only in its scaled-down size and the wine grapes in the parking lot. Wander the 40,000 square feet of stalls and taste your way through the region. Must-try stops include bittersweet chocolate or strawberry balsamic ice cream at Three Twins Organic Ice Cream, a rich espresso from Ritual Coffee, airy lemon cupcakes at Kara's Cupcakes, and a half dozen oysters on the half shell from Hog Island Oyster Co. Other artisan stalls sell organic produce, fine tea, loose spices, sustainably raised beef and seafood, local olive oil, Napa Valley wines, and more. Gott's Roadside operates a satellite burger stand outside. True to the market's mission, everything is served on eco-friendly, recyclable tableware. Community and sustainability here are more than just buzzwords—they're a way of life.

KNOW: *Get even more of a local flavor at the Napa Farmers Market held in the parking lot (Tue and Sat, 7:30a–noon), and Tuesday "Locals Night" (6–8p), which features live music and a block party atmosphere.*

 Fatted Calf Charcuterie

6446 1st St, Napa

MILE/EXIT: NAP-11

707.256.3684

www.fattedcalf.com

OPEN: *Mon–Sat 9a–7p, Sun 10a–6p*

Technically this artisan charcuterie and butcher shop is part of the Oxbow Market, but a pork palace as fine as this one deserves its own entry. Meat lovers will feel like kids turned loose in a candy store, from the fragrant blast of smoked meat on your way in, to the staff that greets you with a smile and a simple question: "What do you want to try?" I couldn't say no to a slice of the house-cured salumi (the aging room is visible behind the counter), or a spoonful of the creamy duck rillettes, which was so good I involuntarily exclaimed, "This makes me happy." The man behind the counter smiled knowingly and said, "It's my job." It's better than being Santa Claus. After sampling, it takes a will of steel to walk away without filling a shopping basket. Why resist temptation? The beef jerky is lighter and fattier than I've ever tasted, made with local grass-fed beef, with a kick from bourbon and sweetness from blackstrap molasses. The miniature salumi are worthy road trip companions, more delicate than their closest cousins, German *landjaeger.* It's been months since I've had it, but I can't stop thinking about the Petit Sec aux Herbes stick, an otherworldly blend of pasture-raised pork, organic garlic, white wine, and French herbs, that snaps when you bite into it before releasing moisture that you know is pure fat, but you don't care. Sandwiches are also very good, especially the smoked-to-perfection pork shoulder with coleslaw and spicy mayo, on rustic bread with just the right amount of chew.

KNOW: *Fatted Calf opened a store in San Francisco's Hayes Valley in late 2010 (320 Fell Street; 415.400.5614).*

CALIFORNIA

Marshall's Farm Honey

159 Lombard Rd, American Canyon

MILE/EXIT: NAP-5

DISTANCE FROM HWY: *7 miles from Hwy 121 junction*

800.624.4637

www.marshallshoney.com

OPEN: *Mon–Fri 9a–5p, Sat–Sun 11a–4p*

If you've never thought much about honey, this homespun roadside farm stand is a good place to start. Husband-and-wife team Spencer and Helene Marshall have set up honeycombs all around the Bay Area, with the singular goal to create raw, 100 percent pure local honey using the most basic methods possible. (He tends to the bees, she tends to the business. How cute is that?) The Marshalls produce 25 seasonal honey varieties by hand and on the spot, sometimes out of the hive and into a jar within hours. The uninitiated will be surprised at the marked difference between honeys from different places and different sources—like wine and cheese, honey depends on the *terroir*, and versions from Marin County and the East Bay will taste as different as versions made from blackberry and sage flowers. All tasting is conducted in the homemade farm stand on the farm property, and the goal is to guide you to a honey purchase you feel good about—it's available for takeaway in jars, plastic bears, and sticks. Weekend tours give a much more in-depth look at the honey-making process, including a honeycomb tasting right out of the beehive. If a trip to the stand isn't in the cards, the Marshalls also sell their honey at many Bay Area farmers markets.

KNOW: *Since this is a honey farm there are, well, honeybees flitting around the property. They generally keep to themselves, but be on the lookout if you have allergies.*

TOURS: *Offered Sunday afternoons, March through November (2 hours; $25 adults, $10 kids 4–16). Make reservations and find exact times on the website.*

Sebastiani Vineyards & Winery

389 4th St E, Sonoma

MILE/EXIT: SON-37

707.933.3230

www.sebastiani.com

OPEN: *Daily 10a–5p*

Even if you don't recognize the name, you'll recognize the label from grocery store shelves—this historic winery was bought by the marketing powerhouse Foley Family Wines in 2008 (the company also owns Firestone Vineyards). Despite a slick corporate veneer, this large-scale winery still has elements of its old-world roots. It was among the first wineries in the region, started in 1904 by Tuscan immigrant Samuele Sebastiani, who first worked as a stonemason creating cobblestones for San Francisco streets before he made the switch to winemaker. Sebastiani was the only winery in the county to stay in business during Prohibition, by selling sacramental and medicinal wine. The tasting room befits the label's history, with stone walls, a cathedral-like coved ceiling, marble bar, and roaring fireplace—it would feel intimate if it weren't for the wine accessories for sale in every corner. Still, big wineries can be a relief sometimes; the staff is used to volume and has a hands-off approach, and the sheer range of available wines trumps smaller production houses. Sebastiani has vines in most of the sub-appellations of Sonoma County, and it's a treat to compare chardonnays from Russian River, Sonoma County, and Carneros, or cabernets from the Alexander Valley and Sonoma County.

KNOW: *Don't leave without checking out the fabulous hand-carved barrels in the aging room just beyond the tasting bar, created by Samuele Sebastiani's son, August.*

TOURS: *Available daily 11a, 1p, and 3p (free).*

Vella Cheese Company

315 2nd St E, Sonoma

MILE/EXIT: SON-37

707.938.3232

www.vellacheese.com

If you haven't tried Dry Jack cheese, prepare to get your world rocked. Dry Jack is America's answer to aged Gouda and Parmesan, probably created by accident when a San Francisco wholesaler allowed his inventory of soft Monterey Jack to age too long. The result was a hard, pale yellow cheese with a nutty flavor, embraced by the American public when World War I cut off its supply to European aged cheeses. Vella Cheese founder Tom Vella is widely heralded as one of the country's original and best artisan cheesemakers, and has been producing high-moisture, partially

Monterey Jack Cheese

The common mild white cheese was likely adapted from an old Spanish recipe, but dairy baron David Jacks was the first to produce it at scale and sell it to a San Francisco market. Dry Jack is a California specialty, and probably created by mistake when a wholesaler in San Francisco didn't refrigerate it, resulting in a dry, nutty cheese. Vella Cheese Company (see page 201) produces some of the best in the state.

dry, and dry Monterey Jack cheeses since his factory opened its doors in 1931. He didn't stop there, however: in 1935, with backing from cheese mogul J. L. Kraft, Vella bought a small nonoperational cheese plant in Southern Oregon that became the Rogue Creamery (see page 90). Tom Vella's incredible legacy is carried on by his son, Ignacio "Ig" Vella, who has expanded the factory's repertoire to Jack cheeses seasoned with pesto, rosemary, and garlic, along with cheddar and a short list of Italian cheeses. Snap up the chance to try the mildly sweet Toma, a soft cheese from Piedmont rarely found in the states. All tasting is conducted in the original stone-walled factory building. If you're lucky, Ig Vella himself will be holding court behind the counter.

KNOW: *It doesn't seem right to mention Tom Vella without a passing nod to his former business partner and crosstown rival Celso Viviani, who opened the touristy Sonoma Cheese Factory on Sonoma's main plaza.*

Buena Vista Winery

18000 Old Winery Rd, Sonoma

MILE/EXIT: SON-37

707.252.7117

www.buenavistacarneros.com

OPEN: *Daily 10a–5p*

Any self-respecting Wine Country tour needs to pay homage to the state's oldest winery. In 1857, flamboyant Hungarian count Agoston Haraszthy arrived in Sonoma as a representative to the state legislature, but his interest in grapes quickly outpaced his interest in politics. He bought some land and disappeared on a fact-finding mission to Europe, returning with 10,000 vine clippings of varietals previously unknown to the New World—and thus secured his place in history as the father of the California wine industry. Raise a glass to Haraszthy 's legacy in the ivy-draped stone tasting room that once housed the winery's original press house. Pinot noir and chardonnay from the winery's 500-acre Carneros vineyard are the wines to try here, though the syrah is definitely worth a spin. No Buena Vista visit is complete without a trip to the mezzanine museum followed by a stroll around the grounds, scattered with antique fountains, an original wine barrel, and an exquisite picnic area shaded by old oaks. Though it's only minutes from the bustling Sonoma plaza, it feels like centuries away.

KNOW: *The parking lot is outside the winery grounds, and getting to the tasting room requires a five-minute walk down a tree-lined lane.*

 Swiss Hotel

18 W Spain St, Sonoma
MILE/EXIT: SON-37
707.938.2884
www.swisshotelsonoma.com
OPEN: *Daily 11:30a–9p*

There's something about old hotel bars. Maybe it's the constantly rotating cast of characters, always on their way somewhere else, or maybe it's the history contained in the walls—the tales they could tell, if they could talk. This particular bar on Sonoma's main plaza has seen more action than most. The two-story Monterey Colonial adobe was originally built by General Vallejo's brother in 1840 to serve as a family home. Later, it was converted into a hotel for weary passengers coming into town on the stagecoach, then the railroad. History is present and accounted for in the yellowing photographs on the walls, the pre-Prohibition dark wood bar, and the appropriately dim lighting. To put it another way: it's the kind of watering hole that reminds you that good bars, like good men, are hard to find.

KNOW: *Despite its name, the Swiss Hotel has been owned by the Italian American Marioni family for four generations, and the food at the bar and adjacent restaurant is strictly old-world Italian, with nary a fondue fork in sight.*

CALIFORNIA

(🍴) the girl & the fig

110 W Spain St, Sonoma
MILE/EXIT: SON-37
707.938.3634
www.thegirlandthefig.com
OPEN: *Mon–Thu 11:30a–10p, Fri–Sat 11:30a–11p, Sun 10a–10p*

The girl is proprietress Sondra Bernstein, who has carved out a Sonoma culinary empire around French countryside cuisine using local, seasonal ingredients. What started as her small cafe in Glen Ellen now encompasses three restaurants, a catering outfit, and a cookbook. The fig is the star of the menu, popping up in cocktails, salads, and daily specials when it's in season. The girl & the fig's butter-colored dining room and peaceful patio are open for lunch and dinner, but the weekend brunch knocks one out of the park. In my mind, a good brunch must have three elements: sweet, savory, and alcoholic. Go sweet with the outstanding mascarpone-stuffed French toast, topped with fresh berries. Savory is covered with the seasonal Fig & Arugula Salad, a masterpiece of chèvre, pecans, fresh figs, and crispy explosions of pancetta that will give you new appreciation for bacon bits, all tossed in a not-too-sweet port-and-fig vinaigrette. And then there's the brunch cocktail. House-made fig liquor is a major player—the star of the fig royale, a play on the kir royale, and a champagne cocktail that retains the subtle dryness of the sparkling wine in a way a mimosa never manages. If you sit at the flapper-era mahogany bar and ask nicely, the bartender will tell you how to make the liquor in your own kitchen. Beyond cocktails, the award-winning "Rhone Alone" wine list offers local glasses and flights—perfect for pairing with cheese at the "salon de fromage," a hybrid tasting bar/cheese shop in the front room.

KNOW: *Make reservations, track your cheese favorites, and more on the restaurant's own iPhone app.*

(🏠) Artisan Bakers

750 W Napa St, Sonoma
MILE/EXIT: SON-37
707.939.1765
www.artisanbakers.com
OPEN: *Mon–Sat 6:30a–3p, Sun 7a–2p*

To step into this delightful bakery is to enter a European twilight zone; its chalkboard menu, baskets holding more than a dozen bread varieties, mismatched vintage tables, and Provençal mural on one wall bring you into a continental state of mind. For a moment you wonder if you should be ordering in English. Most bakeries that excel at bread-baking usually have a heavy hand with pastries, and vice versa; Artisan Bakers is the rare exception that does both equally well. Bread is made from old-world methods, using three different natural starters (sourdough, poolish, and riga, if you want to get technical), formed by hand, and baked in a stone oven. These are attractively scored rustic loaves covering a pantheon of baking traditions: Italian country, Pugliese, classic French, sour rye, and American ingredients like jalapeno corn and Dry Jack and roasted garlic sourdough. On the other end of the spectrum are the pastries—rows of danishes, croissants, tea cakes, and éclairs that are so light, buttery, and ephemeral they could have been formed by fairies. This being Sonoma County, all flour is organic and ingredients are local whenever possible. If you're feeling peckish, there's a small but mighty lunch menu, including pizza, quiche, and inventive sandwiches like poached pear and blue cheese.

KNOW: *Pick up some of the house-made granola—you'll thank yourself tomorrow morning.*

Sonoma Springs Brewing Co.

750 W Napa St, Sonoma

MILE/EXIT: SON-37

707.938.7422

www.sonomaspringsbrewing.com

OPEN: *Mon 3–8p, Thu–Sat 1–8p, Sun 1–6p*

Germans take their beer very seriously, a lesson I learned the hard way while visiting a Bavarian friend a couple years back. We were conducting a taste test of local brews in her kitchen, and I committed the cardinal sin of pouring Bamberg's famous smoked ale into the wrong type of glass. The table went silent; my friend was so embarrassed she could barely look me in the eye, and a later glance in her cupboard revealed two shelves devoted entirely to beer glasses of all shapes and sizes. Anyway, all I'm saying is that it takes a brewer with moxie to attempt authentic German-style ales in the states—and brewmaster Tim Goeppinger is the man for the job. He earned his chops for nearly two decades at California breweries like Goose Island and Firestone before opening this small Sonoma brewery with his wife in 2009. Most Northern California brewpubs focus on hop-heavy ales that are big on flavor and big on alcohol; Goeppinger makes these too, but his passion lies in subtler, nuanced German styles such as the pilsner-like Kolsch, rye-based Roggenbier, dark Dunkel lager, and a traditional banana-and-clove-scented hefeweizen. He also experiments with barrel aging to great effect, like a recent Mission Bell sour wheat. Try a tasting flight of the four or five beers offered at the moment, neatly laid out on a chalkboard, or go big with the 24-ounce "Hourglass" stein.

KNOW: *There's no food available at the moment, but who needs bar snacks when you have Artisan Bakers two steps away?*

🍴 El Molino Central

11 Central Ave (17999 Hwy 12), Boyes Hot Springs
MILE/EXIT: SON-35
707.939.1010
www.elmolinocentral.com
OPEN: *Daily 7a–7p*

Bay Area food fans rejoiced when the hugely popular Primavera Tamales—previously available only at farmers markets and certain specialty stores—found a permanent home along Sonoma Valley's main highway in 2010. The tamales, I'm pleased to report, haven't suffered a bit since the expansion, probably because they're still handmade with such care by owner/chef Karen Taylor Waikiki. She starts with raw corn kernels sourced from a single Nebraska organic farm, which she painstakingly grinds into masa meal every day to serve as the base for her tamales and handmade tortillas. (See her in action around 11am.) After putting in the labor, Waikiki doesn't desecrate her food with less-than-worthy ingredients, only selecting high-quality sources like Niman Ranch and local, organic producers. Origins this noble don't come cheap, and though a single tamale costs $5, it is so, so worth it. The corn flavor of the masa shines in the chicken mole tamales, which incidentally have the best mole I've tasted outside of Oaxaca. Other Mexican regional dishes are similarly well executed—Waikiki spent time in Mexico learning from Mexican cooking authority Diana Kennedy, and it shows in her crisp potato tacos, Swiss chard enchiladas, and outstanding morning chilaquiles. The cafe's Spanish Colonial look and feel summon thoughts of Mexico with its vibrant tile floor, whitewashed walls, and bright colored accents. Plus there's Blue Bottle coffee and a quiet back patio.

KNOW: *Die-hard foodies can buy Waikiki's masa and make their own tamales at home, without the labor of grinding the corn themselves.*

Oak Hill Farm

15101 Sonoma Hwy, Glen Ellen
MILE/EXIT: SON-32
707.996.6643
www.oakhillfarm.net
OPEN: *April–Christmas Wed–Sun 10a–6p*

It doesn't get more legit than this organic farm stand, located down a sunflower- and apple tree–lined lane in a red barn straight out of the storybooks. Oak Hill has more than 200 crops on 45 acres of protected farmland, which has been farmed organic and sustainably since the Teller family bought the farm in the 1950s. The Tellers aren't just any family: Otto Teller was a renowned conservationist who founded the Sonoma Land Trust with his wife, Anne. The Red Barn Store is in the 100-year-old dairy barn, and overflows with a cornucopia of peak-of-season produce identified by chalkboard signs. What you'll find depends on the time of year. Spring brings salad greens, carrots, and broccoli; summer is an explosion of vegetables and fruit; and fall offers pumpkins, gourds, and fresh and dried herbs. The farm also has a large array of flowers, which are put to gorgeous effect in the popular handmade decorative wreaths and bouquets.

Fig Café

13690 Arnold Dr, Glen Ellen
MILE/EXIT: SON-30
707.938.2130
www.thefigcafe.com
OPEN: *Mon–Thu 5:30–9p; Fri–Sat 10a–3p, 5:30–9:30p*

Equally good for a pre-wine tasting brunch or a post-tasting dinner, this friendly cafe is the lower-key offshoot of Sonoma's the girl & the fig. It's

CALIFORNIA

a favorite spot of winemakers, both for the unpretentious, well-crafted food and the lack of corkage fee. The menu is a scaled-down version of its sister restaurant: comfort food done Sonoma style. An extremely popular entrée is the grilled top sirloin burger, topped with caramelized onions and your choice of white cheddar or cambozola cheese, served on a toasted brioche bun. Other favorites include steamed mussels and interesting thin-crust pizzas, such as one topped with grilled lamb, feta, red bell peppers, spinach, and marjoram. Brunch offerings include a duck confit omelet and brunch pizza. The casual dining room echoes the colors of the surrounding valley with its high A-frame light wood ceiling, pale green walls, and yellow tablecloths casually covered with butcher paper. If you haven't fallen in love with the place by the end of the meal, there's something wrong with you.

Benziger Family Winery

1883 London Ranch Rd, Glen Ellen
MILE/EXIT: SON-30
888.490.2739
www.benziger.com
OPEN: *Daily 10a–5p*

Benziger threw down the gauntlet for eco-friendly wineries in 2000, when it became the first Demeter-certified biodynamic vineyard in Sonoma County. What is a biodynamic farm? What is Demeter certification? Find out everything you want to know, and probably more, during the 45-minute tram tour of one of the winery's four certified-biodynamic vineyard estates. The tour gives a comprehensive overview of the certified-sustainable program Benziger asks its grape producers to follow, the three types of natural farming methods, what producing wines to these specifications means, and walks you through the wine-making process from start to finish. I'll be honest: after a while, I started to space out and gaze at the sweeping scenery instead, located as we were on the slope of Sonoma Mountain. When we visited the fermentation facility and barrel caves, I had flashbacks to high school chemistry class. But I stuck it out, and walked away with a much more solid idea of what went into wine-making. After all, when did high school homework ever include wine tasting?

 **Loxton Cellars**

11466 Dunbar Rd, Glen Ellen

MILE/EXIT: SON-29

707.935.7221

www.loxtonwines.com

OPEN: *By appointment, roughly 11a–5p daily (call ahead)*

F. Scott Fitzgerald's oft-quoted phrase about second acts in American lives clearly doesn't apply to Australian-born winemaker Chris Loxton. He came to the states to get a PhD in physics and intended to return Down Under shortly thereafter to become the third-generation winemaker on his family's shiraz vineyard. Instead, he found himself drawn to Sonoma, and here he remains, growing the same grapes on the other side of the world. Syrah is the French name for shiraz, and Sonoma syrah is a blend of the two wine-making styles: it doesn't have all the bold spices of Australia, but has a certain brashness not usually found in French wine. Loxton Cellars' tasting room is in the barrel aging and production facility, a warehouse-like building surrounded by a sea of vineyards and decorated with Australian tourism posters. The setting ceases to matter once the wine tasting begins; these are amazing wines, and Loxton himself is often the man behind the tasting bar, walking you through the wines and wine-making process like an old friend, and often gesturing to the vineyards through the window to punctuate his point that wine and land are inexorably intertwined. For a small tasting room, it has many stylish touches: the award-winning port and surprisingly sweet Late Harvest zinfandel are served with different grades of dark chocolate, and if you buy a bottle, he'll write you a personalized note with a gold pen. Such access to a winemaker is rare, and Loxton has a mind like a steel trap and is super-nice to boot. My heart broke a little when it was time to leave him and the winery behind.

Figone's of California Olive Oil Company

9580 Hwy 12, Kenwood

MILE/EXIT: SON-27

707.282.9092

www.figoneoliveoil.com

OPEN: *Daily 10a–5:30p*

Frank Figone's great-grandfather emigrated from Italy in the 1920s with the bare essentials: his wife, children, and an olive tree sapling from their native Lucca, a revered olive oil region. The tree was transplanted to the family's asparagus farm; a few generations later, the tree had become a grove and Figone got the idea to start an olive oil production company in his great-grandfather's asparagus packing shed. The company flourished and now makes single-press olive oil from 4,000 trees, including Mission and Manzanillo along with seven Tuscan varietals. In 2010, Figone's moved from a storefront in Glen Ellen to a bigger tasting room along a scenic stretch of Highway 12, which showcases the oil-making process and state-of-the-art Rapanelli machinery in a glassed-in room behind the tasting bar. Figone and his wife greet customers and guide them through thimble-sized samples in plastic cups, ranging from classic Mission/Manzanillo and Tuscan blends to eight flavored oils including Meyer lemon, blood orange, porcini mushroom, Persian lime, chili, and garlic. The company also makes an assortment of flavored balsamics. The original Lucca sapling still provides oil for the special La Visione blend.

KNOW: *At press time, plans were in the works for a picnic area complete with a brick barbecue on the unused land north of the winery.*

Landmark Winery

101 Adobe Canyon Rd, Kenwood

MILE/EXIT: SON-26

707.833.0053

www.landmarkwine.com

OPEN: *Daily 10a–4:30p*

A horse-drawn carriage greets visitors to this peaceful winery on Saturday afternoons in the summer, ready to transport them on a short tour of the estate vineyards led by a seasoned winemaker. It's a strange choice for a winery started by the great-great-granddaughter of tractor making icon John Deere—until you learn that Deere was a country blacksmith before inventing the steel plow that revolutionized the agriculture industry long before the automobile was invented. The family's deep agrarian roots are present in every aspect of the winery, which embraces winemaker Eric Stern's "less is more" philosophy by forgoing the common practice of destemming and crushing the grapes before pressing (which can lead to bitterness) and letting indigenous yeasts do the heavy lifting for the primary fermentation. The resulting chardonnays—which *Wine*

Spectator called "among the most exciting wines made in California"—and pinot noirs, all sourced from cool-weather regions like the Sonoma Coast, Russian River Valley, and Santa Barbara County, achieve a rare harmony of balance and richness. Get the all-chardonnay tasting, which includes the winery's award-winning Overlook chardonnay. Do linger on the landscaped grounds, which include a free bocce ball court and shady patio with views of the vineyards set against the backdrop of the Mayacamas Mountains.

KNOW: *Stay a night, or a week, at the small cottage on the property, which offers reasonable rates and a hard-to-beat Wine Country location.*

DETOURS & DESTINATIONS

Scenic Route: Silverado Trail

EXIT: NAP-37

LENGTH: 29 miles (Calistoga to Napa)

www.silveradotrail.com

Open fields, tree-coated mountains, rows of vineyards, no visible commercialism . . . this 29-mile road on the eastern edge of Napa Valley is what you dream of when you dream of Wine Country. More than 40 wineries are hidden along this stretch, including prestigious spots like Mumm Napa Valley and Stag's Leap Wine Cellars (one of the wineries that put Napa on the map in the Judgment of Paris). Though it's now a side route running parallel to the more popular Highway 29, the Silverado Trail was once the most important, as the first permanent road between Napa and Calistoga and site of Black Bart's infamous stagecoach holdups. What it lacks in the excitement of the olden days, it makes up in serene views and a more intimate look at life in Napa Valley. And, when traffic backs up on Highway 29—which it does frequently—the Silverado Trail is usually wide open.

KNOW: *Fill up or find picnic supplies at the Soda Canyon Store, a deli and gourmet grocery with a shady picnic area overlooking a creek and vineyards (4006 Silverado Trail, Napa; 707.252.0285).*

CALIFORNIA

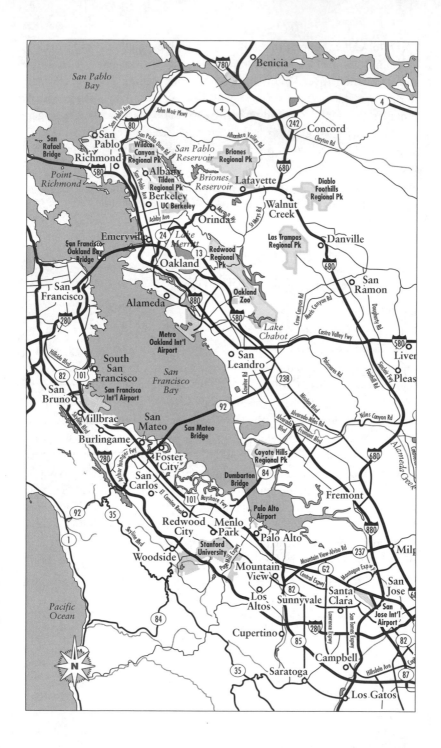

San Francisco

City Stats

LOCAL FLAVOR: Italian food, Mexican food, beer, Asian food.

BEST TIME: Fall—San Francisco enjoys gorgeous, warm Indian summers.

WORST TIME: Summer, unfortunately—cold fog blows in from the bay, and Mark Twain's oft-quoted quip, "The coldest winter I ever spent was a summer in San Francisco," certainly applies.

LOCAL FOOD FESTIVALS: San Francisco Beer Week (February). A massive celebration of all things beer.

MORE INFO: San Francisco Travel (www.onlyinsanfrancisco.com)

Despite L.A.'s grandstanding, San Francisco is probably the more important city when it comes to the development of what's known today as "California cuisine"—the cultural immigrations to California and their accompanying foods helped develop the state, and it's possible to eat your way through the whole history of California in a day.

Get dim sum in Chinatown—thousands of Chinese workers poured into California to work on the railroad and other development projects, and this is the oldest and best established Chinatown in the country. Snack on artisan meats and cheeses at the Ferry Building—a restored 1890s Beaux Arts ferry terminal that now houses a who's who of the best the Bay Area offers. Eat pizza and cannoli in North Beach—San Francisco's vibrant Little Italy, childhood home of Joe DiMaggio and fave hangout of the Beat poets. Wolf down a burrito in the Mission District—birthplace of the modern burrito. And head over to the East Bay—home of Alice Waters, the woman who pioneered local cuisine.

San Francisco was—and still is—a significant port town, and its proximity to Sutter's Mill ensured its place in history when gold was discovered in 1848. That was the year the city's population swelled from 1,000 to 25,000 residents. Sixty years later, the 1906 earthquake leveled half the town, left 250,000 homeless, and prompted Jack London to write in an eyewitness account for *Collier's*, "San Francisco is gone. Nothing remains

CALIFORNIA

of it but memories." He was wrong. The spirit of San Francisco survived, even if many of its buildings did not. And a century later, it's not only survived, but grown up.

KNOW: *All in-city entries, unless otherwise noted, are within 5 miles of Hwy 101, which runs north to south through San Francisco on surface streets: Doyle Dr, Lombard St, and Van Ness Ave. It's a good idea to have a GPS or detailed city map handy when driving through San Francisco.*

🍴 Boudin Bakery

160 Jefferson St, San Francisco
415.928.1849
www.boudinbakery.com
OPEN: *Sun–Thu 8a–9p, Fri–Sat 8a–10p*

San Francisco sourdough owes its legend to this historic bakery, one of the city's oldest. It was opened in 1849 by Isadore Boudin, who combined his French family's bread-baking prowess with the local sourdough popular with gold rush prospectors. Many have tried, but none have succeeded at replicating the bread's famous tang—and they never will, because Boudin has used the same starter since the beginning, and it's now imbued with a century and a half of San Francisco history. The flagship store on Fisherman's Wharf might cater to a tourist crowd, but it's anything but touristy. For starters, the food is better than you'd expect. Clam chowder in a sourdough bowl is worth the visit alone, as are the sourdough-crust pizzas and grilled sandwiches. More interesting than the meal, for a food nerd like me, is the on-premises museum, which walks you through the history of sourdough bread as well as the unique history of the bakery. (Was any other sourdough starter saved from the wreckage of the calamitous 1906 earthquake in a bucket? Didn't think so.) Don't leave before you've seen the 5,000-square-foot demonstration bakery where bakers still form loaves by hand, visible through 30-foot display windows and a glassed-in catwalk.

KNOW: *Experience more California history at the upper-level Buena Vista Carneros Tasting Room, an offshoot of the state's first commercial winery, still operating in Sonoma.*

🍴 Caffe Trieste

601 Vallejo St, San Francisco
415.392.6739
www.caffetrieste.com
OPEN: Sun–Thu 6a–11p, Fri–Sat 6:30a–midnight
Cash only

Around the corner from legendary Beat poet hangout City Lights Bookstore sits this Italian espresso bar, where Kerouac, Ginsberg, and the gang used to hold court. Caffe Trieste is said to be the first espresso bar on the West Coast, opened in the 1950s by Italian immigrant Giovanni Giotta, who was nostalgic for the coffee bars of his native Trieste. It still retains that old-school European feel, from the long espresso bar to the large Italianate mural along one wall—the only thing missing is the old men paying backgammon in the corner. An entire wall is covered in framed black-and-white photos showing the history of the place (including a few snapshots of Francis Ford Coppola, who wrote most of the original *Godfather* screenplay here), but the coffee shop's not resting on its laurels or trading on the past. It's as relevant today as it was back then, serving up some of the best espresso you'll have this side of the Aegean, enjoyed at the crowded tables inside or out on the sidewalk in the company of North Beach hippies and hipsters. A food menu of panini, thin-crust pizzas, and other specialties is also available.

KNOW: *Come Saturday afternoons between 1pm and 5pm for the city's longest-running musical show, a mix of jazz, show tunes, vaudeville, and big band that's a whole lot of fun.*

🍴 Tommaso's Restaurant

1042 Kearny St, San Francisco
415.398.9696
www.tommasos.com
OPEN: Tue–Sat 5–10:30p, Sun 4–9:30p

The line starts forming before this legendary North Beach pizzeria even opens its hunter green doors—there's a strict no-reservations policy, and to snag a seat you have to get there early or be prepared to wait. But the waiting is part of the experience: Put your name on the list, order a glass of Italian wine, talk to the people next to you in line, and let the communal anticipation build as you watch charred brick-oven pizzas pass by on their way to happy recipients. Eventually, you are seated at a table in the crowded dining room, and then you can get down to business. There's a reason this place has gotten accolades from pretty much every food publication in the world—the food is, in a word, transcendent. The pizza comes charred and bubbly, topped with enough cheese to make the middle almost too soggy to pick up (the hallmark of a great wood-fired pizza), and high-quality toppings like spicy pepperoni and sausage are sourced from Italian delis. If you can tear yourself away from the pizza, the lasagne is a light, creamy dream, and the pasta dishes feature sauces you can tell have simmered all day. If your stomach can handle it, the super-authentic tiramisu is incredible.

KNOW: *Tommaso's had the first wood-fired brick pizza oven on the West Coast, thanks to its Napolese owners, and has been the model for similar ovens in the kitchens of heavy-hitting chefs like Alice Waters and Wolfgang Puck.*

🍴 Golden Gate Fortune Cookie Factory

56 Ross Alley, San Francisco
415.781.3956
OPEN: *Daily 8a–8p*

It's easy to miss this tiny fortune cookie factory in a narrow alley in Chinatown, but you'll know it from the warm vanilla scent of baking cookies wafting from the open door. Inside, watch the Chinese proprietors as they manipulate the machines that bake the cookies, then manually insert the fortunes and fold them by hand with such deftness that it looks like they've been doing this since time immemorial. The room is small—only fits about a half dozen people—and it can get crowded, but you'll have enough time to take a peek inside, try a sample hot off the griddle, and buy a bag of cookies to go. You'll never look at fortune cookies the same way again—one bite of these babies, fresh out of the oven, and you're spoiled on the stale versions in Chinese restaurants forever. Buy bags of 'em to go in traditional, chocolate, and "adult," which come with (slightly) racy fortunes.

🍴 Ferry Building Marketplace

1 Ferry Building, San Francisco
415.983.8030

www.ferrybuildingmarketplace.com
OPEN: *Mon–Fri 10a–6p, Sat 9a–6p, Sun 11a–5p*

The city of San Francisco spent $110 million to restore the soaring 1898 Beaux Arts building on the Embarcadero, which now houses one of the best food markets on the West Coast along with a ferry terminal that serves more than 11,000 commuters each day. The best and brightest of Bay Area cuisine have set up shop here, among them Cowgirl Creamery, Blue Bottle Coffee, Hog Island Oyster Co., Gott's Roadside, Boccalone Salumeria, and Scharffen Berger Chocolate. The thronging Saturday Farmers Market is a must-visit: dozens of fresh farm stands, restaurant stalls, artisan producers, and all of San Francisco society on display (8a–2p). For a slower scene, try hitting up the market on Tuesday and Thursday mornings (10a–2p). Free walking tours are offered at noon on weekends if you're interested in the historical details; if, like me, you're only interested in the food, it's much more fun to make your own tasting tour. You'll find something to eat, even if you're not hungry.

Burma Superstar

309 Clement St, San Francisco
415.387.2147
www.burmasuperstar.com
OPEN: *Sun–Thu 11:30a–3:30p, 5–10p; Fri–Sat 11:30a–3:30p, 5–10:30p*

I don't know what secret ingredient goes into this Burmese restaurant's signature Tea Leaf Salad, but I do know that everyone who's ever eaten here, myself included, is absolutely addicted to the thing. The salad's made from soaked tea leaves imported from Burma, which sounds off-putting until you realize that they're combined with crispy fried garlic, peanuts, and lemon and prepared tableside; this is one of those cases where the whole is greater than +the sum of its parts, and the whole is sublime. No less addictive are the veggie samusas, deep-fried and wonton-like, filled with a slurry of vegetables and spices and enhanced by a dunk in the accompanying tangy red sauce. If you've never eaten Burmese food, don't be intimidated. It's sort of a cross between Indian and Thai cuisines, with earthy curries, spicy noodle dishes, and traditional dishes like a chicken casserole with cardamom cinnamon rice. Wash it all down with a pitcher of Burma Coolers—a combo of beer, ginger, and lemonade that will go far to alleviate the burn of the spices.

CALIFORNIA

KNOW: *This place is as legendary for its waiting list as it is for its food. Come early, write your name and cell number on the clipboard outside the door, and head out to browse the foggy Inner Richmond's Asian shops until your phone rings.*

🍴 Blue Bottle Coffee

66 Mint St, San Francisco

MILE/EXIT: 2C (from I-80)

415.495.3394

www.bluebottlecoffee.com

OPEN: *Mon–Fri 7a–7p, Sat 8a–6p, Sun 8a–4p*

The first thing you notice when you walk into this modern downtown coffee shop is the Japanese siphon coffee-making system, a glass apparatus that looks like it would be more suited to a chemistry lab than a coffee shop. But this is a laboratory in its own right, and founder James Freeman is its requisite mad scientist. He opened Blue Bottle in 2002 with the single-minded dream to roast beans and have them in customers' hands within 48 hours, and he still manages to do exactly that despite massive Bay Area and Brooklyn expansions. Freeman takes coffee beans more seriously than just about anyone on earth, experimenting with vintage equipment and new technology to produce the perfect cuppa. The aforementioned Japanese brewing system has the capacity to brew up to three single-origin beans at once; if you're with friends, order a few different varieties and taste the differences that a grower and roaster make. The cafe also offers fresh sandwiches and other baked goods that go well with coffee.

🎂 Tartine Bakery

600 Guerrero St, San Francisco

415.487.2600

www.tartinebakery.com

OPEN: *Mon 8a–7p, Tue–Wed 7:30a–7p, Thu–Fri 7:30a–8p, Sat 8a–8p, Sun 9a–8p*

The morning roll from Tartine is the stuff dreams are made of. It's a ball of sweet croissant dough, baked in muffin tins with a meld of brown and white sugars, butter, and grated orange zest, and emerges from the oven with a caramelized outer shell that simply must be tasted to be believed. It's deceptively simple and thoroughly delicious, especially paired with a European-style latte bowl from the coffee bar. Tartine is rightfully known as one of the best bakeries in the city, nearly always with a line. This gives you plenty of time to scope out your options before you need to order, but it's not uncommon to witness (or experience) paralysis at the counter—the kind of crisis of choice that comes in the face of too much good stuff. Close your eyes and point if you have to—you can't go wrong with the superbly executed pastries, tarts, pressed sandwiches, and luscious-looking slices of quiche, all made from local, organic ingredients, of course. The bakery's cornerside location and European technique could easily outscale the neighborhood, but local art on the walls and a laid-back attitude bring in just the right amount of Mission grit.

KNOW: *Don't come before 5pm if you're looking for a loaf of bread—the bakery's oven is occupied with pastries for most of the day and only starts turning out loaves in the evening.*

 La Taqueria

2889 Mission St, San Francisco
415.285.7117
OPEN: *Mon–Sat 11a–9p, Sun 11a–8p*

You could argue all day about which Mission District taqueria invented the Mission-style burrito—that enormous, foil-wrapped creation that's been popularized by chains like Chipotle. Or you could just head to this no-frills taqueria and eat one. La Taqueria might not be the originator of the outsized burrito, but it still offers one of the best around, as evidenced by the dazzling array of plaques, awards, and framed clippings that cover one wall. These accolades are even more incongruous because of the setting: a simple adobe building, with a casual takeout counter and tables, does not exactly scream fine dining. But the burrito is fantastic— an authentic, giant-sized meal that would take a Herculean effort to finish. Grilled meat is the thing to order, either in a burrito or on the excellent tacos—carne asada and carnitas are strong choices.

KNOW: *The Mission District can get pretty rough around the edges at night— exercise caution after the sun goes down.*

🍴 Wat Mongkolratanaram

1911 Russell St, Berkeley
MILE/EXIT: 10 (from I-80)
510.849.3419
www.watmongkolberkeley.com
OPEN: *Sun 10a–1p*
Cash only

It doesn't get any more "Berkeley" than Sunday brunch at this Thai Buddhist temple, where the people watching is second to none if you're lucky enough to be in town during the Sunday "weekly food offering," aka brunch. Since it's not a working restaurant, visitors—an equal mix of starving students, flower children, and normal middle-class folks—first need to exchange their money for tin tokens to be able to gain access to the steam trays. Food offerings include traditional Thai items like curries over rice, fried chicken, noodle soup, and a mango and sticky rice dessert. Snag one of the picnic tables under a blue-and-white awning or find a grassy knoll nearby, look the other way when the dude next to you accidentally dips his dreadlock in his curry, and then dig in, as pleased by the food as the fact that you're having a quintessential Bay Area experience.

CENTRAL CALIFORNIA

Drive through the agricultural heart of the state to see the garlic, lettuce, apricot, olive, and asparagus capitals of the world—or go wine tasting in Paso Robles and Santa Barbara.

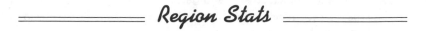 *Region Stats*

LOCAL FLAVOR:

- **Wine:** Santa Barbara and Paso Robles are known for pinot noir, chardonnay, and zinfandel.

- **Produce:** Between the fertile Salinas and Central Valleys, this region is a farming powerhouse.

- **Beef:** From the steaks of Harris Ranch to Santa Maria–style barbecue of the Central Coast, this area is beef-heavy in a way much of California is not.

I was surprised to find Central California deeply working class at its core, despite a veneer of tourism and money. Lifeguards and beach babes aside, this is what most people imagine when they think about California; this is the essence of the state, the land that wars were fought for, the land that has brought it the prosperity it enjoys today. It's also achingly scenic, not with the same takes-your-breath-away gorgeousness of its northern counterpart, but with the tame beauty of a place that has been lived, farmed, and experienced.

California is often considered extremely new, but this is where the new meets the very old. It's where it's possible to have regions like Santa Barbara Wine Country, paradoxically the oldest and newest wine region in the state, because history has played out many times over, even its limited time frame. It's because this is the heart of California; the place where there still truly is the capacity for reinvention.

CALIFORNIA

Trips in Central California

I-5: Sacramento to Los Angeles

There's more to the endless monotony of the Central Valley than meets the eye. (Page 223)

Highway 101: San Francisco to Los Angeles

Explore the microclimates and agricultural diversity of a region with storied, deeply agrarian roots. (Page 239)

Highway 1: Central Coast

Breathtaking scenery, barking sea lions, and top-notch seafood make this a drive to remember. (Page 269)

Santa Barbara Wine Country

Spend an hour or a weekend in one of the state's most exciting and laid-back wine regions. (Page 283)

I-5: Sacramento to Los Angeles

🖊 Trip Stats

START: Sacramento

END: Los Angeles

LENGTH: 384 miles

LOCAL FLAVOR: This is ranch country, and the cuisine is naturally very beef-heavy. Expect to find beef every which way. But there are also apricots and tons of other produce.

BEST TIME: Spring and fall.

WORST TIME: Summer, when the temperatures can be cripplingly hot, and winter, when the temperatures are impossibly cold.

LOCAL FOOD FESTIVALS:

- **Stockton Asparagus Festival:** Stockton (April). Try asparagus deep-fried or in a martini at this festival celebrating the green veggie. (www.asparagusfest.com)

- **Patterson Apricot Fiesta:** Patterson (June). Apricots in ice cream and deep fried are just some of the treats at this annual harvest fair.

WORD OF WARNING: Keep your windows rolled up around Harris Ranch.

MORE INFO: Central Valley Tourism (www.visitcentralvalley.com)

The long rural stretch of freeway through the Central Valley is known to most Californians for two reasons: it's the quickest route between San Francisco and Los Angeles, and there's a spot exactly between the two cities at the 800-acre Harris Ranch feedlot where the stench of cow manure becomes nearly unbearable.

I have driven through the Central Valley many times before, in various moods and various stages of life, but I've always driven it with the singular goal of getting through it as quickly as possible. The valley seems almost lunar in its barrenness. If you drive very fast the monotony only

CALIFORNIA

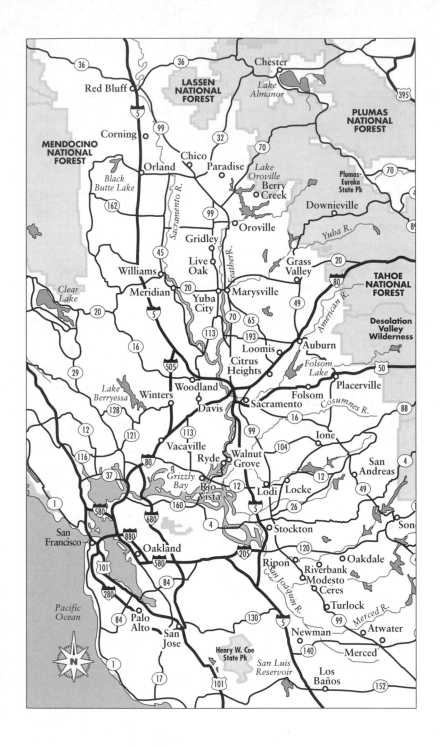

lasts four hours. It is always dusty and always hot. It is the only place I have never felt guilty about stopping at service plaza Taco Bells.

California's Central Valley is one of its most profitable regions, thanks to its Mediterranean climate and rich soil. You pass trucks loaded with tomatoes and watermelons and onions leaving a paper trail of skins in the air like snow. Crops line either side of the freeway: fruit trees, grapevines, low rows of cabbage and strawberries, bales of hay stacked like bricks.

For all its bounty, it is a superficial, mirage abundance. The Central Valley is not an easy place to survive—unless you're one of the crops chosen for mass production. Wild sunflowers struggle for life in cement cracks by the side of the road. Billboards offer inspiration, distraction, salvation. Aqueducts slash the dry earth and tractors kick up tremendous clouds of dust. Signs remind you that water is a political issue in these parts, and whoever controls the rights controls the destiny of the region. This is where Dorothea Lange took her photograph "Migrant Mother." You wonder what made people ever settle here, and what makes them continue the struggle.

I never stuck around long enough to find out, until I started taking the nowhere exits to forgotten towns in search of fabled burgers and hidden taco stands. Driving two-lane highways through orchards to these towns opened up a whole universe beyond the freeway, a complex interplay between water, survival, and struggling farms. As I drove over aqueducts and canals, I saw a glimpse of local society in the family-owned restaurants and farm stands. It gave me a small taste of how the whole place functioned—as a culture, as an economy, as an ecosystem. Getting off the road gives you a whole new appreciation for the struggle.

Eventually the Tehachapi Mountains appear purplish-blue in the distance and you know you've made it through the punishing valley. As you climb through the Grapevine to Tejon Pass, one of the highest points on all of I-5, the sagebrush scrub and baked hills look like they could go up in flames at any second. The first suburbs seem to blend in with the land itself, but then you see the neon fantasy of Magic Mountain and you're suddenly back in civilization. And as you descend into the crowded Los Angeles basin you're glad to be somewhere again, even if part of you suddenly wishes you were back there, out on the open road.

CALIFORNIA

ON THE ROAD

Sacramento Farmers Market

Corner of 8th and W Sts, Sacramento
MILE/EXIT: 519A
916.688.0100
www.california-grown.com
OPEN: *Sun 8a–noon*
Cash only

Sacramento is the distribution and marketing center of the country's most fertile agricultural regions, and this large year-round farmers market is the best place to experience the bounty. Fruit, vegetables, wine, cheese, honey, nuts, olive oil—it's all available, along with the opportunity to talk to the farmers and artisans who produced it. The market is part of the California Grown Certified Farmers Market collective, whose mission is to support family farms, cut out middleman costs, and rigorously inspect all producers before letting them sell their goods. The freeway underpass location might seem strange at first, but the concrete provides shade that's priceless on a hot afternoon. Take your produce and head to Southside Community Park across the street—it's got a lake, shady trees, and makes a very good place for a picnic.

KNOW: *Avoid the parking lot, which can be gridlock. Park on W Street instead.*

Blue Diamond Nut & Gift Shop

1701 C St, Sacramento
MILE/EXIT: 519B
916.446.8438
www.bluediamond.com
OPEN: *Mon–Fri 9:30a–5p, Sat 9:30a–4p*

Don't be deterred by the industrial setting, which looks more like a detainment camp than a friendly nut-processing facility. This almond processing and marketing cooperative has been making things easier for local growers since 1910, and now serves more than 3,000 growers from its headquarters in downtown Sacramento. In the gift shop, sample your way through flavors like wasabi, soy, habenero, barbecue, lime and chili, and more along one wall (including flavors that you can't buy in the supermarket), and marvel at all the different uses that people have found for almonds over the years. If you want to learn more about the ins and outs of production, check out the short video and interpretive exhibits about the process.

How to Soothe a Tired Tummy

Research trips always took a certain toll on me, gastronomically speaking, but never so much as the weekend I spent in the Central Valley. A day on a nearly all-beef diet left me with a bad case of the meat sweats and a bottle of Pepto-Bismol in the cup holder from Los Gatos to Sacramento. Here are my personal remedies when eating on the road gets the better of me.

Fizzy water: The easiest and least intrusive defense. Pick up a bottle of seltzer or sparkling water at a gas station or supermarket and let the bubbles work their magic.

Alka-Seltzer and Brioschi: Mild antacids that neutralize excessive acid in your stomach that causes heartburn, upset stomach, and indigestion. Unlike calcium-based tablets like Tums, these "effervescent antacids" activate when dissolved in water and work instantly. Alka-Seltzer contains aspirin to ease pain; Brioschi is all-natural and my personal favorite (I never travel without it).

Pepto-Bismol: Also an antacid, but a harder-core version—the pale pink liquid provides relief from nausea, heartburn, indigestion, upset stomach, and diarrhea.

Body cleanse: Multiple days of unfettered eating just compounds the problem. Give your body a break with steamed or sautéed veggies, brown rice, vitamin-packed smoothies like Odwalla SuperFood and Bolthouse Green Goodness, green tea, kombucha, and lots and lots of water.

CALIFORNIA

Jim-Denny's Hamburgers

816 12th St, Sacramento
MILE/EXIT: 519B
916.443.9655
www.jim-dennys.com
OPEN: *Tue–Sat 7a–3p*

Locals have been hitting this downtown burger joint since 1934, equally for its nostalgic ambiance as for the incredible burgers, made from a custom ground beef mix by the Del Monte meat company. Sit at one of the 10 stools at the scuffed lunch counter, if you can grab one, and order one of the menu's eight specialty burgers. The one-pound Megaburger ($9) will challenge even the heartiest appetites, and the "5-cent burger," now $5.50, is still a bargain. Hot dogs, sandwiches, and old-fashioned milk shakes and malts are also available. The burger joint's retro architecture is a welcome anomaly in Sacramento's corporate downtown, and the Depression-era interior is enhanced with framed and faded newspaper articles, photos, and menus on the walls. All remind you that there was once a time when burgers cost 20 cents, men wore three-piece suits and hats, the nation was united around radio broadcasts . . . and if life wasn't simpler in practice back then, it's at least nice to imagine it was.

KNOW: *Jim-Denny's isn't just a lunch spot. Many come for the comprehensive breakfast menu—especially the massive pancakes, which, as the menu boasts, are truly "bigger than your head." (Breakfast is served Mon–Fri 7–10:30a, Sat 7a–noon.)*

 # Rubicon Brewing Co.

2004 Capitol Ave, Sacramento
MILE/EXIT: 519B
916.448.7032
www.rubiconbrewing.com
OPEN: *Mon–Thu 11a–11p, Fri–Sat 11a–12:30a*

You have to respect a brewery that offers a beer called Monkey Knife Fight. This pale ale with a serious bite is just one of the beers in the hard-hitting lineup at this lively downtown brewpub, which is as well known for its hoppy IPA as for its addictive chicken wings. These are hot wings good enough to satisfy even the most die-hard enthusiast, deep-fried and covered in a tangy, slow-burning red sauce made from a secret recipe. Rubicon's interior is the standard-issue brick-and-corrugated-metal decor that's favored in brewpubs up and down the West Coast. For something new, snag a seat on the sidewalk patio and watch the life of Sacramento saunter by.

Squeeze Inn

5301 Power Inn Rd, Sacramento
MILE/EXIT: 518
DISTANCE FROM HWY: 7.4 miles
916.386.8599
www.thesqueezeinn.com
OPEN: *Mon–Fri 10a–7p, Sat 10a–6p*

The Squeeze with Cheese is a local legend, an experience more than a burger, a heart attack on a plate. Here's how it's done: Take a third-pound beef patty, cook it on a flattop grill, cover it with a third-pound of shredded cheese, and cap the gooey mess with the top of a hamburger bun. Then the culinary magic happens. Add ice chips to the hot grill, cover with a hood, and cook until the alchemy of the ice-turned-to-steam has melted the cheese into a glorious "cheese skirt," something akin to a Parmesan wafer. Serve to the table in a cardboard box, and watch customers try to attack it. Some eat the skirt separately, some fold it into the burger, and all have trouble putting it into their mouth in one bite. The novelty would attract crowds in itself, but the burger's also so addictively delicious that the masses flock to this place. (A shout-out on *Diners, Drive-ins, and Dives* certainly didn't hurt.) On Saturday afternoons, the wait can be up to an hour. Trust me: it's worth it.

KNOW: *Ask for a free bumper sticker and proudly display your love for the Squeeze with Cheese everywhere you go.*

Al's Place

13936 Main St, Locke
MILE/EXIT: 498
DISTANCE FROM HWY: 5.6 miles
916.776.1800
OPEN: *Hours vary; call for details*
Cash only

Formerly called "Al the Wop's," this cafe clearly dates back to a less-than-politically-correct time. Locke is the only rural community in America built and settled by the Chinese, and this simple wood frontier structure was built in 1915 as a Chinese restaurant before colorful local character Al Adami took it over and turned it into an institution. He had no menu, he just asked how you liked your steak and went from there. Steak's still the thing to get all these years later, which is massive and comes with Texas toast, supplemented by the marmalade and peanut butter on the tables. Sit at rugged benches surrounded by taxedermied heads and various knickknacks. Ask about the dollar bills stuck to the ceiling—I know what the story is, but I wouldn't want to ruin the surprise.

KNOW: *If you want to learn more about the region's Chinese-American past, check out the Dai Loy Museum down the street.*

Lodi Wine & Visitor Center

2545 W Turner Rd, Lodi
MILE/EXIT: 487
DISTANCE FROM HWY: 5 miles
209.365.0621
www.lodiwine.com
OPEN: *Daily 10a–5p*

Get the scoop on this up-and-coming California wine region, known for its zinfandels, at this tasting room and interpretive center run by the Lodi Winegrape Commission. The tasting bar offers nine wines at a time on a weekly rotation, usually grouped by a common theme like varietal. After tasting your way through the counter's wines, check out the interactive exhibits on grape-growing and wine-making, including a flyover map of the region. If you like what you taste, there are more than 200 wines to buy.

Manny's California Fresh Cafe

1612 Pacific Ave, Stockton
MILE/EXIT: 473
209.463.6415
OPEN: *Daily 9a–9:45p*

Most road food is hearty and cholesterol-laden by nature; Manny's is the rare exception where you can get a healthy and satisfying meal on the road. The ambiance is exactly right for a casual cafe: big wood booths, Spanish tiles, wood ceilings, and an old-school feel, with jumpy jazz playing in the background. Grab a table and mingle with the locals, or order to go and wait on a wooden bench for your number to be called. Manny's offers a shaved turkey sandwich that rivals day-after-Thanksgiving leftovers—all moist and fresh from the free-range bird they use, piled on a thick and chewy French bun with an unhealthy amount of mayo. The iceberg lettuce is there for textural contrast more than any nutritional value, but you appreciate the thought. The quarter-pound burger's two patties are cooked well-done, then glued together with cheese, slathered in secret sauce, and set on a toasted bun. You'll decimate a small forest's worth of napkins as you eat it, but it's worth it.

🏪 Ghirardelli Factory Outlet

11980 S Harlan Rd, Lathrop
MILE/EXIT: 465
209.982.9304
www.ghirardelli.com
OPEN: *Mon–Thu 8a–8p, Fri–Sun 8a–9p*

A half century before Milton Hershey became America's favorite chocolatier, Domingo Ghirardelli set up his now-famous chocolate shop on a San Francisco street corner in 1852. In his native Italy, Ghirardelli had been apprentice to a local confectioner, and when he turned 20 he sailed to Uruguay to learn about the South American chocolate trade. Lured to California by the gold rush, he struck out as a prospector and turned to what he knew instead. Today, Ghirardelli Chocolate is the country's longest continuously running chocolate manufacturer, and the only one that controls the entire manufacturing process, from selecting the beans to refining the bars. You can't miss this roadside outlet—a huge sign in front that spells out the Ghirardelli name in lights. Outside, the air smells like cattle and chocolate; inside, it's pure cocoa. Seemingly every product Ghirardelli has ever made is here, at prices 10 to 20 percent off retail. There's also an ice cream counter with the shop's "world-famous" hot fudge sundaes. The key to a good hot fudge sundae is the quality of the chocolate. This sauce uses 60 percent cacao bittersweet chocolate, so it's not too sweet, but has an intensely chocolate flavor. Unsurprisingly, the place is filled with children, but for those who want to escape the little ones, there are tables outside and good coffee to take for the road.

KNOW: *Stop stumbling over the pronunciation forever. It's "Gear-ar-delly."*

🍶 Stewart & Jasper Orchards Company Store

2985 Renzo Ln, Suite D, Patterson

MILE/EXIT: 434

209.895.9463

www.stewartandjasper.com

OPEN: *Daily noon–7p*

California produces 95 percent of the country's apricot crop, and most of it comes from the Stanislaus County fields around Patterson—where Stewart & Jasper Orchards has been in business since 1948. The third-generation family farm's dedication to history and community is reflected in its logo, an old-school fruit truck. Head back to the wine bar and try the apricot wine, worth the stop alone. It's sweet without being syrupy or saccharine, and served cold enough to quench the thirst as it tickles the taste buds. The wine bar also offers a number of area wines and a knowledgeable staff; it's usually not crowded, so you can get an intimate experience with plenty of personal attention. Browse in the store after wine tasting for better-than-average snacks, including chocolate-covered apricot chunks and almonds dusted with cocoa and spices reminiscent of Mexican hot chocolate.

KNOW: *If you're traveling to visit friends or family, a fully loaded Stewart & Jasper gift pack would make an excellent hostess gift.*

🍴 Wolfsen's Meat & Sausage

358 S Ave, Gustine

MILE/EXIT: 418

DISTANCE FROM HWY: 5.8 miles

209.854.6456

www.wolfsensausage.com

OPEN: *Mon–Fri 8a–6p, Sat 8a–5p, Sun 8a–3p*

Wolfsen's is a really excellent meat market hidden away in a farming community. When you walk in, you're greeted by more than 60 types of sausage in a refrigerated case, along with baskets of pepperoni sticks, beef jerky, and other unperishable edibles. Buy some for later, but for now, indulge in Wolfsen's incomparable hot sausage sandwiches. The small-but-mighty menu offers the usual favorites like hot Italian and bratwurst, but those in the know order the linguica, a garlicky Portuguese sausage that's kind of smoky and not too spicy. For all sandwiches, sausages are sliced down the center, piled with peppers and onions, slathered with mustard, on a very pillowy sweet bun that holds it all together nicely. It's a pretty messy endeavor, but that's why napkins were invented.

KNOW: *There's no inside seating, but you can eat at tables in the tented area next to the store, which manages to remain cool even when outside temperatures are 85 degrees.*

Wool Growers Restaurant

609 H St, Los Banos

MILE/EXIT: 403A

DISTANCE FROM HWY: 6.8 miles

209.826.4593

OPEN: *Tue–Sat 11:30a–2p and 4:30–9p; Sun 11:30a–8p*

Bring a healthy appetite to this French Basque institution, where all the food is served family-style at communal tables, and one serving is enough to feed a family of four. The welcoming spirit of the dining room is reflected in its history—it's on the ground floor of an 1890s hotel that once provided a safe haven for Basques emigrating to the Central Valley. You'll only hover awkwardly at the entrance for a moment, as I did, before a waitress in traditional Basque garb gestures to an empty chair and offers you a choice of tri-tip, roast lamb, pork chop, chicken, steak, roast lamb, or prime rib before you even have a chance to get settled. Each would be big enough to be dinner in itself, but you've no sooner ordered than the sides start coming, which include lamb stew, vegetable soup, salad, French fries, bread, potato salad, and a big bowl of baked beans, all plopped on the table with little to no ceremony. It's a bewildering amount of food—especially for $18—but just roll up your sleeves, give in to the gluttony, and get friendly with your neighbors. (Wine from the communal jugs on the table helps.) The night I visited, my immediate company included a local couple celebrating a birthday and a ranching family indulging in a night out. Across the room, a tough-looking man in a cowboy hat played with a baby. I don't know if it was the food, the wine, or the feel-good community vibes, but I left feeling sated, happy, and surprisingly rejuvenated.

KNOW: *You'll want to pace yourself, but be prepared to cry "uncle" before your plate is clean and risk disapproving clucks from the waitresses. Plastic baggies are provided for takeout.*

(🏠) Apricot Tree

46271 W Panoche Rd, Firebaugh

MILE/EXIT: 368

559.659.2028

OPEN: *Daily 7a–9p*

The apricot shake at this roadside diner is nothing special, but it's as good an excuse as any to stop and stretch your legs. A fresh fruit shake should taste like the ripeness of summer; this one tastes like sugary ice cream with occasional bursts of apricot, but it's really all you need after miles of interstate driving. The rest of the menu offers thoroughly mediocre American standards, divided into cutesy sections like "Everything Between the Slices." An on-site gift shop sells apricot fudge, dusty bottles of California wine, and knickknacks like Daniel Boone hats and Native American dream catchers. The coolest thing about the place is the decor—a surprisingly comprehensive collection of vintage metal lunch boxes and thermoses, representing pop culture from Howdy Doody to Evel Knievel.

KNOW: *Stop for dried local fruit, nuts, and snack mixes at The Palms market, located in the same complex.*

(🍴) Harris Ranch

24505 W Dorris Ave, Coalinga

MILE/EXIT: 334

800.942.2333

www.harrisranch.com

OPEN: *Daily 6a–10p*

You smell Harris Ranch before you see it. The notorious 100,000-cow feedlot—located exactly halfway between San Francisco and Los Angeles—has gained the nickname "Cowschwitz" for its size and stench, but don't let the tangy odor of cow manure stand between you and one of the best steaks of your life. You won't get in and out of Harris Ranch in less than an hour, but it's worth the time investment, both for the food and the old-fashioned California ranch interior. There's an extensive menu, but not ordering beef is like not getting a hot dog at a baseball game. Try the baseball-cut top sirloin and eggs, the third-pound Black Angus beef burger, or the "restaurant reserve" 14-ounce New

York striploin. The beef speaks for itself, but like an upscale Cheesecake Factory, the bound, booklike menu actually does offer something for everyone, and most of the produce comes from the Harris family's 230-acre "backyard garden." Though more food is the last thing on your mind after you polish off a pound of beef, stop in the old-fashioned country store and bakery on your way out for apricot squares, cookies, and beef jerky. You'll thank yourself in 100 miles. (The store is open Sun–Thu 8a–8p, Fri–Sat 8a–9p.)

KNOW: *Harris Ranch can be crowded at peak mealtimes, but the restaurant has the system down to a science. Wander the grounds or sit on a bristly cowhide couch while you wait for your electronic thingy to buzz.*

Chris Meat Market

36539 S Lassen St, Huron

MILE/EXIT: 334

DISTANCE FROM HWY: 9 miles

559.945.2902

OPEN: *24/7*

Sausages hang from the ceiling at this Mexican meat market in a way that seems like it can't be sanitary, but you need to check any squeamishness at the door in order to enjoy some of the best tacos in the Central Valley. Pick your poison, meat-wise, from the short menu of Mexican standards—carne asada, *al pastor*, carnitas, *lengua*—and watch the counter staff warm your tortillas and assemble your tacos on the spot. Word to the wise: when they warn you the salsa is spicy, they aren't messing around. It's the kind of slow burn that tingles on the lips long after the taco is gone. Pick up a coconut popsicle in the freezer case next to the cash register for relief. If you're not a taco fan, the simple menu also includes *tortas*—grilled sandwiches popular in Mexico City.

KNOW: *The drive from I-5 is a very scenic 10-minute jaunt along a small highway lined with orchards, fields, and farm stands. Despite the short distance, you feel amazingly removed from the culture of the interstate and more connected to day-to-day life in the Central Valley.*

CALIFORNIA

 **Debbie's Place**

429 Skyline Blvd, Avenal

MILE/EXIT: 319

DISTANCE FROM HWY: 5.6 miles

559.386.0477

OPEN: *Mon–Fri 11a–8p, Sat 11a–7p*

Cash only

You first glimpse the town of Avenal from above, as you crest the Kettleman Hills on Highway 269 and see it spread out in the narrow valley below. The highway is a graveyard of rusted oil derricks, frozen since the day someone decided that there was no more value in these hills, and Avenal's wide, empty main drag has a similar forlornness. You get the sense that this is kind of a desolate, left-behind corner of the world . . . until you see the crowd around Debbie's Place. The locals are at this unassuming roadside dive for the same reason you are: the hamburger, which is messy and sublime. Imagine a fist-sized quarter-pound patty of high-quality beef cooked to medium-rare perfection, with cheese melting into the chilled red onion, lettuce, and tomato. It's a perfect study in contrasts—the yielding warmth of the burger and cheese meets the crisp, cool veggies for a bite that you won't soon forget. My ketchup-smeared research notes say, in letters that take up at least four lines, "OH MY GOD." Eat in the no-frills dining room, which has, somewhat inexplicably, a racing car theme—the bathroom is called a "pit stop," and decor consists of black-and-white checkered curtains, a matchbox-car mobile, and framed drawings of legendary racecars, including a Hummer called the Humbler. Or order at the outside takeout window and join local teenagers sitting on the curb.

KNOW: *If you need cash, there's an ATM at the Circle K across the street.*

 **Tita's Papuseria**

20643 Tracy Ave, Buttonwillow

MILE/EXIT: 257

661.764.5111

OPEN: *Daily 6a–11p*

This permanently parked taco truck provides a welcome respite from the usual fast-food dining establishments that dominate the I-5 food

---
Stellar Sandwiches

Porchetta: Salumi, WA

Dungeness Crab Melt: Ecola Seafoods, Cannon Beach, OR

Muffaletta: Olive Pit, Corning, CA

Tri-tip: Los Olivos Market, Los Olivos, CA

The Godmother: Bay Cities Italian Deli, Santa Monica, CA

---

scene. Papusas are the tacos of El Salvador—thick tortillas filled with meat, beans, and cheese, covered with vinegary cabbage slaw and red salsa. Tita's papusas are the real deal—the filling is warm and pliable underneath a pile of tangy slaw, with a hint of heat from the salsa roja. Choose from traditional fillings like *loroqo* (an edible Central American flower), squash, and beans and cheese, along with the usual meat offerings. One papusa is usually enough for me unless I'm ravenous (like pancakes, they expand in your stomach), but at $3 a pop, you can afford to be extravagant. Top the meal off with a refreshing *agua frescas* in flavors like watermelon and pineapple, or a Mexican Coke. A complete menu of tacos, burritos, and other Latin American standards is also available.

KNOW: *Tita's has two locations in Buttonwillow—the other is a kind of grimy sit-down restaurant. For speed and a bit of fresh air, I've always preferred to order at the truck and dine freewayside at the covered picnic tables.*

ⓧ Murray Family Farms

9557 Copus Rd, Bakersfield
MILE/EXIT: 228
661.858.1100
www.murrayfamilyfarms.com
OPEN: *Daily 9a–5p*

If the monotony of the road starts getting to you, this nice mom-and-pop farm stand at the southern end of the Central Valley makes a nice diversion. The Murray family produces more than a million pounds of fruits and vegetables a year on their 360-acre Kern County farm, and

CALIFORNIA

you can sample the fruits of their labor at this freeway-side farm stand. Perfectly in-season produce like this hardly needs a sales pitch, but the Murrays always put out free samples of their goods, which might include several varieties of cherries (the farm grows eighteen), stone fruits like peaches and apricots, every berry under the sun, and veggies and fruits like asparagus, artichokes, and tomatoes. Bags of nuts and dried fruit, jars of homemade jam, baked goods, fudge, and convenience store favorites round out the offerings. It's all housed in a friendly room with country trim wallpaper. The farm stand also offers U-pick berries and fruit (May–July, Fri–Sun 8:30a–5p), but if it's a million degrees outside you're better off going prepicked.

KNOW: *This is just a satellite location—the Murray's much bigger "Big Red Barn" Farm is 40 miles east, and also offers a petting zoo, weekend hay rides, and a play area for children. (6700 General Beale Rd, Bakersfield; 661.330.0100)*

Highway 101: San Francisco to Los Angeles

Trip Stats

START: San Francisco

END: Los Angeles

LENGTH: 430 miles

LOCAL FLAVOR: Wine, produce, olive oil.

BEST TIME: Spring and summer, for the full effect of all the produce.

WORST TIME: Winter, when the fields are bare and there's nothing much going on in Wine Country.

LOCAL FOOD FESTIVALS:

- **California Strawberry Festival:** Oxnard (May). Kick off summer at this sweet festival that offers everything from strawberry pizza to beer.

- **Paso Robles Wine Festival:** Paso Robles (May). The region's biggest celebration puts all its wineries and more in one place.

- **Gilroy Garlic Festival:** Gilroy (July). What does garlic ice cream taste like? Who will be crowned Miss Gilroy Garlic? Attend the festival in the "Garlic Capital of the World" to find out.

WORD OF WARNING: Watch for traffic pileups around San Jose through Silicon Valley, and Santa Barbara to Los Angeles.

B efore I-5 was built in the 1960s, Highway 101 was the main artery between Los Angeles and San Francisco. The highway, one of the nation's oldest, was built in the 1920s and followed the trail of the old California missions. This was the golden age of the automobile, and a motorist tourism trade quickly sprung up along the highway. Highway 101 is the site of the world's first motel, and the fantastic spectacles of the Madonna Inn and the Dutch windmills of Buellton and nearby Solvang.

The road's fantastic elements are in some ways completely at odds with its agrarian past. This is farming territory—and always has been—and

CALIFORNIA

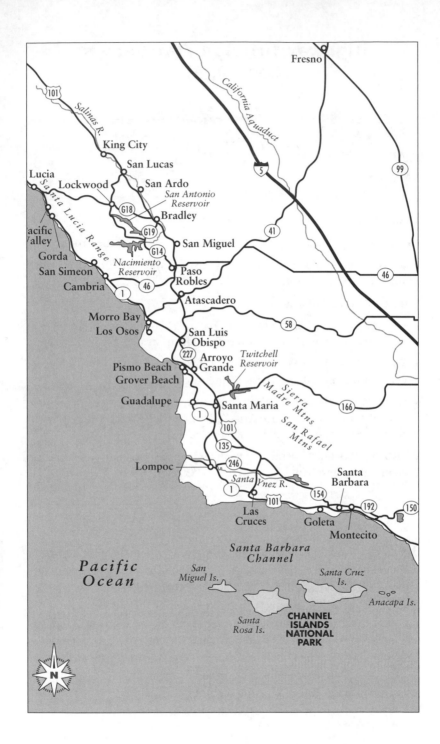

has a diversity uncommon to its relative size. The difference is in geology: this isn't one long sedimentary valley like its partner to the east, but a series of ups and downs, a landscape scarred by collision of faults and trenches. Every hill and valley is different, and each has its own microclimate and soil composition, which provide an unrivaled agricultural and viticultural range.

Highway 101 takes you past the cypress trees of Hitchcock's *Vertigo*, through the Salinas Valley ("The Salad Bowl of the World"), through a landscape of tawny hills marked with dark green California oaks, picture-perfect small Colonial towns built around missions. The highway hits the ocean north of Santa Barbara, and you're treated to a pastoral tableau so beautiful it seems staged: a herd of cows grazing in a golden pasture, framed by the ocean and silhouetted in the late afternoon sun. It's the beauty of potential.

To understand the area's character, visit the town of Gilroy—"The Garlic Capital of the World"—located 80 miles south of San Francisco. A faint, pungent whiff of garlic hits you as you drive through, if your car windows are down and the breeze is just right. Gilroy is fittingly known for its annual Garlic Festival, which includes such delicacies as garlic ice cream.

It also houses Gilroy Gardens, the country's only agriculture-themed amusement park. The park has food-themed rides modeled after childhood favorites and is the perfect synthesis of the quiet earthiness of Northern California and the playful whimsy of Southern California. It's kitschy and ridiculous, in a small-time way, the kind of place where if you think you'll have fun, you probably will—and it's also a fitting stop along the road that connects the two very different halves of the state.

CALIFORNIA

Gilroy Gardens

3050 Hwy 152, Gilroy
MILE/EXIT: 360
DISTANCE FROM HWY: 5.7 miles
408.840.7100
www.gilroygardens.org
OPEN: *Hours vary by season; call ahead for details*

If Walt Disney had been a foodie, he might have designed a theme park like this. The 40-plus rides include the usual amusement park suspects, but are themed so charmingly—the Artichoke Dip swaps in artichokes for Disney's teacups, the Banana Split is a sweet variation on the popular pirate ship attraction—that the old standards seem new again. Take a breather from the rides with a stroll through the park's well-tended display gardens, or take a spin in an antique car through the two-acre "South County Backwoods Garden" that shows the land as it looked in the early half of the twentieth century. The park is also educational: Learn about farming techniques in models of old-fashioned apple packing sheds and watch honeybees at work in the Honey Bee Hut. If all the food imagery has gotten you hungry, there are plenty of local specialties on hand, including fried artichoke hearts, Gilroy garlic fries, tri-tip, Mexican food, and funnel cakes, along with the usual slew of burgers, corn dogs, personal pizzas, and ice cream.

KNOW: *Kids will enjoy the "Tree Top Sprayground" waterpark in an 18-foot replicated citrus tree.*

 La Casa Rosa

107 3rd St, San Juan Bautista
MILE/EXIT: 345
831.623.4563
www.lacasarosarestaurant.com
OPEN: *Wed–Mon 11:30a–3p*

A decade before Alice Waters was even a twinkle in her mother's eye, Bertha Campbell Cole opened this pink-hued restaurant serving original "California Cuisine"—a humble collision of Mexican and Midwestern cooking made with fresh, local ingredients. Cole's claim to fame was the California Casserole, a tasty mess of corn, sharp cheddar, and red meat sauce, made from a recipe given to her family by the daughter of General Vallejo. Though the restaurant has changed hands a few times over the past 50 years, Cole's casserole is still the star of the four-item menu, rechristened as the Old California Casserole to differentiate it from the New California Casserole—a modern update made with Monterey Jack cheese and mild Ortega green chiles. Light soufflés are the only other lunch option; all come with a salad and are a steal at around $12. La Casa Rosa's historic pedigree, proximity to moneyed Carmel, and pretty, vine-covered 1858 building have brought the restaurant its fair share of celebrities and luminaries over the years, including Alfred Hitchcock and Kim Novak, who frequented the cafe often while filming scenes from *Vertigo* at the nearby Mission San Juan Bautista.

Gutierrez and Rico Drive-In

61 Sherwood Dr, Salinas
MILE/EXIT: 329
831.424.8383
OPEN: *Mon–Fri 9a–9p, Sat 8:30a–9p, Sun 8:30a–9p*

The sign outside claims *"especialidad en carnitas y mariscos."* Trust it. Locals have headed to this no-frills taco stand for more than 20 years for some of the best Mexican food in the region (and there's no shortage of competition, thanks to the valley's migrant worker population). If you order one thing, order carnitas—doesn't matter if it's in a taco, burrito, or even just piled on a plate, it's some of the best carnitas I've ever had: super tender and juicy, not overly greasy, just an explosion of pure pork flavor. Adventurous types can take it one step further by ordering *chincharrones*, fried pork skins, also done very well. But don't overlook the *mariscos*, or the seafood platters—Salinas is just over the mountains from the ocean, and the seafood here, cooked Mexican-style, is eminently satisfying. I'm a fan of the sharable *pulpo* platter—octopus cooked tender with sautéed chiles and other spices, served with a generous portion of fresh tortillas. Wash it down with a Mexican beer and make sure to visit the salsa bar.

ⓘ Steinbeck House

132 Central Ave, Salinas
MILE/EXIT: 329
831.424.2735
www.steinbeckhouse.com
OPEN: *Tue–Sat 11:30a–2:30p*

John Steinbeck covered a lot of ground in his 27 published literary works, but one subject he kept coming back to was the relationship between farmers, migrant workers, and the land they tended in his native Salinas Valley. Gain more context for the author's life at his birthplace and childhood home, a Queen Anne–style house in Salinas that has been lovingly restored to its former glory and and opened to the public as a non-profit restaurant. Servers in period costume give you the day's menu, which highlights produce from the valley—dishes might include cream of lettuce soup, vegetable frittata, crepes stuffed with local veggies, and desserts like peach pie. Head to the basement Best Cellar Gift Shop for new and vintage Steinbeck books, the *Steinbeck House Cookbook*, and a collection of memorabilia that includes the headboard from the bed in which the writer was born.

KNOW: *Learn more about Steinbeck at the National Steinbeck Center in Salinas, which has a collection of the author's artifacts, photographs, and letters, as well as a permanent exhibition on the history of agriculture in the Salinas Valley (1 Main St; 831.775.4721; www.steinbeck.org. Open daily 10a–5p)*

TOURS: *Volunteers take visitors through the Steinbeck House on Saturday afternoons (Memorial Day through Labor Day; 1–3p; $5 adults, $3 students and seniors).*

ⓘ The Farm

7 Foster Road, Salinas
MILE/EXIT: 329
831.455.2575
www.thefarm-salinasvalley.com
OPEN: *Mar–Dec; hours vary by season—call for details.*

This farm stand tells the story of contemporary farming in the fertile Salinas Valley through its fresh produce stand, demonstration farm, and an agricultural tour that lets you get down and dirty with the crops.

California's Missions

The year was 1776. America's founding fathers were gathered in Philadelphia signing the Declaration of Independence. And Father Junipero Serra and his crew of Spanish missionaries were trekking across Central California, setting up the first nine missions of a system that would grow to 21 missions and shape much of modern California society.

The mission's role in California culinary history cannot be overemphasized. Missionaries brought the first grapevines and olive trees to the region, and grew the roots of the agrarian culture that still flourishes today. They introduced European fruits, vegetables, horses, cattle, and livestock to the region. The Spanish and then the Mexican government also set up a system of land grants given to cattle ranchers for raising livestock and cultivated the soil. These land grants have not only shaped the culture of the region (giving birth to traditions like Santa Maria BBQ, page 257), but also its physicality. Many of today's boundaries and streets are based on the original land grants.

It was all because of the land, of course, a land so lush and valuable that blood was shed in its honor. American interest took hold in the mid-1800s and we fought a war with Mexico for ownership of Texas and California. Many of the battles for California were fought on and for these hills and waters, in places of strategic importance: Monterey, San Francisco, Santa Barbara, Los Angeles.

America officially gained control of Alta California in 1848 at the Treaty of Guadalupe Hidalgo. The U.S. government promised to honor the Mexican land grants, and put the remaining land up for grabs for anyone who wanted to develop it. That same year, gold was discovered in Sutter's Mill near Sacramento, and California changed overnight. Over the next two years, more than 90,000 people came to the state seeking instant fame and fortune. Homesteading was a good alternative if getting rich turned out to take longer than they'd expected.

Central California contains nine out of ten of the state's most prolific agricultural counties, and is the nation's sole provider of artichokes, almonds, raisins, and walnuts. It's a working-class culture at heart—step off the tourist track and take a look around.

CALIFORNIA

It's worth a stop just for the produce, much of which is grown on the premises and organically certified. While you're there, you might as well check out the five-acre demonstration farm's dazzling array of lettuce, broccoli, celery, artichokes, beets, and herbs, and visit with the farm animals, which vary by season but usually represent a token array of goats, chickens, rabbits, etc. Flowers are also grown on the premises and sold in reasonably priced bouquets. The best feature of the farm, however, is the hands-on tour—a 60-minute foray into the fields where you'll learn agricultural techniques and then harvest and sample the produce yourself. Gardeners might learn a few new tricks.

TOURS: *Available Tue and Thurs, 1p (45 min to 1 hour, $8 for adults 16+, $6 for kids 2–15).*

 La Plaza Bakery

945 Front St, Soledad
MILE/EXIT: 302
831.678.1452
www.laplazabakery.com
OPEN: *Daily 5a–8:30p*

Guanajuato Jesus immigrated to Soledad in 1969 with his wife and 10 children, worked long hours in the fields, and longed for the tradition of Sunday morning bread and chocolate in his hometown of San Jeronimo. In 1982, he brought his dream to the Salinas Valley when he opened this no-frills *panaderia* on Soledad's main drag. Try traditional Mexican pastries like *pan dulce* (sweet breads with a crust of sugar on top), cakes, and flan—I've found the best ordering strategy is just to point at what looks good, and it's always worked out. Savory lunch items like tortas, burritos, tacos, and enchiladas are available at the deli counter.

VARIOUS LOCATIONS *in Salinas, Gonzales, and Greenfield*

 Hahn Estates

37700 Foothill Rd, Soledad
MILE/EXIT: 301
831.678.4555
www.hahnestates.com
OPEN: *Daily 11a–4p*

Set on a hillside overlooking the Salinas Valley and its surrounding mountains, this winery is an excellent escape for an hour, or for the afternoon. The land was once divided into neighboring horse and cattle ranches, but the owners joined forces and turned to vineyards when they realized that Monterey County had the soil and climate for growing top-notch wines. (Like other wine-growing regions in Central California, Monterey County has the warm days and foggy nights necessary to produce cool-weather grapes like chardonnay and pinot noir.) All Hahn wines are made from grapes grown on 1,200 acres of estate vineyards, which range geographically from the Santa Lucia Highlands to Paso Robles. In addition to the wines, the tasting room also offers house-made jams, mustards, sauces, and dips, including a heavenly chocolate wine sauce.

Monterey County Agriculture & Rural Life Museum

1160 Broadway, King City
MILE/EXIT: 282B
831.385.8020
www.mcarlm.org
OPEN: *Thu–Fri 10a–4p (Main Exhibit barn; outbuildings open Fri noon–4p, Sat–Sun 11a–4p)*

Nerd out on old farm equipment and learn about the development of agriculture in the valley. There are six buildings on the property: Start at the exhibit barn, which traces agricultural and rural life from the late nineteenth century through WWII. Then head to the Olson Blacksmith Shop, a real-deal blacksmith workshop moved from its original location, to learn about the importance of blacksmiths to successful farmers (who else would sharpen their plows, repair farm machinery, and make hinges and other useful implements?). Don't leave without stopping at the Sprekels House, once owned by the Sprekels Sugar Company (as marked by the wooden sugar beet on Building 91). It depicts a typical Salinas Valley farmhouse and shows what life was like for an employed farmer at the time. Also on the premises is a schoolhouse and a Southern Pacific Railroad train depot. Super-nerds can call ahead to view the newest addition, the History of Irrigation Museum, which features a topographic map of the drainage of the region.

CALIFORNIA

KNOW: *Admission is free, but there's a fee to enter San Lorezno Park where it's housed (Mon–Fri $5 per car, Sat–Sun $6 per car, walk-ins free).*

 Eberle Winery

3810 Hwy 46 E, Paso Robles
MILE/EXIT: 231B
805.238.9607
www.eberlewinery.com
OPEN: *Apr–Sept daily 10a–6p, Oct–Mar daily 10a–5p*

Founder Gary Eberle brought syrah to the people of California, though it came about as a matter of chance. While pursuing his doctorate of enology at UC Davis, Eberle met winemaker Brian Crozer, who introduced him to the syrah grape—widely popular in Crozer's native Australia and virtually unknown in California. Eberle procured a vine from UC Davis's extensive collection, and became the first winemaker in the United States to produce a 100 percent syrah wine in 1978, which became the winery's flagship. Eberle's syrah is indeed a beauty—lush, fruity, and well structured—but all the wines are excellent: a row of ribbons above the tasting counter is a testament to their quality and reputation. Though the initial tasting is free, it's worth buying a glass of your favorite and heading out to take in the vineyard views from the tasting room's sunny deck, or make an afternoon of it and play a game of bocce ball on the court near the front entrance. Keep a lookout for Gary's two poodles, Cabernet and Roussanne (look to the right of the front door for his memorials to former winery pups).

KNOW: *Gary Eberle grills outside on summer Saturdays, and it's worth stopping by for his duck sausage and other meats. Otherwise, if you're looking for food you can order a gourmet picnic lunch 48 hours in advance.*

TOURS: *Unless you're claustrophobic, do take the free, every-half-hour tour of the winery's 16,000-square-foot underground storage catacombs, lined with oak barrels as far as the eye can see.*

Panolivo Family Bistro

1344 Park St, Paso Robles
MILE/EXIT: 231A
805.239.3366
www.panolivo.com
OPEN: *Daily 7:30a–8:30p*

Set on a corner in downtown Paso Robles, this upscale casual bistro serves breakfast, lunch, and dinner to locals and wine tourists. The royal purple color scheme is perhaps a little much—I'll give it the benefit of the doubt and assume the color's a nod to the region's viticultural roots—but its garishness is mitigated by sunny yellow walls and big picture windows. The French-inspired menu highlights the best food of the region, from wine to produce. Breakfast and brunch offer a few French twists on the usual standards, including a croque-monsieur, herbal breakfast sausage imported from France, and a grown-up breakfast sandwich on high-quality sourdough. True to its name, the "family bistro" has an ambitious kids' menu, including cannelloni, meat loaf, fish-and-chips, and, in the mornings, Mickey Mouse–shaped pancakes. If you're in a rush, order baked goods and coffee or choose from the to-go menu at the bakery counter.

KNOW: *Make your dining experience even more continental by requesting a sidewalk table.*

We Olive

1311 Park St, Paso Robles
MILE/EXIT: 231A
805.239.7667
www.paso.weolive.com
OPEN: *Mon–Sat 10a–6p, Sun 11a–4p*

Sidle up to the long wooden tasting bar and get a crash course on the diversity of California's new liquid gold. We Olive's mission is twofold: to educate the public on California olive oil, and to provide a place for serious producers to market and sell their goods (the shop only promotes olive oils certified by the California Olive Oil Council). One tasting can include up to 20 olive oils and vinegars, ranging in flavor from bold and peppery to smooth and mild. Knowledgeable staff guide you through the flavors and patiently answer all questions, no matter how basic. Pitchers of olive branches around the shop lend a casual grace to the ambiance. Along with the oil itself, We Olive also stocks jars of olives, condiments and spreads, and olive oil ice cream.

VARIOUS LOCATIONS *in San Francisco, San Luis Obispo, Fresno, and Ventura*

CALIFORNIA

Firestone-Walker Brewing Co. Tasting Room

1400 Ramada Dr, Paso Robles
MILE/EXIT: 228
805.238.2556, ext. 15
www.firestonewalker.com
OPEN: *Sun–Fri noon–7p, Sat 11a–7p*

What's in a name? The Firestone family, of tire fame, has made their fortune and reputation on their capacity for invention, and this microbrewery isn't any exception. Adam Firestone, the grandson of Harvey S., and his brother-in-law David Walker started this brewery in a small facility on the family's Firestone Vineyard. They soon outgrew the modest space and moved to the current location in 2002. Because of their wine-making roots, the brewers ferment their beer in an oak barrel system they developed based on the famous Burton Union system in England. (Oak infuses the beer with a smokiness and fullness that stainless steel tanks don't provide—the brewers use medium or heavy toast oak depending on the beer.) The resulting brews fill the palate with the mature taste of hops and the clean briskness that's found in the best British pale ales. If you aren't familiar with the beer, the six-beer sampler is a good place to start. To-go growlers are sold for a picnic.

KNOW: *There's a limited food menu available at this tasting room in the commercial operation, but the Buellton offshoot has a full brewpub menu (620 McMurray Rd; 805.686.1557).*

TOURS: *Offered Sat 11:30a, 1:30p, 3:30p, and 5:30p; Sun 1:30p, 3:30p, and 5:30p (free)*

 Peachy Canyon Winery

1480 N Bethel Rd, Templeton
MILE/EXIT: 228
866.335.1918
www.peachycanyon.com
OPEN: *Daily 11a–5:30p*

Paso is best known for its zinfandels, and this winery located inside an old schoolhouse focuses on the region's specialty almost exclusively. Except for a couple white and red outliers, the wine tasting menu is mostly zins, which range from bold and peppery to smooth and mellow (make sure to try the 2007 Especial Estate Zin). The winemakers expanded and remodeled the circa 1886 Old Bethel School House to build their tasting room—the bright room no longer has a real connection to its schoolhouse roots, but the staff can show you a picture taken when it was a working classroom. Overall, the atmosphere is homey, with a fireplace and curtains, and the grounds have a few picnic tables and a gazebo. The tasting fee is reasonable—$5 for six wines—and it's refunded with a bottle purchase.

KNOW: *If you want to make a more extended wine-tasting side trip after visiting Peachy Canyon, there are a number of other fine wineries to visit just a few miles off of Hwy 101. See page 264, Side Trip: Paso Robles Wine Country, for more details.*

🏠 Apple Farm

2015 Monterey St, San Luis Obispo
MILE/EXIT: 204
805.544.2040
www.applefarm.com
OPEN: *Thu–Mon 10a–4:30p*

Eat ice cream churned by nature at this working replica of a turn-of-the-century grist mill over San Luis Creek, where a 14-foot waterwheel powers an ice cream maker and cider press. The patio next to the creek is a pleasant spot to sit, eat your cone, and ruminate on the endless forward march of technology. Or skip the philosophy and hit up the on-site bakery specializing in all things apple (pies, dumplings, muffins, you name it). The adjacent restaurant is a popular tourist spot, serving up homestyle favorites like chicken and dumplings, turkey pot pie, pork chops with house-made applesauce, and big country breakfasts. It's all a little dowdy and skews toward a slightly older crowd, but like the food it serves, it's comforting to know such places still exist.

CALIFORNIA

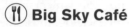 Big Sky Café

1121 Broad St, San Luis Obispo

MILE/EXIT: 202A

805.545.5401

www.bigskycafe.com

OPEN: *Mon–Thu, Sun 7a–9p; Fri 7a–10p; Sat 8a–10p*

This friendly downtown cafe is wholly of the West—from its decor, with stars painted on the wood-beam ceiling and big copper pots with tomatoes outside the door, to its menu, with influences from the Southwest, Mexico, and Asia. It's one of those confident cafes that knows exactly what it is and where its place is in society. Chef/owner Charles Myers sources primarily organic local food, and features more than 20 by-the-glass selections on the super-local wine list. Dinner options might include a fresh market vegetable plate, ancho chile glazed salmon, adobo-rubbed steak, or filling salads like the warm bacon, lettuce, and tomato chopped salad. Brunchtime selections are equally inventive, including a blue cheese, apple, and smoked bacon omelet, served with warm, crumbly cornbread muffins with a hint of heat from jalapeno. Also popular are whole-grain pancakes, filled with bananas and pecans, chocolate chips, Swiss cheese, or fresh berries, served with the cafe's own blend of maple syrup.

KNOW: *There can be a wait for a table, but there's a comfortable front area with couches to accommodate the rush. Free coffee is available in the mornings for would-be cranky brunchers.*

The Madonna Inn

100 Madonna Rd, San Luis Obispo

MILE/EXIT: 201

805.543.3000

www.madonnainn.com

OPEN: *Daily 7a–10p (Bakery and Copper Café), 5–10p (Gold Rush Steak House)*

I can say with absolute confidence that there is nowhere on earth like the Madonna Inn. Adjectives like "gaudy" and "over-the-top" don't even begin to do it justice; the spectacle defies description, and please forgive me for saying that you really just need to see it for yourself. First, it's a hotel—one of the most outrageous in the country, with guest rooms that include out-of-the-ordinary touches like rock walls and waterfall showers. Second, the Madonna Inn is a restaurant—actually four restaurants—resplendent with hand-carved wood accents, elaborately painted walls, giant wine goblets, and curiosities like a hand-carved marble balustrade from Hearst Castle. The food is decent, but your senses will be so engaged elsewhere that you will hardly notice what's on your plate. Grab cream puffs and danishes in the bakery and pastry shop, sit down for a casual meal at the horseshoe-shaped bar in the Copper Café, or have a steak and martini in the Gold Rush Steak House and adjacent Silver Bar. Either way, expect a lot of pink, and so much visual razzle-dazzle that you'll leave, blinking a little in the sun, completely confused about what just happened. Don't miss a chance to gawk at the enormous pink cakes in the display case next to the front door; they bring confection-making to new heights.

KNOW: *Pay a visit to the downstairs men's bathroom. To say more would ruin the surprise, but it's probably the most famous bathroom in California.*

🍨 Doc Burnstein's Ice Cream Lab

114 W Branch St, Arroyo Grande
MILE/EXIT: 187A
805.474.4068
www.docburnsteins.com
OPEN: *Sun–Thu 11a–9:30p, Fri–Sat 11a–10:30p*

Every Wednesday at 7pm, owner Greg Steinburner and employees invent new flavors of ice cream in the shop's glassed-in "lab," putting on a show that delights both kids and parents. ("Tickets" are distributed at the counter, or you can just show up.) Some of the shop's most popular flavors have been invented in these sessions, like the banana-and-peanut-butter Elvis Special. The newbies join the long list of tried-and-true flavors, ranging from the usual (simple and perfect vanilla made with real vanilla beans—the mark of a good ice cream place) to the unusual (Merlot Raspberry Truffle, made with real wine, and Root Beer Marble). The ice cream is superlative because Doc Burnstein's sources hormone-free cream from Sacramento, classified as "super-premium" for the percentage of butterfat, along with

CALIFORNIA

using real fruit. Kids will love the model train that travels around the store's perimeter near the ceiling.

KNOW: *Even if you can't make it to the storefront, Doc Burnstein's ice cream pops up on restaurant menus up and down the Central Coast.*

🍴 Jocko's Restaurant

125 N Thompson Ave, Nipomo
MILE/EXIT: 179
805.929.3565
www.jockosmix.com
OPEN: *Sun–Thu 8a–10p, Fri–Sat 8a–11p*

This is a deeply strange restaurant, as any self-respecting local dive should be, and also happens to offer some of the best Santa Maria barbecue around. A sign outside the front door invites guests to "come in and monkey around," which throws you off a little before you even enter the cinderblock structure. Inside, ranchers talk horses around the so-dim-you-can-barely-see-your-glass bar, or share table space with the foodies who flock here from hundreds of miles away. The people-watching is a full-time diversion, but once the steak comes a reverential hush falls over the table. Cooked over a massive oak barbecue pit in back, the steak lives up to the hype: beefy, salty, smoky, and with the subtle spices characteristic of Santa Maria–style 'cue. Tri-tip is equally tasty, and the ginormous burger, also flame-grilled, is a messily delicious treat.

KNOW: *The symbols in the wooden trim around the bar are local cattle brands.*

🍴 Pea Soup Andersen's

376 Avenue of the Flags, Buellton
MILE/EXIT: 140A
805.688.5581
www.peasoupandersens.net
OPEN: *Daily 7a–10p*

When Highway 101 ran right through town, Pea Soup Andersen's was *the* place to stop on the road, and has been a waypoint for travelers for generations since. The billboards start miles away—entertaining road diversions showing the illustrated mascots Hap-Pea and Pea-Wee about to hit one another over the head with an outsize hammer. Once you finally arrive, the standard Andersen's order is a bowl of endless pea

Unusual Ice Cream Flavors

They may seem to cross the line between sweet and savory, but these ice creams borrow flavors from other cultures to stretch the boundaries of America's favorite frozen dessert.

Cayenne Pepper: The combination of spicy and sweet has long been a signature of Mexican desserts. Here it brings a subtle, spicy kick to a cup or cone. (Mallard Ice Cream, Bellingham, WA, page 9)

Mushroom: It's not as disgusting as one might imagine. The mushrooms in question are candy caps, and you'd be hard-pressed to distinguish it from maple in a blind taste test. (Cowlick's Ice Cream Co., Fort Bragg, CA, page 173)

Lavender: This flowering herb is gaining notoriety in kitchens around the world, and its floral sweetness makes you wonder why lavender ice cream isn't in grocery stores everywhere. (Screamin' Mimi's Ice Cream, Sebastopol, CA, page 165)

Strawberry Je Ne Sais Quoi: The mystery element of this fresh, organic strawberry ice cream is a splash of balsamic vinegar—a flavor combo that's popular in Italian desserts. (Three Twins Organic Ice Cream, Napa, CA, page 198)

Champagne: Technically a sorbet, this classic palate cleanser has all the crisp dryness of an expensive bottle of bubbly. (Doc Burnstein's Ice Cream Lab, Arroyo Grande, CA, page 253)

soup that comes with sides like cheese, green onion, bread crumbs, ham, and bacon bits; the menu also offers breakfasts and American standards like Monte Cristo sandwiches. The soup itself, which is canned and sold across California, is nothing to write home about, but it's the legend of the place that matters—everyone of a certain age who lived in this part of California has a story about it from their youth.

KNOW: *The life-size cut outs of Hap-Pea and Pea-Wee at the front entrance make a great photo op.*

CALIFORNIA

🍴 Hitching Post II

406 E Hwy 246, Buellton
MILE/EXIT: 140A
805.688.0676
www.hitchingpostwines.com
OPEN: *Daily 4–9:30p*

Only proprietor Harley Ostini knows what's in the "magic dust," the culinary pixie dust that has made his steaks taste magically delicious for the past 50 years. These are some of the most flavorful steaks you'll have anywhere: corn-fed Midwestern beef, grilled Santa Maria–style over an open fire fueled by red oak. The grilled artichoke appetizer is a must, all smoky from the fire and savory from the magic dust—the flavors especially pop when dipped in the smoked tomato mayonnaise. When it comes to steak, the prime top sirloin is the cheapest cut on the menu and to my taste is the best—it's grainier than its more refined counterparts, but the grain holds up well to the fire and gives the seasonings more surface area to permeate. Affordable house wines under the Hitching Post label are designed to complement the meal—pinot noir is a good starter that pairs well with appetizers, and Generation Red, a blend of mostly cabernet franc, holds up to the meat without trying to steal the show. And yes, this is the restaurant where Maya worked in the movie *Sideways*. It can get crowded, but the bar is a welcoming hang while you wait. Ask for a seat in the main dining room—you want to be near the grilling action.

KNOW: *You can buy the magic dust at the counter, along with smoked tomato pesto if you want to make the mayonnaise at home.*

OstrichLand USA

610 E Hwy 246, Buellton
MILE/EXIT: 140A
805.686.9696
www.ostrichlandusa.com
OPEN: *Daily 10a–dark*

Want to make a splash at your next brunch? Try cooking up an ostrich egg—the equivalent of 18 to 24 chicken eggs—that you bought from this offbeat roadside attraction. The zoolike stop features more than

Santa Maria Barbecue

The local specialty of steak grilled over a red oak flame dates back to the Spanish rancheros. There are as many different ways to prepare it as there are producers; some only season with salt and pepper, some use special spice blends—either way, the smokiness of the wood gets into the beef and makes for a truly superlative steak or tri-tip sandwich. Try it at Jocko's, Far Western Tavern, Hitching Post, or at any of the sidewalk stands that spring up on weekends, at farmers markets, and during festivals.

50 ostriches and emus trained to play nice with visitors and even to accept food from the hands of strangers. Being surrounded by that many ostriches can only be described as a once-in-a-lifetime experience. After getting to know the birds, head to the gift shop for ostrich and emu eggs, frozen ostrich meat (don't worry, it's not from your new feathered friends; the owners have it shipped in), ostrich jerky, and other items like ostrich feather dusters, blown ostrich and emu eggshells, and emu oil (supposedly does wonders for the skin).

il Fustino

3401 State St, Santa Barbara
MILE/EXIT: 101A
888.798.4720
www.ilfustino.com
OPEN: *Mon–Sat 11a–6p*

The olive oil bar is a new concept in the states, but it's an old one in Europe—an observation owner Jim Kirkley made while traveling in Italy, and decided to bring the concept home with him. He imported handsome stainless steel tanks called *fusti*, made specifically for olive oil storage and distribution, which serve as the centerpiece of the shop and house il Fustino's California extra-virgin olive oil blends. Taste your way through different oils to see the difference the olives make, guided by the store's expert staff. There's the popular, peppery Tuscan blend; the green and smooth Frantio, made from an Italian olive grown near San Francisco; and the mild, buttery California blends made from organic

Mission and Manzanillo olives. Some are infused with ingredients like basil, garlic, rosemary, jalapeno, lemon, and orange; Kirkley adds an extra burst of flavor to these by crushing the fruit and herbs with mild Mission olives right at the mill. The shop also makes balsamic and flavored vinegar (in varieties like fig balsamic, cherry, pear, and late-harvest riesling), and avocado, walnut, and sesame oil.

KNOW: *All olive oils are certified by the California Olive Oil Council, a governing body that ensures quality and consistency of extra-virgin olive oils across the state.*

(👨‍🍳) McConnell's Ice Cream
210 W Mission St, Santa Barbara
MILE/EXIT: 99
805.569.2323
www.mcconnells.com
OPEN: *Sun–Thu 10:30a–10:30p, Fri–Sat 10:30a–11p*

Everyone's in the business of making fresh ice cream from local ingredients these days, but this beloved ice cream shop has been playing the local game since 1949. Founder Gordon F. "Mac" McConnell was an Air Force pilot during WWII and sampled ice creams across Europe during his tour of duty. McConnell became enamored with the "French pot" method—ice cream mixture is put in a chilled, spinning pot and scraped off the walls of the bowl as it freezes, resulting in a very creamy final product—and he was one of the first to import it stateside. However, method is nothing without good ingredients. McConnell's is careful about sourcing the very best, using fresh cream, bourbon vanilla beans, Guittard chocolate, and local produce. The shop's ice creams are some of the richest around with 17 percent butterfat, and come in usual and unusual flavors like macadamia nut, California lemon zest, Elberta peach, and Bordeaux strawberry.

VARIOUS LOCATIONS *in Isla Vista, Goleta, and Ventura*

 Joe's Café

536 State St, Santa Barbara
MILE/EXIT: 98
805.966.4638
www.joescafesb.com
OPEN: *Daily 7:30a–11p*

With its dark high-backed booths, checked tablecloths, big wooden bar, framed silver prints of old-school California, and high copper ceilings, this is the kind of bar that wouldn't be out of place in a Raymond Chandler novel. Joe's has been a local institution since 1928, and if it weren't for the large arched windows looking out onto State Street, it would be easy to forget that we are well into the twenty-first century. The food is chophouse standard: French dip, steaks, lettuce wedge with blue cheese dressing, fried chicken. Joe's even has the kind of shady past proper for an institution of its pedigree—when Santa Barbara was a haven for rumrunners during Prohibition, rumors abounded that the bar was a speakeasy.

Santa Barbara Shellfish Co.

230 Stearns Wharf, Santa Barbara
MILE/EXIT: 97
805.966.6696
www.sbfishhouse.com
OPEN: *Daily 11a–8:30p (open until 9p in summer)*

Yeah, it's kind of a tourist trap out there at the end of the pier, but sometimes a tourist trap is just fine. This seafood shack offers steamed clams, mussels, oysters, and other shellfish, as per the name, and a first-rate list of local wines and local microbrews on tap, including Santa Barbara Blonde, Firestone Double Barrel, and Anchor Steam. Eat inside in the crowded, nautical-themed dining room, or order from the takeout window on the south side and commandeer a picnic table with sweeping views of Santa Barbara and the bay. The restaurant will validate pier parking, too.

🍴 La Super Rica

622 N Milpas St, Santa Barbara
MILE/EXIT: 96B
805.963.4940
OPEN: *Mon, Tue, Thu, Sun 11a–9p; Fri–Sat 11a–9:30p*

One of Julia Child's favorite restaurants late in life, which is endorsement enough in itself because the woman valued a tasty meal more than almost anything else on earth. The food at this Mexican stand is, indeed, *super rica* (very rich). Number 18 is a bowl of melted cheese and bacon that will clog your arteries just by looking at it, but when mopped up with fresh corn tortillas it becomes an amazing thing—a dish you'll find yourself yearning for later, even though you're simultaneously ashamed to be lusting after *a bowl of melted cheese and bacon*. (Sorry to harp on it, but it was one of the most delicious things I've ever eaten, and also one of the most calorifically horrifying. Especially since I ate the whole bowl.) Anyway, you can't go wrong with anything on the menu, and don't overlook the daily specials—one afternoon featured posole with a broth so bright-red from chiles that just looking at it made my taste buds quiver in fear and anticipation. Faced with such spicy food, you realize why Mexican beer and *horchata* were invented. Seating is on a covered deck next to the restaurant.

KNOW: *Expect a line, but it will move quickly, and watch the chefs ball masa for fresh tortillas and grill piles of green onions while you wait.*

🍸 Santa Barbara Winery

202 Anacapa St, Santa Barbara
MILE/EXIT: 96B
805.963.3633
www.sbwinery.com
OPEN: *Daily 10a–5p*

Pay your respects at the oldest winery in Santa Barbara County. If you're in downtown Santa Barbara, you don't have much of an excuse—the tasting room has an enviable location two blocks from bustling State Street and one block from the beach, which makes it a breeze to stop in and sample the excellent Italian-style reds that the winery consistently turns out. Sip your way through syrah, grenache, pinot noir, zinfandel, sangiovese, nebbiolo, and other big reds at the U-shaped tasting bar with friendly staff and a mix of locals and wine tourists.

🍽 Jeannine's American Bakery Restaurant

1253 Coast Village Rd, Montecito
MILE/EXIT: 94A
805.969.7878
www.jeannines.com
OPEN: *Mon–Thu 6:30a–4p, Fri 6:30a–4:30p, Sat–Sun 7a–4:30p*

Ladies lunch in expensively "casual" clothes, a tinkly jazz soundtrack plays, huge wall photos display a moneyed California lifestyle that you never had and never will have—the display of wealth and class at this upscale Montecito cafe provides an interesting glimpse into how the other half lives. You are reminded that this is the part of Santa Barbara where Oprah resides. Despite the pretension, Jeannine's is a very good bakery, turning out treats worth ruining a diet for. Pick from cookies, muffins, scones, croissants, quick breads, coffee cakes, and one of the best lemon bars I've ever had, sweet and tart in all the right ways. If you do stay for lunch, expect pricey salads like Cobb or California chicken, fancy sandwiches like house-roasted turkey breast with house-made cranberry chutney, and a daily quiche with a side salad. Jeannine's has locations scattered around the city, making it easy to pick up baked treats without going out of your way.

🏛 Ortega Adobe

215 W Main St, Ventura
MILE/EXIT: 71
805.658.4726
OPEN: *Daily 9a–4p*

Nothing much to see these days. The building's on the lonely end of Ventura's main drag and kinda derelict and run down, and the modern cleaning supplies leaning up against the wall definitely take something away from the nineteenth-century ambiance. But this is a reproduction of the Ortega family home where they first roasted chiles for salsa in 1857, so if nothing else, it's interesting from a purely historical perspective. (You look into the rooms and wonder what the Ortega family would think of its massive displays in supermarkets today.) A visit also helps you imagine Ventura in the 1800s, when adobe homes like this lined the main street.

 Snapper Jack's Taco Shack

5100 Telegraph Rd, Ventura
MILE/EXIT: 70A
805.642.5111
www.snapperjackstacoshack.com
OPEN: *Daily 11a–9p*

You know you've entered Southern California when you hit this taco shack. The interior is decorated with beach cruiser bicycles, surfer memorabilia, a TV showing surfing videos, tables decorated like surfboards, and a sign above the door with a finger pointing west that says, "To beach." Order fish tacos and choose between a corn or crispy tortilla, and grilled or fried fish. The fried fish tends to fall apart when you bite into it, but the grilled is in such a flavorful marinade you don't miss the batter—and if you order grilled fish in a fried shell you still get that deeply satisfying snap, crackle, and pop. All tacos come slathered in secret sauce and crowned with fresh veggies, but don't miss out on the totally radical salsa bar. If you need a break from the "hang-ten" atmosphere and Jeff Spicoli look-alikes, there are picnic tables out front. All food is free of trans fat, MSG, and lard.

KNOW: *There's a second location off the 101 at exit 52 in Camarillo (4850 Verdugo Way; 805.384.0334).*

Andria's Seafood

1449 Spinnaker Dr, Suite A, Ventura
MILE/EXIT: 68
805.654.0546
www.andriasseafood.com
OPEN: *Sun–Thu 11a–9p, Fri–Sat 11a–10p*

All of Ventura is here, it seems: teenagers and retirees, families and singles, UCLA and USC fans, everyone bonding over huge portions of fish-and-chips and other seafood specialties from this shack on Ventura harbor. You can still taste the sea in the lightly breaded, fried-to-perfection fish-and-chips, which are nicely complemented by the house-made tartar. The clam chowder, made from a family recipe, is peppery and smooth, with celery, carrots, onion, and large chunks of potato—the only thing it's light on is pieces of clam, making it more like a clam-scented potato soup. Get out of your comfort zone by ordering one of the unusual burgers, including scallop, salmon, and the "Fabulous Fish Burger," aka a deep-fried angel shark fillet. Avoid the bustling interior, decorated with neon beer signs and framed photos of fishing boats, and snag a deck chair outside under the blue tarp ceiling, or out on the dock overlooking Ventura harbor.

KNOW: *Andria's gets insanely busy on weekends, but the line moves quickly and a team of servers takes orders while people wait.*

Mrs. Olson's Coffee Hut

117 Los Altos St, Oxnard
MILE/EXIT: 68
DISTANCE FROM HWY: 7.5 miles
805.985.9151
OPEN: *Mon–Sun 7a–2p, dinner served Thu–Sat 5–8p*

Experience the cultural collision of beach bums and military types at this beachside coffee shop, which turns out huge breakfasts to bleary-eyed twentysomethings and hungry sailors from the nearby naval bases. It's not only the clientele that showcases the cultural divide, it's also the decor: patriotic Americana mingled with hand-painted murals of beach scenes. Try the gigantic breakfast burrito, or chilaquiles that come with an ungodly amount of cheese. There's often a wait on weekend mornings; leave your name with one of the toned surfer-girl waitresses, and pass the time on one of the weathered wooden benches in front. Afterward, burn off the calories with a walk on Hollywood Beach a half-block away.

DETOURS & DESTINATIONS

Side Trip: Paso Robles Wine Country

MILE/EXIT: 232

LENGTH: 45 miles (for the whole loop)

Paso Robles, known to locals as simply "Paso," has finally emerged from the shadow of Napa and Sonoma and come into its own as an exciting wine region. It was bound to happen sooner or later: Paso is located half-way between San Francisco and Los Angeles, and enjoys a long growing season of warm days and cool nights aided by breezes from the Pacific wafting over the Santa Lucia Mountains. Paso Robles Wine Country is divided in half by Highway 101: The warmer eastern side is known for producing big reds like zinfandel and cabernet sauvignon, while the more famous western side, closer to the ocean, is known for its Rhone-style wines like syrah, and proprietary Bordeaux and Rhone-style blends. The wine route road skirts the city and goes up into the hills, where it twists and turns past wineries, vineyards, ranches, and oak trees draped with Spanish moss.

KNOW: *If you don't want to make the drive to see the wineries, let them come to you—there are a dozen tasting rooms within walking distance of downtown.*

JUSTIN Vineyards & Winery

11680 Chimney Rock Rd, Paso Robles

MILE/EXIT: 232

DISTANCE FROM HWY: 16.2 miles

805.238.6932

www.justinwine.com

OPEN: *Daily 10a–5p*

You can tell this winery takes itself seriously as you walk past the vine-yards that lead up to the Craftsman-style tasting room building. Each row ends with an embossed plaque informing visitors of its type of trellis system, grape varietal, clone, and rootstocks—if you don't know much about wine, it's easy to get intimidated. Especially when you step into the dark wood-paneled tasting room, done up like the library at a French estate, all deep maroon and royal purple, with velvet flags identifying JUSTIN's flag-ship wines. All this severity and attention to detail produces deep, rich, and complex award-winning reds that the winery assertively spells with all caps—like the mighty ISOSCELES, a Bordeaux-style blend of cabernet sauvignon, merlot, and cabernet franc, and the even bigger JUSTIFICATION, a St. Emilion–style blend of cabernet franc and merlot. On the lighter side, Deborah's Delight is an orange muscat dessert wine that's not too sweet, surprisingly light, and redolent of orange blossoms.

KNOW: *The price tag can be hefty, but a meal at Deborah's Room, the on-site restaurant, is a pleasant experience with very good food. It's not worth the splurge if you're on a tight budget, but if you can swing it, it'll be a very nice escape. There is also an on-site bed-and-breakfast.*

TOURS: *Learn about the sustainable, biodynamic growing practices the winery uses for its 160 acres of estate vineyards on the 45-minute tour. (Daily 10:30a, 2:30p, and 5p; $15 per person, includes tasting fee)*

Tablas Creek Vineyard

9339 Adelaida Rd, Paso Robles

MILE/EXIT: 232

DISTANCE FROM HWY: 12.2 miles

805.237.1231

www.tablascreek.com

OPEN: *Daily 10a–5p*

Paso's wine-making reputation was sealed when established French winemakers started to open vineyards in the neighborhood, like this joint venture with the Perrin family of France, fifth-generation proprietors of Chateau de Beaucastel. The family recognized the region's similarity to their native Rhone estate—limestone clay soils, hot days and cool nights, lots of rainfall in the winter—and brought over cuttings of red and white Rhone varieties from their renowned French vineyard. They also imported the wine-making process: all wine is aged in barrels from France and fermented with French native yeasts. Tablas Creek is one of the most educational tasting rooms in the region—the pourers know about wine and know how to share their knowledge, including using nifty visual aids like a handout that shows the grapes and their characteristics to help explain the science and art of blending. Tablas wines are good for drinking now, but these are also wines that can be cellared—try the simple Cotes de Tablas, their take on French table wine, and the lush Espirit de Beaucastel.

KNOW: *The tasting room is makeshift now, but the winery is at work on a new one, opening date undetermined.*

TOURS: *Covers the 120-acre organic estate vineyard, grapevine nursery, and winery. Call ahead for reservations and more information.*

Pasolivo

8530 Vineyard Dr, Paso Robles

MILE/EXIT: 228

DISTANCE FROM HWY: 12.2 miles

805.227.0186

www.pasolivo.com

OPEN: *Fri–Sun 11a–5p, Mon & Thu 11a–4p*

It's quiet, rustic, and still at this small-scale olive oil boutique, set in an old farmhouse shaded by a grove of oaks. Inside the light-filled tasting room, staff guide you through award-winning olive oils like the signature Pasolivo, an extra-virgin olive oil with a peppery, slightly bitter finish characteristic of the Tuscan olives it's made from. The California blend, made from local olives Mission and Manzanillo, is very bold and green. It's amazing to discover how different oils from the same 45-acre olive ranch can be. Pasolivo also makes citrus-flavored oils in tangerine, lime, and Meyer lemon, along with a white and dark balsamic. The rapid-fire tastings can get a little overwhelming to the palate, but don't miss the olive jams. These chutneylike concoctions blend olives and apples with spices and perfectly walk the line between sweet and savory. I like the mild, allspice-hinted green variety; the black variety is bolder. The shop also sells jars of olives, olive oil–based hand lotion, and more.

KNOW: *If you buy oil, make sure you get instructions for how to open it—the mechanism's a little tricky and easy to break.*

Farmstand 46

3750 Hwy 46 W, Templeton

MILE/EXIT: 228

DISTANCE FROM HWY: 4.6 miles

805.239.3611

www.farmstand46.com

OPEN: *Daily 7a–7p*

"Get the Goat" is what everyone said when they recommended this stop on Highway 46 in an attractively rusting corrugated metal hangar. I was a little apprehensive, but the Goat turned out to be a sandwich made with slow-cooked pork shoulder layered with melted fontina and red onion. It's greasy, but if you want something to sustain you while wine tasting, it's the Wine Country equivalent of drunk food. Equally big toasted sandwiches like the Badger—roasted vegetables, squash, zucchini, eggplant, peppers, onions, herbed goat cheese, and basil—sit on the menu alongside breakfast burritos and sandwiches. There's also a coffee bar, and picnic supplies like premade salads, a cheese counter, and local produce. An on-site organic garden, visible to the west of the parking lot, provides all the greens and herbs for the salads and sandwiches. The whole place is very stylish, and inside the cement floor is painted with slogans like "Do egalitarians eat animal crackers?" and "Cheese is milk's leap toward immortality."

KNOW: *The picnic tables up front under the umbrellas can get very busy and finding one can be a fierce competition, but those tucked down in the garden offer a bit more privacy.*

Jack Creek Farms Country Store

5000 Hwy 46 W, Templeton
MILE/EXIT: 228
DISTANCE FROM HWY: 6.2 miles
805.239.1915
www.jackcreekfarms.com
OPEN: *Hours vary by season; call ahead for details*

Jack Creek Farms sprung out of the Barlogio family's heartfelt love of farming and fervent need to share it with others. You might write it off as a tourist trap after seeing the Wild West movie-style façade, but there's more to the fifth-generation family farm than initially meets the eye, and it's hard to know where to start. First, there's produce: heirloom varieties of vegetables rarely seen elsewhere, including 300 fruit trees, 40 varieties of pumpkins, and 40 varieties of squash. There's food: apple cider, pomegranate slushies, and jugs of local cider; home-baked pies and baked goods made from farm eggs and honey; jars of local honey; grape juice made from zinfandel; fudge and saltwater taffy. And then there's stuff to do: U-pick berries, flowers, veggies, and herbs; tours of antique farm equipment; plenty of activities for kids, especially in the fall. You could stop in for a second and pick up something to go, or you could stay all day.

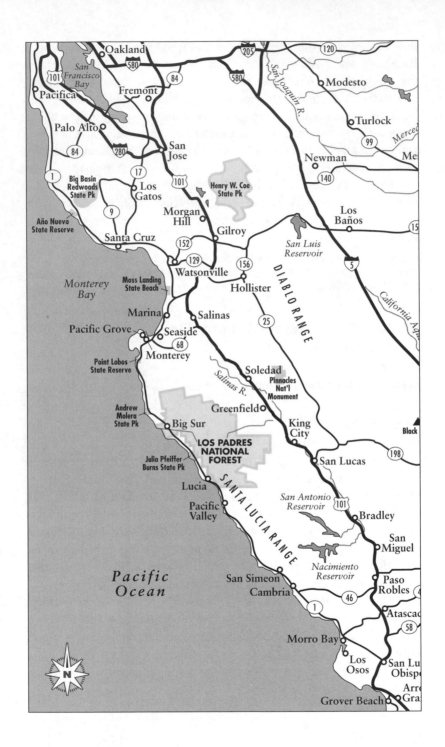

Highway 1: Central Coast

Trip Stats

START: Pescadero

END: Pismo Beach

LENGTH: 225 miles

LOCAL FLAVOR: Seafood shacks, artichokes, and bakeries catering to weary travelers in search of coffee and sugar.

BEST TIME: Spring and summer, when the sun's shining and beach-frolicking is a given.

LOCAL FOOD FESTIVALS: **Castroville Artichoke Festival**, Castroville (May). Artichokes every which way, cooking demos, and a colorful parade.

WORD OF WARNING: The road around Big Sur can be treacherous in the winter and occasionally closes for days at a time. Look up road conditions before you go to avoid any unpleasant surprises.

MORE INFO: Central Coast Tourism Council (www.centralcoast-tourism.com)

This drive sure must've been something in the 1950s. Back then, derelict buildings were all Cannery Row had to offer; writers, painters, and bohemians defined the community of Carmel; Henry Miller and Jack Kerouac scribbled furiously in Big Sur cabins; and the small fishing towns of the south remained untainted by tourism.

Times change, I suppose. The past half century has been good to the Central Coast, infusing it with the money and opportunity brought by sun-seeking tourists. But the mantle of tourist destination is a new one, and the region wears it uneasily. Past glories are certainly rosier through the gauzy film of nostalgia—but, simply put, the Central Coast is going through an identity crisis.

Identity crisis isn't quite right—it's more like a culinary and cultural coming-of-age. Vestiges from the past still live on in both unassuming seafood shacks and four-star restaurants, but there's a new

CALIFORNIA

self-consciousness about their place as relics from a time before this one. Many haven't figured out what newfound fame means to them—or how to take their day-to-day existence to the next level. Some have become mediocre tourist traps; some expanded too early and failed; some closed due to internal stresses; and a very few have kept calm and carried on as they always have. These were the spots I was interested in finding, and they were harder to uncover than I'd imagined.

The one thing that has remained constant all these years is the road: a two-lane highway hugging a coast so beautiful and barely tamed that you wonder how people managed to settle here at all. The waters of Monterey Bay seem tranquil compared to the crashing surf and weather-worn coast down by Big Sur. Things calm down as you near Southern California, and impenetrable harbors smooth into the peaceful waters of Pismo Beach.

The craggy, mountainous coast will, too, eventually change over time, evening out into the sea and losing its uniqueness. Lucky for us, geology works on a slower timeline. Central Coasters have about 15 million years to figure out where they're headed before they lose their most distinctive feature.

ON THE ROAD

🍴 Duarte's Tavern

202 Stage Rd, Pescadero
MILE/EXIT: SM-13
DISTANCE FROM HWY: 2 miles
650.879.0464
www.duartestavern.com
OPEN: *Daily 7a–9p*

This well-known roadhouse, famous for its cream of artichoke soup, crab cioppino, and historical pedigree, has been featured in every magazine and food-travel TV show out there and received the James Beard Foundation's American Classic award. Duarte's opened in 1894 when Frank Duarte put a barrel of whiskey on the bar and declared it a local watering hole. Four generations of Duartes later, the saloon's salt-of-the-earth atmosphere prevails even in the face of foodie invasion. The food is definitely worth the pilgrimage. Cream of artichoke soup is a revelatory balance of subtle woodsiness and velvety creaminess; crab cioppino comes to the table literally overflowing with claws and hunks of meat. The rest of the menu items are worth investigating, including artichoke dishes, seafood specials (try the crab melt), and down-home classics like pork chops with house-made applesauce. Don't miss the pies, made fresh every morning. They're bursting with local produce and are anything but dainty.

KNOW: *The short drive from Highway 1 into the all-American small town of Pescadero is a treat in itself. It gives you a visual preview of your upcoming meal as you drive through acres of farmland that showcase the region's specialties: artichokes, brussels sprouts, and strawberries.*

🐟 Dolphin Restaurant

71 Municipal Wharf #A, Santa Cruz
MILE/EXIT: SCR-19
831.426.5838
OPEN: *Daily 8a–9p*

The quintessential Santa Cruz evening in three easy steps: 1) Take a ride on the historic wooden Big Dipper roller coaster on the Santa Cruz boardwalk. It was built in 1924 and was the fifth roller coaster in the country. 2) After you've had your fill of the boardwalk's chasing lights and penny arcades, walk to the end of Santa Cruz wharf, past the gift shops and amateur fishermen. Sea lions hang out below the pier, and there are special openings created for tourists to watch them swim and nap. 3) Walk a few feet north to the Dolphin, a small, end-of-pier seaside shack that serves up some of the best clam chowder on the coast. It's not as touristy as many of the other restaurants on the pier, but feels local, with its weathered wooden walls, sea blue booths, and mounted-marlin decor. The clam chowder has the perfect clam-to-potato ratio and is creamy and thick without being overwhelming. The fish-and-chips is fine, but I recommend avoiding any of the fancier seafood dishes or pastas. A selection of bottled microbrews rounds out the equation. When the weather's nice, sit on the sizeable outside deck, as big as the dining room itself, and soak up the views of Monterey Bay and the boardwalk.

KNOW: *A side takeout window caters to tourists on the run.*

Cannery Row

"A poem, a stink, a grating noise, a quality of light, a tone, a habit, a nostalgia, a dream." This is how John Steinbeck described Cannery Row, once one of the most productive sardine-canning communities in the world and home to the lab of famed marine biologist Ed Ricketts (fictionalized as Doc in Steinbeck's novel *Cannery Row*). When the sardines more or less ran out in the 1950s, the abandoned factory buildings fell into disrepair until an urban rejuvenation in the mid-'80s turned them into a tourist attraction. Today, Cannery Row is a Disneyfied version of its once-gritty self. Casual fish-and-chips stands abound on the waterfront main drag; for sit-down dining, Portola Restaurant at Monterey Bay Aquarium can't be beat. The aquarium is the brains behind the Seafood Watch sustainable seafood program, and the fish served in the restaurant all falls within their high standards. Besides—tables come with binoculars for wildlife viewing outside the big picture windows. (886 Cannery Row; 831.648.4870)

 Cliff Café

815 41st Ave, Santa Cruz
MILE/EXIT: SCR-14
831.476.1214
OPEN: *Mon–Fri 8a–1p, Sat–Sun 8a–1:30p*
Cash only

A regular crowd of locals shoots the breeze with waitresses in this small breakfast spot, equally popular for its beach-casual ambiance as for its tofu scrambles. Tofu crops up in many dishes in the vegetarian-friendly menu, which features delicious omelets and scrambles made with fresh local ingredients. Try eggs "Gal's Way," an oh-so-California scramble with tomatoes, green onions, Monterey Jack, and optional hot sauce. Good, too, are the pancakes, with a wheaty cinnamon wholesomeness to them. The beachy paintings on the walls bring in sunshine even on foggy mornings, and overall I can't think of a more pleasant place to start your day. With only a handful of tables and a small staff, getting seated takes a while and service can be a bit slow. Pass the time at the green chairs in front, or hit up the coffee shop across the street and take a ramble.

KNOW: *Santa Cruz is the birthplace of O'Neill Wetsuits, Santa Cruz Surfboards, and Santa Cruz Skateboards, and home to a large community of surfers, skateboarders, and other extreme-sports fanatics. After your meal, drive down to Capitola's beach to see the legendary surfing culture in action.*

Giant Artichoke Restaurant

11261 Merritt St, Castroville
MILE/EXIT: MON-92
831.633.3501
OPEN: *Daily 7a–9p*

Take a picture next to the world's biggest artichoke at this road food institution, located right past the downtown core of Castroville, the self-proclaimed "Artichoke Center of the World." After your requisite photo op, head into the dusty green restaurant for deep-fried artichoke hearts, a local specialty. Crunchy on the outside, creamy on the inside, and dipped in garlicky aioli, these deep-fried delights will ruin you on regular-old steamed artichoke hearts forever. The edible thistle shows up in many other surprising places on the menu, including soup, omelets, and a bread reminiscent of zucchini quick bread. The rest of the menu

CALIFORNIA

is ho-hum diner fare—it's best to skip the dining room and grab and go from the prepackaged items on the main counter. A farm stand next door showcases the astonishing array of local produce in cute bins painted to look like various fruits and veggies.

A Taste of Monterey Wine Visitors' Center

700 Cannery Row, Suite KK, Monterey
MILE/EXIT: MON-78
831.646.5466
www.tastemonterey.com
OPEN: *Daily 11a–6p*

Monterey County has an ever-expanding list of boutique wineries, and this visitor center is a great way to sample them without driving through the winding back roads of the Coastal Range. The region is known for its cooler weather whites like chardonnay, sauvignon blanc, and riesling—choose from more than 70 of them at the tasting bar, or browse the wine shop for exclusively Monterey County wines. The center also has educational exhibits and a dedicated staff on hand to answer questions, ranging from "Why isn't white wine colored red?" to specific queries about a winemaker's particular growing philosophy. Its Cannery Row location makes the center a convenient, and popular, tourist destination, and the large windows give a panoramic view of Monterey Bay.

KNOW: *The shop has a second location in Old Town Salinas (127 Main St; 831.751.1980).*

Compagno's Deli

2000 Prescott Ave, Monterey
MILE/EXIT: MON-78
831.375.5987
OPEN: *Mon–Fri 10a–5:15p, Sat–Sun 10a–6p*

A short drive up the hill from Cannery Row takes you to this unassuming sandwich shop, which has some of the best and heartiest Italian subs this side of the Mediterranean. The military theme and customer base throw you for a moment, but Monterey has always been a military town, and the imposing Monterey Presidio is only a block away. You stop noticing all surroundings, anyway, once you get your hands on

History of the Agricultural Fair

Agricultural fairs have been around almost as long as agriculture—the Book of Ezekiel mentions a fair in the trading city of Tyre in scriptures dating back to 500 BC—and have always been important places for geographically dispersed farmers and tradesmen to gather, exhibit, barter, and sell merchandise. The fair came to North America in 1765 in Windsor, Nova Scotia (a festival that carries on today), and became widely celebrated in the United States thanks to the efforts of a scrappy New England farmer named Elkanah Watson. He organized the country's first fair—a cattle competition, complete with prize money, held in Pittsfield, Massachusetts in 1811—and spent the rest of his life helping communities develop their own events. By the end of the nineteenth century, almost every state had at least one agricultural fair. These featured competitions for the best agriculture, horticulture, and livestock; industrial exhibits and demonstrations; entertainment for visitors; and an overall celebration of the region's bounty. These agricultural fairs are the foundation of the more than 3,200 fairs held in North America every year, including iconic West Coast events like the Gilroy Garlic Festival, Stockton Asparagus Festival, and Castroville Artichoke Festival.

one of the deli's enormous sandwiches. A half sandwich is enough for a full meal; you'll probably be sorry if you finish a whole one in one sitting. Try No. 2, with turkey, ham, bacon, avocado, and the works, or the Army Special, piled high with roast beef, turkey, and pepperoni. All are made with fresh, high-quality ingredients and just-baked French bread sturdy enough to withstand the onslaught of ingredients. As if the sandwiches weren't enough, Compagno's also has thrillingly rich chocolate cake in the bakery case by the cash register, and a deep selection of sodas you've never heard of.

CALIFORNIA

🍴 Carmel Bakery

Ocean Ave & Lincoln, Carmel
MILE/EXIT: MON-73
831.626.8885
www.pepeinternational.com/carm_bakery
OPEN: *Daily 6:30a–9:30p*

Carmel is famous for its fierce individualism and lack of street addresses, but this bakery's easy to find even without an address: Look toward the Pacific on Ocean Avenue and you'll see the bakery's pretzel-shaped sign and display window showing a carb lover's fantasy of baked goods. The bakery was established in 1906 and is one of the town's longest-running businesses, specializing in shortbread, scones, pretzels, and biscotti, along with Starbucks coffee and soups and sandwiches at lunchtime. It's also refreshingly down-to-earth; the warm yellow walls are welcoming, and the staff is friendly and accommodating. An excellent place to stop and get some goodies before you wander the beach.

🍴 La Bicyclette

Dolores St at 7th, Carmel
MILE/EXIT: MON-73
831.622.9899
www.labicycletterestaurant.com
OPEN: *Daily 11a–10p*

Nothing snooty about this rustic French bistro, which oozes charm from the moment you spot the vintage bicycle parked outside the entrance. Inside, copper pots hang from the ceiling, daily menu specials are written on chalkboards, and a whimsical small-scale reproduction of a thatched-roof building contains three cozy tables perfect for couples. The cuisine is French comfort food, with an emphasis on simple flavors made from local, organic ingredients, many sourced from a garden at Carmel Middle School. A daily changing menu might feature dishes like roasted chicken, duck confit crepes, and the beloved soups of the day, ladled tableside from a communal copper pot. The real surprise, though, is the price. It certainly couldn't be classified as a "cheap eat," but all menu items are at least $10 less than other French bistros of its stature and quality, and the wine list has a number of by-the-glass selections for under a tenner. If you want the upscale Carmel experience of a nice lunch with a glass of wine, this is the spot. Both à la carte and prix fixe menus are available.

 Big Sur Bakery & Restaurant

47540 Hwy 1, Big Sur
MILE/EXIT: MON-75
831.667.0520
www.bigsurbakery.com
OPEN: *Mon 8a–3:30p; Tue–Thu, Sun 8a–8:30p; Fri–Sat 8a–9p*

Don't let the remote location of this rustic bakery and restaurant fool you—it's run by a seasoned ex-waiter and two CIA-trained chefs from Los Angeles, who decided to leave the proverbial rat race and open a country bakery together. The trio's culinary talent and decades of experience shine in everything they create, from the morning pastries to the evening dinners. Baked goods include famous chocolate chip cookies, croissants, and muffins, along with strong coffee and fresh-squeezed juices. Lunch and dinner focus on fresh, local ingredients, including pizzas and entrees fired in a wood-burning oven. All of it exists in a world the trio has built themselves in a 1930s farmhouse in the wilds of Big Sur, the kind of world you'd create if you were given the chance. Inside has the feel of an upscale country cabin, all dark wood and sage walls, and the leafy outdoor patio lets you avoid missing even a moment in the sun. It's a culinary commune humming away by itself in the woods, made complete by a vintage gas pump out front (pricey, but the only gas for miles)and an offbeat hippie shop and enclave next door.

KNOW: *The restrooms are little more than upscale outhouses, located down a short path on the north side of the cabin.*

Nepenthe

48510 Hwy 1, Big Sur
MILE/EXIT: MON-44
831.667.2345
www.nepenthebigsur.com
OPEN: *Daily 11:30a–10p*

It's rather unfashionable for foodie-types to like Nepenthe these days. "Overrated" is liberally bandied about on message boards, along with "tourist trap" and "way too expensive." Nepenthe might very well be all these things and more, but one needs to understand the context behind such damnations. If Nepenthe is overrated, it's only because it was *the* celebrity spot for decades, host to Henry Miller, Kim Novak, Joan Baez, and countless more, and it's set in a wooden building designed by a Frank Lloyd Wright prodigy, on land that once belonged to Orson Welles. Before writing it off as a tourist trap, consider that the thousands of travelers who pass by the driveway every year are more or less a captive audience, who know enough of Nepenthe's reputation to know they're guaranteed a good meal. And expensive . . . well, guilty as charged. Entrees climb into the $30 range; the famous Ambrosiaburger is still pricey at $14. But the modern, glassed-in dining room is literally perched on the edge of the continent, surrounded by old-growth forest and far above the crashing surf. Is an evening in such a room, eating an impressively good dinner and watching the sun set over the Pacific, really something you can put a price on?

KNOW: *Breakfast, baked goods, and coffee are available in the significantly cheaper Café Keva, on an outdoor terrace in the lower half of the restaurant. Open Presidents Day weekend to New Year's Day.*

🥧 Linn's of Cambria

2777 Main St, Cambria

MILE/EXIT: SLO-46

805.927.0371

www.linnsofcambria.com

OPEN: *Daily 8a–9p*

Thank the olallieberry. This raspberry/blackberry hybrid was virtually unknown in California before Renee Linn started selling olallieberry preserves, pies, and other specialties from the Central Coast orchard she owned with her husband. Three decades later, their empire has expanded from their original farm stand to a cafe, bakery, and specialty food store. If you only get one thing, get a slice of olallieberry pie, an oozing, sweet/tart, jammy masterpiece with a perfect crust. Better yet, buy a whole one, or try another flavor (Linn makes several pies depending on the season). Linn's Easy-as-Pie Café (4251 Bridge St; 805.924.3050) is a quicker, cheaper stop than her Main Street cafe, but both offer menus of modern comfort food (think mac-and-cheese with asiago and fontina cheeses), paired with simple soups and salads. Olallieberries appear in surprising places like lemonade and a turkey-cranberry sandwich. Don't leave without a jar of homemade olallieberry preserves.

🍪 Brown Butter Cookie Co.

250 N Ocean Ave, Cayucos

MILE/EXIT: SLO-35

805.995.2076

www.brownbuttercookies.com

OPEN: *Daily 10a–5p*

Butter is one of the most comforting and delicious substances on the planet, and this sister-owned business has managed to capture all its goodness into one bite-sized cookie. Co-owners Traci Nickson and Christa Hozie brown butter to golden perfection before adding it to a sugar-cookie dough, and finish each cookie with a pinch of sea salt after baking. The resulting cookie is crunchy, course, salty-sweet, nutty, addictive, sublime. A peek in the bakery's kitchen—watching the chefs form cookies or brown butter—will get you salivating like one of Pavlov's dogs. Other cookie flavors include cocoa, espresso, and honey. You'll know the bakery by its bright-red farmhouse exterior.

🍖 Ruddell's Smokehouse

101 D St, Cayucos

MILE/EXIT: SLO-35

805.995.5028

www.smokerjim.com

OPEN: *Daily 11a–6p*

Like a carnivorous Ahab, Jim Ruddell spent years on a monomaniacal quest to find the best smoked meat and fish on earth, before concluding that he made it himself and decided to get serious about his craft. Choosing Cayucos as his laboratory for its proximity to fresh seafood, he spent so much time smoking fish in the sun that he gained the nickname "Smoker Jim." At the storefront he eventually opened at the end of the boardwalk, peruse the whiteboard menu and see what's fresh out of the smoker. As far as food is concerned, Ruddell's offers tacos and sandwiches made from his legendary smoked pork loin, chicken, albacore tuna, or salmon, along with all the meats available to go. Smoker Jim hasn't let fame go to his head, either; the sign is hand-lettered, the press

CALIFORNIA

clippings displayed are preserved in loose plastic, the plastic picnic tables in front look like they've seen better days. Trust me: After one bite of the sandwich, none of it will matter. This is meat that truly can't be beat.

Ⓐ Avila Valley Barn

560 Avila Beach Dr, San Luis Obispo
MILE/EXIT: On Hwy 1, 2.2 miles south of Avila Beach
805.595.2810
www.avilavalleybarn.com
OPEN: *Daily May–Dec; hours vary by season. Call ahead for details.*

Instead of asking what you can do at Avila Valley Barn, ask what you *can't* do—which, judging from the sheer range of opportunities, isn't much. This collection of wooden barn buildings is actually a small-scale rural commune, containing an ice cream bar, candy store and bakery, cafe, farm stand, petting zoo, hay rides to U-pick berries, and, in the fall, a hay maze. It can all be pretty overwhelming, especially on summer weekends when it's crowded with families, but it's definitely a good place to pick up local produce, a restorative cup of coffee, or a cup of house-made ice cream. Relax away from the crowds on the deck outside the ice cream shop, overlooking the fields of berries. During the summer months, don't miss the straight-from-the-garden grilled corn, served with plenty of dripping butter.

Ⓕ The Splash Café

197 Pomeroy Ave, Pismo Beach
MILE/EXIT: SLO-15
805.773.4653
www.splashcafe.com
OPEN: *Mon–Thu, Sun 8a–8:30p; Fri–Sat 8a–9p*

Locals and travelers alike line up for a bowl of award-winning clam chowder at this casual Pismo Beach cafe, a local institution since 1989. It's astonishingly good stuff, a perfect combination of ingredients that you can't analyze; like the beginning of a great relationship, you just have to accept its goodness on faith. Beyond chowder (get the bread bowl, topped with bay shrimp), the cafe also offers a seafood-centric menu of fried fish, fish fillet sandwiches, steamers, and seafood salads, along with burgers and deli sandwiches. All is housed in a charmingly homemade storefront, with a retro neon sign and surfer murals outside, and a large undersea mural and patio furniture inside. In 2000, the cafe expanded to a second location in San Luis Obispo (1491 Monterey St; 805.544.7567).

KNOW: *Don't leave Pismo Beach without paying a visit to the "world's largest clam" at the Chamber of Commerce. (Actually, you could skip it. It's made out of cement and pretty much underwhelming. But hey—at least you've seen what an oversize clam could look like.)*

Giovanni's Fish Market & Galley

1001 Front St, Morro Bay

MILE/EXIT: SLO-28

805.772.2123

www.giovannisfishmarket.com

OPEN: *Daily 11a–6p*

Pretty much your standard no-frills seafood shack: order at the window and head to the wharfside patio and wait for your number to be called. While you wait, the local gang of sea lions makes an excellent diversion, framed by views of Morro Rock and the fishing fleet in the small historic harbor. Clam chowder is excellent here, chock-full of clams, with a nice balance of saltiness and creaminess. Fish-and-chips is nothing extraordinary, but fried fish is like pepperoni pizza—"just fine" is better than none at all. Less successful are two of the signature menu items. Fish on a stick sounds promising, but turns out to be a long fillet of greasy fried fish that slides off its wooden skewer almost immediately. The crab quesadilla might get your attention, but the delicate flavor of Dungeness crab is lost in the onslaught of Jack cheese, cilantro, and onion—I ended up taking the crab out like a picky 10-year-old and eating the quesadilla without it. The family-owned business also operates a popular fish market; there's not a whole lot to offer travelers without a cooler, but fresh-baked bread and smoked fish are appealing options. (Fish market open daily 9a–6p.)

KNOW: *Don't go here on a cold, blustery day. The back deck is it—there's no inside seating.*

Ⓨ Far Western Tavern

899 Guadalupe St, Guadalupe

MILE/EXIT: SB-49

805.343.2211

www.farwesterntavern.com

OPEN: *Tue–Thu 11a–8:30p, Fri–Sat 11a–9p, Sun 9a–8:30p*

Successful in establishing itself as one of the best spots for Santa Maria–style barbecue in all of California, this tavern is the opposite of rough-and-tumble Jocko's (see page 254). While its rival is working class, the Far Western Tavern is upscale, the place where local ranchers dress up to go to dinner on Saturday nights. Padded leather chairs, white tablecloths, scarlet wallpaper with dark wood wainscoting, and mounted steer horns above the door complete the old-school steakhouse look—but don't think for a second it's inauthentic. Owner Clarence Minetti first started eating at the tavern in the 1930s, when he could get a steak and spaghetti dinner on a field hand's salary. When his favorite spaghetti place closed, he bought the business with his wife, Rosalie, the daughter of a locally renowned ranch cook who once hosted Cecil B. DeMille for dinner (the director was in town to film *The Ten Commandments*). Clarence Minetti's first love, a 14-ounce rib eye called Bulls Eye Steak, is still the thing to order, especially since it comes with traditional Santa Maria sides like pinquito beans, salsa, and grilled garlic bread. The Minettis' children are now getting in the family game, and have successfully introduced modern menu items like fried polenta and bottled house barbecue sauce without ruining the place's old-school flavor.

Santa Barbara Wine Country

Trip Stats

LENGTH: 30 miles as the crow flies, but this road is made to meander. The trip can take an hour or it can take all day.

LOCAL FLAVOR: Pinot, chardonnay, syrah—also apples and wine region stuff. Farm-fresh, organic cuisine.

BEST TIME: Thanks to the temperate climate, there's year-round sun, cool nights, and average temperatures ranging from 40 to 76 degrees (summertime highs in the 80s, winter lows in the 40s, rainfall no more than 12 inches).

LOCAL FOOD FESTIVALS: Celebration of Harvest (October). Try the latest wines from local wineries at this party in the middle of harvest season.

WORD OF WARNING: Winding roads—watch for drunk driving. And for cyclists.

MORE INFO: Santa Barbara County Vintners' Association (www.sbcountywines.com)

Sometimes a book colonizes a place. It's hard to picture the Salinas Valley without conjuring Steinbeck; San Francisco without summoning Kerouac. "A place belongs forever to whoever claims it hardest, remembers it most obsessively, wrenches it from itself, shapes it, renders it, loves it so radically that he remakes it in his own image," Joan Didion once wrote.

In 2004, Santa Barbara Wine Country was claimed by the indie flick *Sideways*, based on the Rex Pickett novel with the same title. The story was a bromance that followed two friends through a week in Wine Country, and had a ripple effect that instantly brought the under-the-radar region into the spotlight.

For one thing, the film so thoroughly captures the place at its best, it's hard to get out of your mind (and makes you think director Alexander Payne should have been on the tourism board's payroll). Beautiful

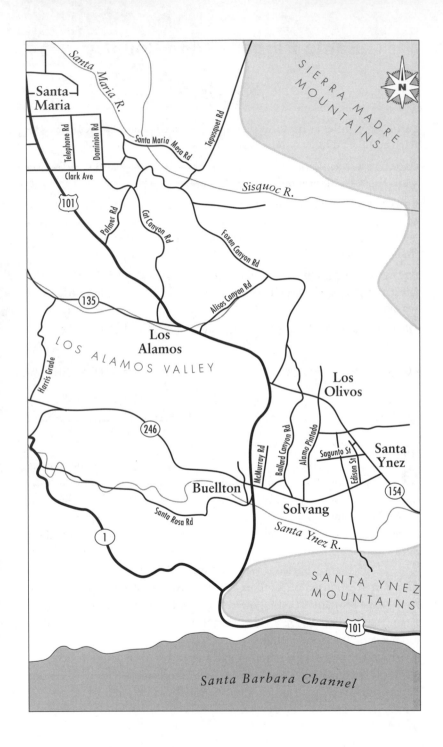

montages convey a love and respect for grapes, wine, and the road in a way few films can achieve. And then, the movie shows up everywhere. The Santa Barbara Wine Country website offers a downloadable *Sideways* wine trail map, and almost every winery or restaurant has a memento from filming: a publicity still, a framed opening night pass, even signs out front that say, "As seen in *Sideways*."

Though it's only recently come of age, Santa Barbara Wine Country is one of the oldest wine regions in California. Grapes were first brought to the Santa Barbara Mission by Father Junipero Serra in 1782, and rancheros in the late 1800s made wine for their own enjoyment (there were 45 vineyards back then). Unfortunately, Prohibition killed the burgeoning industry, and it took several more decades for the prolific wine region to get back on its feet.

And it did because Santa Barbara Wine Country is geographically unique. Unlike most in California, Santa Barbara's valleys run east-west instead of north-south, which means they get all the benefit of the cool ocean breezes at night. This makes them the perfect region for pinots and chardonnays, which can only be grown to their full potential in cool climates. In 1970 there were 171 acres of vineyards; today there are more than 20,000 acres growing more than 65 grape varieties, 60 percent of which are chardonnay. Go ahead, call it a comeback.

The roads meander here, the culture is casual. You see farm stands that are little more than handwritten signs with someone sitting there under an umbrella. Sunbaked hills dotted with oaks. Grapes at angles on the hills, some covered with netting because of the impending harvest. Some roads cut through valleys so small you feel like you're the only person left in the world. Fields of strawberries and kale, at the ready to feed a hungry nation. And the food is good—fresh, local, in season, meant to complement the wine. It's the kind of place that puts a goofy smile on your face.

Los Olivos is the cultural hub of the region, a well-preserved Victorian town whose main streets are lined with art galleries, tasting rooms, and organic cafes, which coexist peacefully with saddlery shops that service the area's sizeable rancher population. It's also a good place to consolidate your wine tasting if you don't have a lot of time. Grand Avenue is lined with small tasting rooms, in many cases the only place to try a winemaker's wine. Pick one and take your chances, or head to Los Olivos

Tasting Room & Wine Shop, which specializes in pinot noir from dozens of wineries around the region.

Our visit turned out to be a halfhearted *Sideways* tour—we slept at the Windmill, ate at the Hitching Post, and walked along an uneasy trail following the movie's footsteps. It wasn't intentional—it's just what you *do* in the region. The movie followed the local rhythms of life so beautifully that it made them immortal.

Note: The mile/exit numbers in the following section refer to Highway 101.

ON THE ROAD

Rancho Sisquoc Winery

6600 Foxen Canyon Rd, Santa Maria

MILE/EXIT: 169

DISTANCE FROM HWY: 14 miles

805.934.4332

www.ranchosisquoc.com

OPEN: *Mon–Thu 10a–4p, Fri–Sun 10a–5p*

A visit to this charming, low-key winery is an escape from the modern world and a chance to see the valley as it was 150 years ago. The turnoff is marked by a whitewashed adobe chapel left over from the Spanish empire—the same chapel that graces this winemaker's labels. Follow the short road past cattle pastures and rows of dusty kale blocked from the wind by shimmering olive trees. The road ends at the tasting room, an old wood-plank building under an olive tree that looks and feels like it's always been there. It might as well have—the winery is one of the first in the valley, part of a former 37,000-acre land grant that's now owned by the Flood Ranch Company. Inside, the tasting room is nothing fancy, but its charming rusticity is an excellent backdrop to the big, spicy reds the winery is known for, including a soft, juicy Malbec and a very good Meritage blend.

KNOW: *Don't overlook the winery's sweet, palate-cleansing wine crackers, a step up from the pretzels and saltines you find elsewhere.*

Foxen

7200 & 7600 Foxen Canyon Rd, Santa Maria

MILE/EXIT: 169

DISTANCE FROM HWY: 14 miles

805.937.4251

www.foxenvineyard.com

OPEN: *Daily 11a–4p*

Foxen winery is divided into two tasting rooms that may as well represent the division between the past and present of the region's winemaking. It's no coincidence that Foxen is also the name of the canyon, the road through the canyon, and the elementary school you passed on the way in. William Foxen was a homesteader with a Mexican land grant and something of a local hero, who was instrumental in the American takeover of Santa Barbara. You first arrive at his original blacksmith shop-turned-winery, called "7200." The small, dim room could seem oppressive, but it's open to air and light on each side and feels casual, breezy. Keeping with the old-school spirit, the wines poured here are Cal-Italian and Bordeaux-style blends, big on flavor.

7200 does have a new patio, all modern poured cement, with picnic tables decorated with succulents. Those same clean lines and spare aesthetic are carried over in the new solar-powered winery 30 seconds down the road. Inside are pale colors and high ceilings with skylights that seem to capture all the light of California. Appropriately, whites are poured here—chardonnay, pinot noir, Rhone-style wines. Still, it's anchored to the past, literally, by the imposing wrought-iron anchor at the front entrance, which was William Foxen's cattle brand and is now the winery's label.

KNOW: *The winery offers a twofer option, which includes three tastings at one building and three at the other. Or you can go big and do a full round at each.*

CALIFORNIA

Firestone Vineyard

5000 Zaca Station Rd, Los Olivos
MILE/EXIT: 146
805.688.3940
www.firestonewine.com
OPEN: *Daily 10a–5p*

You can tell that this is much more commercial than many of the wineries in the valley as you come up the long driveway—if the sprawling estate vineyards in either direction didn't tip you off, than the tour buses idling in the parking lot certainly will. Firestone has a traditional large-scale winery tasting room, designed by the powerhouse firm that also designed Robert Mondavi Winery, and though it's very elegant and has large windows overlooking the vineyards, it lacks the intimacy of many of the smaller spots. (It's owned by the Foley Family, a corporate giant that also owns Sonoma's Sebastiani.) However, don't judge this winery by its cover. Firestone was started by the son of tire legend Harvey Firestone, who showed his own entrepreneurial spark when he saw potential in Santa Barbara winemaking before anyone else. When it was established in 1972, Firestone was the county's first estate winery. It offers a full library of wines, including sauvignon blanc, chardonnay, merlot, and cabernet sauvignon.

KNOW: *In 2007, Firestone opened a second location in Paso Robles, focusing on Bordeaux-style reds (2300 Airport Rd; 805.591.8050).*

TOURS: *The free 30-min tour gives a good lesson in Wine-making 101. Sideways alert: This is the attractive barrel room where Miles, Maya, Jack, and Stephanie sneak away for some serious canoodling. (Daily 11:15a, 1:15p, 3:15p)*

Rusack Vineyards

1819 Ballard Canyon Rd, Solvang
MILE/EXIT: 146
805.688.1278
www.rusackvineyards.com
OPEN: *Daily 11a–5p*

All too often people barrel through Wine Country, intent on hitting every spot on their list. Why stress on a weekend that's supposed to be leisurely? Instead, spend an afternoon, or at least a significant portion of one, at this bucolic winery, tucked in the foothills behind Los Olivos.

I guarantee the rest of the world will melt away as you sip an excellent pinot noir on the redwood patio, shaded by oaks, gazing out on the estate vineyards and the yellow hills beyond, letting the sights and sounds of Wine Country wash over you. Or, not. If time is of the essence, the tasting room is very pleasant, a cool mix of modern and traditional beach architecture. Large photos show off owners Geoff and Alison Rusack's new Catalina vineyard, the island's first, located next to the Wrigley estate (home of the gum baron), a fact our pourer helpfully supplied. When her back was turned, the man next to me, who had already hit more than a few tasting rooms, leaned over and loudly whispered, "Mrs. Rusack is a Wrigley." Ah. That explains the island cool and the logo, based on a piece of Catalina tile. Whether she meant to or not, Alison Wrigley Rusack designed a winery that's also an island. Slow down and enjoy your time on it.

Los Olivos Grocery

2621 Hwy 154, Santa Ynez

MILE/EXIT: 146

DISTANCE FROM HWY: 5.4 miles

805.688.5115

www.losolivosgrocery.com

OPEN: *Daily 7a–7p*

This small gourmet grocery store is the go-to stop for picnic fixings and other gourmet goodies on the Santa Barbara wine trail. Like Oakville Market in Napa, this started as a normal country grocery store in the 1930s but has since developed into a stop servicing picnickers and local foodies. The grocery store itself is reminiscent of Whole Foods (it was started by a former Whole Foods exec) and has plenty of gourmet items on the shelves—local produce, good bread, a stellar selection of local wine, and fancy regional cheeses with short explanations of each. Most visitors skip the store and head straight to the back deli, which sells sandwiches named for local landmarks (Happy Canyon Club, Valley Veggie), and snacky items like orzo salad, caprese, and dolmades. On the weekends, the Santa Maria–style barbecue grill is fired up, and the grocery turns out tri-tip sandwiches that have become something of local legend. There is also a small restaurant attached to the screened patio; eat a light organic lunch with great views of Wine Country. The shop's slogan— "We've got the good stuff"—isn't far off the mark.

CALIFORNIA

Los Olivos Café & Wine Merchant

2879 Grand Ave, Los Olivos

MILE/EXIT: 146

805.688.7265

www.losolivoscafe.com

OPEN: *Daily 11:30a–8:30p*

Every good town has a place like this: equally good for date night (it's where Miles and Jack have their big double date in *Sideways*), dinner with the parents, or a snack and a glass of wine. The excellent food focuses on Mediterranean-influenced cuisine made from organic ingredients, including a messy eight-ounce beef burger on a brioche bun, elegant pasta dishes, and addictive thin-crust pizzas at lunchtime. But the food is actually the wingman—wine is the focal point of the cafe, which doubles as a stellar wine shop with a tasting bar. Sit inside and admire the shop's bottle selection, which takes up an entire wall and then some, or sit outside on the wisteria-draped patio and watch life in downtown Los Olivos pass by. Either way, the whole atmosphere feels effortless, a simple enjoyment of the pleasures of wine, food, and life. You get the impression that the owners have spent plenty of time on a vineyard, picking grapes in the sun—and though part of you envies them for it, part of you is grateful to join their *joie de vivre* for this one meal at least.

KNOW: *The olive oil dipping sauce that starts the meal is outstanding, and for sale at the wine shop.*

Panino

2900 Grand Ave, Los Olivos

MILE/EXIT: 146

805.688.9304

www.paninorestaurants.com

OPEN: *Daily 10a–4p*

A local chain, Panino offers good sandwiches delivered speedily—isn't that all you ask from a sandwich bar? The panini lineup changes slightly at each location, but it's the same in spirit, offering Italian deli sandwiches on foccacia. Grinders may require a nap after completion, but these are fresh, made from high-quality ingredients, and not loaded down with too much oil or meat. Go simple with a roast turkey, or step outside the box with the roast chicken with pesto, pine nuts, feta, and sun-dried tomatoes, or the popular curried chicken salad. Vegetarians will be pleased with the large selection of veg-friendly sandwiches and salads. Grab a local beer and sit under the umbrella-shaded tables out front, or pack a sandwich for a winery picnic.

KNOW: *The Los Olivos location has no bathrooms, but there are public restrooms across the street.*

VARIOUS LOCATIONS *in Solvang, Santa Barbara, and Goleta*

Corner House Coffee

2902 San Marcos Ave, Los Olivos

MILE/EXIT: 146

805.688.1722

www.cornerhousecoffee.com

OPEN: *Mon–Fri 6:30a–5p, Sat–Sun 7a–5p*

Cash only

In 1962, political philosopher Jurgen Habermas wrote his theory on the importance of the "public sphere," locations outside of one's home and work where social and political issues could be openly discussed and public opinion could be formed. He would have liked Corner House Coffee a *lot*. It's the perfect coffee shop: leather chairs, high ceilings, creaky floors, a large reclaimed wooden table, and a charming outdoor seating area partially shaded by a giant old oak. Locals shoot the breeze over Peet's coffee and breakfast snacks like granola, breakfast burritos, egg sandwiches, and McConnell's ice cream. It all feels very comfortable and welcoming, and you might be tempted to stay and join the conversation if the Wine Country photographs on the walls don't remind you to keep moving.

🍶 Global Gardens

2477 Alamo Pintado Ave, Los Olivos

MILE/EXIT: 146

805.693.1600

www.oliverevolution.com

OPEN: *Daily 11a–5p*

Gourmet artisans often get the short end of the stick—they're regulated to specialty shops or jammed into the corners of wine shops almost as an afterthought. This tasting room puts them into the spotlight. A few bucks gets you samples of local and international olive oils, including the store's own line of oils and fruit-infused vinegars, made with local wine grapes and flavored with strawberries, blood oranges, apricots, and figs. The knowledgeable staff will help you pair olive oils, vinegars, and spice blends to create extraordinary combinations—not only that, they'll make sure you're confident you can re-create the combinations at home. The shop also stocks finishing glazes, appetizer spreads made from local artichokes and olives, organic mustards, and more. It's a good place to swing by when you want something different for a picnic basket.

🍴 Cold Spring Tavern

5595 Stagecoach Rd, Santa Barbara

MILE/EXIT: 146

DISTANCE FROM HWY: 20 miles

805.967.0066

www.coldspringtavern.com

OPEN: *Mon–Fri 11a–2:45p, 5–8:30p; Sat–Sun 8a–8:30p*

It's about a half hour out of your way (and halfway to Santa Barbara), but just think about how long it must have taken the stagecoach passengers who used to frequent this 1866 rest stop-turned-restaurant. The road winds through the hills and over San Marcos Pass—the same pass that Benjamin Foxen led American generals over in 1846. The tavern itself is pretty much what you'd expect, with big stone fireplaces, rough-hewn walls hung with relics from the past, along with plenty of taxidermied animal heads. It's busy at dinner (reservations are pretty much required), but you can drop in for a casual breakfast or lunch and soak up the pioneer atmosphere. Breakfast offers the usual standards along with flapjacks, house-made biscuits, whole wheat–molasses bread, and venison sausage; lunch has a good burger with homemade mayonnaise, the ubiquitous tri-tip sandwich, a buffalo burger, venison steak sandwich, and famous chili.

KNOW: *Stimulate your digestion while you stroll around the grounds—check out the "Road Gang House" where Chinese laborers stayed while building the road, the Ojai Jail, and four storage buildings in the back that are all that's left of the ghost town of Gopherville.*

 Apple Lane Farm

1200 Alamo Pintado Rd, Solvang

MILE/EXIT: 140A

805.688.5481

www.applelanesolvang.com

OPEN: *Daily during apple season, mid- to late Aug–Nov; call for details*

The four-person Lane family owns, operates, and does most of the hard labor on this small apple farm—that is, unless you decide to do some of the apple-picking for them. During apple season, the 1,500 pesticide-free fruit trees are open to anyone with a basket and the willingness to get their hands dirty. The apple variety you pick depends on the month: Galas ripen first, in mid- to late August; Golden and Red Delicious appear in September and the first part of October; later that month is all Fuji and Granny Smith; by November, Granny Smith are the only apples available. Or skip the labor and buy pre-picked apples at the small country store, and pick up some of Peggy Lane's famous apple crisp (the recipe is on the back of an available flier). The Lanes are also very involved with the local community: Peggy leads educational tours for kids and donates apples to the Santa Barbara County Public Library for its reading incentive program.

KNOW: *Like DIY? Also hit up Morrell Nut & Berry Farm down the street, for U-pick raspberries and blackberries from June to September and walnuts in October and November (1980 Alamo Pintado Rd, Solvang; 805.688.8969).*

🍴 The Red Viking Restaurant

1684 Copenhagen Dr, Solvang

MILE/EXIT: 140A

803.688.6610

www.theredvikingrestaurant.com

OPEN: *Daily 8a–8p*

For some reason, smorgasbord—the traditional Scandinavian mezze buffet featuring hot and cold meats and salads—never caught on like tapas in America. (Is it because of the silly name? Are we really that shallow?) At any rate, I find it hard to say I'm eating smorgasbord for lunch with a straight face, and even harder when I'm eating it in a restaurant with an entrance flanked by ginger-haired wooden warriors. I've been told a trip to a good smorgasbord is a study in subtle flavors, textures, and temperatures, but unless you've got a real jones for dishes like pickled herring, you should probably just go with a house specialty like stick-to-your ribs sausages and meatballs covered in gravy, or a *smorrebrod*—traditional Danish open-face sandwiches with things like pork and prunes, liver pâté, and Danish ham and cheese. Wash it all down with a Carlsberg and finish off your meal with *aebelskiver.*

KNOW: *Get more context for Solvang by reading the detailed history of the town printed on the placemats.*

🍴 Solvang Restaurant

1672 Copenhagen Dr, Solvang

MILE/EXIT: 140A

805.688.4645

www.solvangrestaurant.com

OPEN: *Mon–Fri 6a–3p, Sat 6a–5p, Sun 7a–5p*

This kitschy restaurant proudly bills itself as "Home of Arne's Famous Aebelskiver," and, deserving of their fame or not, Arne's *aebelskivers* have spawned a mix, postcard, and short informational video, which plays on a loop in the front window next to the *aebelskiver*-devoted takeout window. The fritters themselves are unappealingly spongy and coated with a raspberry jam sauce that's somehow too sweet and too bitter simultaneously, and the rest of the Danish-American menu is fairly pedestrian. However, it's one of those cases where the food is enhanced by the atmosphere. This is where Miles and Jack eat breakfast in *Sideways*, and the cafe's interior goes all-out for Denmark. It was designed by a master Danish woodworker, who carved Danish proverbs in the ceiling timbers and Danish village crests on the wooden booths, and the walls are covered by murals of Hans Christian Andersen fairy tales.

Wandering Dog Wine Bar

1539C Mission Dr, Solvang

MILE/EXIT: 140A

805.686.9126

www.wanderingdogwinebar.com

OPEN: *Mon–Thu 1–8p, Fri–Sat 11a–8p*

This is where you go to take a breather from Solvang and re-enter the real world. The bar's motto is "Leave your leash behind," and like all good wine bars, Wandering Dog is focused on education. There are more than 200 wines on the menu and nearly 50 by-the-glass choices, with the lion's share sourced from the surrounding valleys. The real value, though, are the themed flights. Having a set of chardonnays, say, side-by-side really helps you understand the variations in flavor, color, and complexity between winemakers—a perspective that you never get in a single tasting. There's also a solid selection of microbrews on tap, and

---

Solvang

It's easy to make fun of Solvang, poor thing. To be fair, a completely over-the-top faux Danish town in the middle of Wine Country is a pretty strange sight. But it's precisely the over-the-top nature that makes it unlike other themed towns, which often seem gimmicky or opportunistic. Solvang was founded in 1911 by an earnest group of Danish educators setting up a colony and Lutheran school, and there's something about their wholehearted initial effort that's stuck around, despite all the tourist kitsch and ridiculousness. Don't leave without sampling *aebelskiver* (fried dough balls), *kringle* (pastry filled with almond paste), and other Danish specialties.

CALIFORNIA

a palate-cleansing pale ale is the best antidote when you feel like you'll scream the next time someone wants to discuss the structured elegance of pinot.

KNOW: *True to its name, the bar is dog-friendly. There's a jar of dog biscuits by the front door, and pups are encouraged on the patio with their owners.*

(¶) Paula's Pancake House

1531 Mission Dr, Solvang

MILE/EXIT: 140A

805.688.2867

OPEN: *Daily 6a–3p*

A close relative of the crepe, Scandinavian pancakes are paper-thin sheets of sweet, yeasty dough, folded upon themselves, and covered with jam and powdered sugar. The pancake at Paula's is so big it hangs over the plate, and it's very sweet—opt for fresh fruit over the cloying warm apples—and though it comes with a glass of syrup, pouring *more* sugar on top would bring on early-onset diabetes. Do at least taste the dollop of fresh, thick whipped cream, and order a side of Danish sausages, which are smoother in texture than their American counterparts and have the same distinct spice as Ikea meatball gravy. Generally speaking, nothing about this breakfast will change your life, but the waitresses are clad in traditional blue embroidered aprons, the room has properly atmospheric dark wood walls and ceiling timbers, and there's a wood-burning stove in the corner halfheartedly decorated with a wooden clog. All in all, it's the kind of place you feel like you *should* eat when you're in Solvang, and on that criterion, it totally delivers.

(🍰) Oleson's Danish Village Bakery and Coffee Shop

1529 Mission Dr, Solvang

MILE/EXIT: 140A

805.688.6314

www.olsensdanishvillagebakery.com

OPEN: *Daily 7a–7p*

This no-frills bakery has bright fluorescent lighting and too many tables, but none of that matters when you step up to the pastry case, which is about a mile long and has nearly every kind of sweet you can think of. The Danes take their pastries seriously—and a bakery like this shows you the full potential of the "danish," which doesn't have to be the effete, pulverized, sugar-delivery system dotted with cream cheese you get at 7-11. These are varied, substantial, delicious; especially the sour cherry "boat," which had light, crumbly pastry encircling a surprisingly tart cherry center. Do try a slice of the house specialty, *kringle*, which is unofficially the Danish national pastry. After that, you can pretty much close your eyes and point—you really can't go wrong. (The same principle can be applied to smorgasbord, come to think of it.) If you're planning a picnic later, the award-winning Shepherd's Bread would make great sandwiches.

KNOW: *Pick up a branded tub of cookies for someone at home. They're a steal at $10 for three, and make great, silly gifts.*

CALIFORNIA

SOUTHERN CALIFORNIA

Sunshine, oranges, and surfers at the southernmost part of the state, home of McDonald's, the fish taco, French dip sandwich, and more.

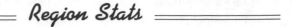 *Region Stats*

LOCAL FLAVOR:

- **Oranges:** This valuable citrus drove a whole nation to move to the coast.

- **Fish tacos:** Brought to the states via San Diego, now a fixture at every taco shack.

- **Road food:** This is the region where road food was invented—and burgers, shake shacks, and other specialties abound.

E uropeans were exploring Southern California before anyone ever settled in Roanoke, but Southern California owes its identity to the twentieth century. This was the century the orange tree blossomed, the Hollywood sign was erected, the automobile was invented, the interstate highway system was developed, Disneyland was created, advertising became king, the Beach Boys released "California Girls." It was the century that introduced the masses to the land of sunshine and oranges—the new American Dream.

It was the railroad that brought the masses of the Midwest. Just as the Oregon Trail had mobilized a generation, so did the completion of the railroad system stretching across the country. But Midwesterners weren't going to come running to an arid desert the way they had poured into the fertile Willamette—they needed to be convinced. Enter the marketing genius of the Southern Pacific Railroad and Los Angeles booster Charles Fletcher Lummis. Lummis published a magazine called *Land of Sunshine* effusively praising Southern California's year-round sunshine and healthful lifestyle, even going so far as to write that Los Angeles was "the new Eden for the Saxon homeseeker." The railroad took a different approach: it went straight to the gut. The railroad's advertising posters of California produce—oversized strawberries, orange trees set on a background of purple mountains—sold the region like no region had been sold before.

And the people bought the marketing vision and came—no longer by covered wagon, but by railroad and then by Oldsmobile wagon over Route 66. Between 1900 and 1940, the population of Los Angeles grew by 1,535 percent (San Francisco only grew a modest 172 percent). Some reached Southern California and thought it was hell. Some thought it was heaven. Most settled down in neat suburban homesteads. By 1930, only a third of the state's population had been born there.

If Southern California fits a stereotype, it's only because it's a consciously constructed one. It's where beach culture and Hollywood collide to make millionaires out of the lucky few, and to absorb the disappointment of others whose dreams were crushed along the Pacific shore. Advertising a dream has its downsides. But at its core, the dream is still alive.

Trips in Southern California

Los Angeles
The hyperreal city is ready for its culinary close-up. (Page 301)

Inland Empire
We couldn't write a book on road food without including Route 66, the original road food route. (Page 311)

Orange County and San Diego
Fish tacos, beachside burger shacks, sun, and surf. (Page 319)

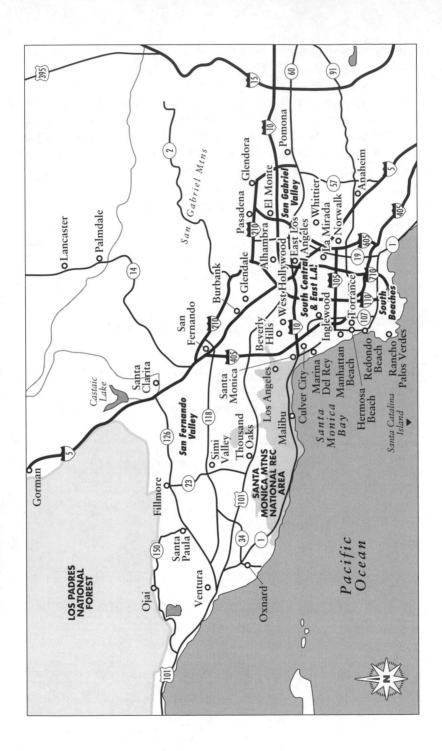

Los Angeles

City Stats

LOCAL FLAVOR: Ethnic food, Mexican food, mobile restaurants, and pretty much every cuisine under the sun.

BEST TIME: Spring, early summer, late September and October.

WORST TIME: Despite popular myth, there is weather in Los Angeles. Best avoided in January, when there are torrential rains; June, when "June gloom" fog permeates the coast and makes everyone depressed; and September, when it is hideously hot and the Santa Ana winds make people irritable.

WORD OF WARNING: There is always traffic. You'll get stuck in it. Get over it.

MORE INFO: The Los Angeles Convention and Visitors Bureau (www.discoverlosangeles.com)

Los Angeles "brings it all together," or so its official city slogan would have us believe. Part urban jungle, part beach bonanza, part Hollywood theme park, Los Angeles plays such a complex role in the American imagination that it's nearly impossible to distinguish fact from fiction, dream from reality. L.A. has been adored, despised, censored, feared, born again—often in the same breath. Like they say, it's complicated.

I have moved away from Los Angeles twice, swearing up and down I'll never return to the land of hour-long commutes, middle-of-the-night traffic jams, and shallow citizens—the common gripes about L.A. And yet I have returned, each time not really knowing why. The simplest explanation is that love it or hate it, L.A. has a hold on me, as it does on the thousands of dreamers who come here with high expectations. It's a city predicated on the idea that anything can happen.

The dark side of a culture built on hope has been exhaustively dissected in novels, essays, movies, TV shows—all decrying the downside of the American dream and the irrigated artificiality of L.A. For me, Los Angeles is most captivating not as a lost paradise, but as an optimistic

CALIFORNIA

search for one. Whether you are coming or going, staying or leaving, L.A. gives you a glimpse of the lengths we will go to make fantasy become reality.

This is true about the food in particular. Los Angeles is the birthplace of the Cobb salad, the French dip sandwich, the Monte Cristo, the chili dog, and most recently, the Korean taco. All foods created on the passing impulse, *What happens when I combine this and this?* Los Angeles is also a city of restaurants in silly buildings. The Brown Derby has long been bulldozed, but there is still Randy's giant doughnut and the original Bob's Big Boy in the Valley. It is the opposite of Northern California's simplicity and finesse.

As a home for drifters and dreamers, Los Angeles houses the greatest variety of ethnic food in the nation. L.A. has exceptional Mexican cuisine spread across the basin, but it also has a lively Koreatown, Thai Town, and Little Armenia. I picked locations that I liked, but they barely scratch the surface. If you're serious about eating around Los Angeles, start with *LA Weekly* critic Jonathan Gold's unparalleled *Counter Intelligence*, a compendium of his restaurant reviews—at press time, Gold is the only food writer to win a Pulitzer Prize.

WESTSIDE (405)

🍴 Bay Cities Italian Deli

1517 Lincoln Blvd, Santa Monica

MILE/EXIT: 55A

310.395.8279

www.baycitiesitaliandeli.com

OPEN: *Tue–Sat 9a–7p, Sun 9a–6p*

Angelenos talk about the Godmother sandwich with hushed, reveren-tial tones, afraid to put words to the beauty of it. It certainly lives up to its name, a superlative creation piled with Boars Head ham, genoa, capicolla, mortadella, and provolone, then covered with "The Works," which includes mayonnaise, mustard, pickles, shredded lettuce, toma-toes, marinated peppers, Italian dressing, and a mild or hot pepper salad. (The hot is medium hot, and can lead to heartburn.) But the Godmother's secret is in the bread, which is baked fresh in-house, some say on the hour, and is chewy in all the right places with a crisp outer shell you have to work for. The resistance of the bread also makes this one of the messi-est sandwiches on earth; eating this while driving is certainly more dan-gerous than texting. Grab extra napkins, a limonata, or cold Illy canned espresso, and take it to the picnic tables outside or head a few blocks west to Santa Monica beach.

KNOW: *The deli is usually busy, but gets very busy on weekend afternoons (the wait for a sandwich can be up to an hour). The staff usually leaves premade Godmother sandwiches out on the deli counter for quick access, or you can call ahead with your order and pick it up in the back left corner of the store, over in the wine section.*

🍐 Santa Monica Sunday Farmers Market

2640 Main St, Santa Monica

MILE/EXIT: 53 (from 405) onto I-10, then exit 1B

310.458.8712, ext. 5

www.smgov.net/farmers_market

OPEN: *Sun 9:30a–1p*

Whenever someone tells me that they "could never live in L.A.," I wish I could somehow explain the feeling of the Santa Monica Sunday Farmers

CALIFORNIA

Market. Santa Monica is known for its Wednesday market, an amazing four-block stretch where the chefs shop, but this is where the people shop, and it is lovely. There is live bluegrass, a number of food stands, so many bicycles there's a bike valet, and since it is always sunny you can get your breakfast fajita and sit in the sun and listen to the music and read the Sunday *Times*. Sometimes there are celebrities there, and sometimes there are obnoxious rich Santa Monicans who have children with names like "Ocean," but you are so mellow on the good vibes that neither affects you very much. It is also two blocks from the beach, so if you eat too much you can walk it off.

Tito's Tacos

11222 Washington Pl, Culver City

MILE/EXIT: 52

310.391.5780

www.titostacos.com

OPEN: *Sun–Thu 10a–10p, Fri–Sat 10a–11p*

Cash only

The best tacos titillate your taste buds with explosions of new flavors in every bite—the sharp tang of raw onion, the smooth burn of salsa, the verdant cool of cilantro. This is not that kind of taco. Visually, these wouldn't be out of place in a middle school cafeteria counter, but appearances can be deceiving. Shredded beef is fried in more lard than you want to know about, scooped into a fresh corn taco shell, topped with iceberg lettuce and grated cheese, and served with tomato salsa that's more like gazpacho. I can't explain exactly what's so delicious about this taco, but most of Los Angeles agrees with me. There's always a crowd at the walk-up window, a blend of Angelenos from all walks of life, but the staff is super efficient and the line always goes quickly. A visit to Tito's is something delightfully democratic and essential, especially while sitting at a picnic table outside in the shadow of the 405 freeway and a few emaciated palm trees. This is what Los Angeles is all about.

KNOW: *Be conservative with your order. These tacos are small-but-mighty gut bombs.*

🍩 Randy's Donuts

805 W Manchester Blvd, Inglewood
MILE/EXIT: 47
310.645.4707
www.randys-donuts.com
OPEN: *24/7*

You may recognize this giant doughnut from such productions as *Iron Man 2*, *The Simpsons*, and *Arrested Development*—the larger-than-life fiberglass treat sits atop a real doughnut stand near the L.A. airport, and is worth a visit just to say you were there. Once upon a time, Los Angeles was crazy for this kind of expressive architecture, where the shape of the building represented the goods it sold. These days, this 1953 doughnut stand is one of the only examples remaining. Once you get over the novelty, you realize this is nothing but a regular doughnut shop, and the doughnuts here are nothing exceptional—order the apple fritter and plain glazed, which is the variety that leaves frosted sugar on your upper lip—but what do you care? You're here to take a picture and put it on Facebook.

Los Angeles Food Trucks

Much has been made about the L.A. mobile food truck explosion, and for good reason. Los Angeles is a city that is built on mobility—always has been—and the idea that a restaurant on wheels could come to you, instead of you having to drive to it, is both revolutionary and obvious at the same time. Taco trucks ("roach coaches") have been around forever, but this latest development takes the basic concept one step further, to the land of gourmet. There are dim sum trucks, pancake trucks, hot wing trucks, margarita trucks, Vietnamese sandwich trucks, and everything else under the sun; it's a citywide celebration of the area's diversity. If you only try one, you should try the one that started the whole craze: Kogi Korean BBQ, Korean-Mexican fusion of the type that could only happen in Los Angeles. The short rib taco, piled with kimchi and a spicy sauce, makes you rethink what a taco means and will make you weep with happiness. The kimchi quesadilla and short rib burrito are also popular options. Track the truck on its website or Twitter feed (www.kogibbq.com; @KOGIBBQ).

EASTSIDE (101)

Galco's Soda Pop Stop

5702 York Blvd, Los Angeles

MILE/EXIT: 3B(exit 30A from 110 N)

DISTANCE FROM HWY: 6.7 miles

323.255.7115

www.sodapopstop.com

OPEN: *Mon–Sat 9a–6:30p, Sun 9a–5p*

You'll never think about soda the same way again after you visit this linoleum-tiled, 1950s throwback shop in Eagle Rock, where owner John Nese presides over his empire of more than 500 arcane, hard-to-find, or downright forgotten glass-bottled sodas from around the world. Discover dozens of variations on cola, root beer, and cream soda, or take a chance on more exotic-sounding flavors like cucumber, rose, and espresso. There is little rhyme or reason to the organization of the aisles, which is part of the place's charm; ask Nese and he'll guide you to the right soda, and give you a hearty primer on soda history, mouthfeel involving variations in bubble size, and his personal vendetta against corn syrup. It all could verge on conspiracy theory dullness, but Nese's childlike delight in soda pop, along with a sizeable vintage candy collection, saves him from veering into obnoxious territory, and makes you hope that the soda you will inevitably walk out with will help restore your own sense of wonder.

KNOW: *There is also a deli in back (Galco's started life downtown in 1897 as an Italian grocery store, and moved to its current location in 1955), which serves perfectly serviceable hoagies.*

Musso & Frank Grill

6667 Hollywood Blvd, Los Angeles

MILE/EXIT: 8B

323.467.7788

www.mussoandfrankgrill.com

OPEN: *Tue–Thu 11a–11p, Fri–Sat 11a–2p*

William Faulkner ate here during his stint as a motion picture screen-writer. So did F. Scott Fitzgerald, Ernest Hemingway, and an entire galaxy of movie stars, directors, and producers. This Hollywood chop-house doesn't wear its historical pedigree on its sleeve. It's got class in the old-fashioned sense of the word, and is a great antidote to the lingering tawdriness of Hollywood Boulevard outside and the garish neon Times Square that Hollywood and Highland, a few blocks down, has become. Musso & Frank hasn't changed much since the days of Faulkner and Fitzgerald, but it's not a museum piece. Much is said about the gin mar-tinis, and rightly so, but be careful: they are strong enough to soothe even the most disillusioned screenwriter. In today's culinary world, the food at Musso's might seem dull, some even say bland, but to dismiss this as a failing is to miss the point. Musso's hearkens back to a time when garlic was considered "ethnic" and Julia Child was just entering elementary school. The steaks and chops are perfectly cooked, but it's fun to order something you'd never ordinarily, like tongue, and a side of creamed spinach. The waiters here are the career variety, reminiscent of when being a waiter was an art, not a stopgap until your acting career takes off, and their professionalism shows in every interaction.

⑪ Philippe's the Original

1001 N Alameda St, Los Angeles
MILE/EXIT: 3A
213.628.3781
www.philippes.com/
OPEN: *Daily 6a–10p*

There is a long, boring debate among Angelenos about whether Philippe's or downtown rival Cole's invented the French dip sandwich. Honestly—who cares? The French dip sandwich was a delicious invention either way, and I'm glad that one of them came up with it. Your personal preference comes down to ambiance. Cole's is great in a sit-down, old-school way (Jonathan Gold wrote of its "romantic, Chandleresque dinginess"), but Philippe's is the working-class version, from the sawdust on the floor to the lines to the old signs on the walls. Coffee is still 10 cents, which is the exact kind of gimmicky throwback that I'm a sucker for. The line for a sandwich can be long, but it's good for people watching and equally good for wondering who orders arcane deli items like pickled pig's feet. Whatever you do, have your order ready when you reach the counter (these people are tired of your nonsense, and have been tired of your nonsense for more than 50 years). Watch as they pull a crispy French roll out, dunk it in au jus (ask for "single dip," "double dip," or "wet"), and pile it high with steaming meat—beef is the traditional order, but pork, ham, turkey, and lamb are also available. Then find a table (there's a whole warren of rooms upstairs if the downstairs tables are full—they are utilitarian, but have a lot of natural light). Augment your sandwich as you see fit with the table mustard, but exercise restraint at first; this is the kind of mustard that gets up your nasal passage and makes your eyes water if you take too much of a snootful at once.

 Olvera Street

845 N Alameda St, Los Angeles
MILE/EXIT: 3A
213.625.7074
www.olvera-street.com
OPEN: *Daily 10a–7p*

The site of the first house in Los Angeles has been turned into a kitschy tourist attraction, but there is something so earnest about its kitschiness that it seems almost authentic. Here you can buy the same sort of junk you can buy at tourist shops in Mexico—bright striped blankets, lucha libre masks, Loteria cards, light-up Jesus statues—and you can also enjoy the same street food. Mr. Churro stands in the main square, and across from him is a fresh-juice cart most days, the kind you would never dare try in Mexico City. (Though locals hardly drink from the tap, Los Angeles water certainly won't make you sick.) Some stands have things like candied yams that make great snacks later. And if you want a hot meal, Casa La Golondrina claims to be the first Mexican restaurant in Los Angeles and still offers perfectly serviceable combo meals and margaritas, with the added bonus of mariachi serenades at night.

 El Tepeyac

812 N Evergreen Ave, Los Angeles
MILE/EXIT: 19 (after merging on to I-10 E)
323.268.1960
www.manuelseltepeyac.com
OPEN: *Mon–Tue 6a–8p; Wed–Thu, Sun 6a–10p; Fri–Sat 6a–11p*

The L.A. River downtown is one of those unspoken lines most white people in Los Angeles won't cross—across the moat lies East L.A., the Latino part of town. Some of the city's most authentic Mexican fare can be found across the bridge, racial boundaries be damned, but El Tepeyac is most famous to Westsiders, and the most accessible to the unadventurous—anything that's been featured in an episode of the Travel Channel's *Man v. Food* has to be safe. The food is outstanding but it's more about the legend: The burrito here is bigger than your head, and I am not exaggerating. Sit at the counter or take one of the tables. Behind the counter there are things like framed high school diplomas and baby pictures curling at the edges; this is a family-owned operation, and has been for dozens of years.

KNOW: *The Manuel Special is a five-pound monster of a burrito, topped with tomato sauce and melted cheese.*

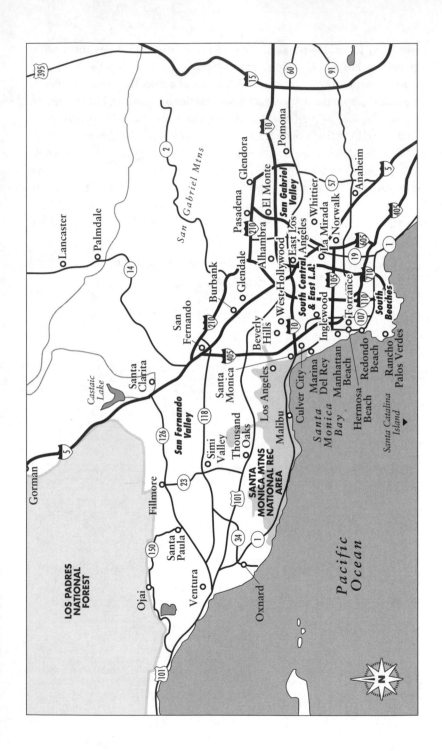

Inland Empire (I-10)

Route 66. Can anything summon up the romance and yearning of the open road as effectively as those two words? This ribbon of highway was one of the first transcontinental roads in America and stretched 2,400 miles from Chicago to Los Angeles. Route 66 is deeply ingrained in the American consciousness, a symbol more than a street, a metaphor for American migration like none other. Songs are devoted to it. John Steinbeck called it the "Mother Road" and made it a central character in *The Grapes of Wrath.*

Route 66 also introduced America to the pleasures and possibilities of the road trip. Billboards lined the highway advertising quirky attractions, kitschy restaurants, themed motels. Novelty was the goal. Much of the iconography of road food comes from "the road of second chance," as people took to calling it: neon signs, diners, mini-marts, drive-ins, blue-plate specials, homemade pies. And in San Bernardino, Route 66 passed by a hopping burger stand called McDonald's—the rest, as they say, is history.

I wish that I could say that you can still travel Route 66 through the Inland Empire, but most of it has been paved over or simply obliterated in the miles of interconnected suburbs and endless freeway interchanges. The Inland Empire was once one of the richest in all the land thanks to the citrus trees that kicked off the state's "second gold rush," but to find evidence you have to do some digging.

That's not to say it isn't worthwhile to pay your respects to the survivors. Drive west from San Bernardino and you'll pass the Wigwam Motel, where you can still rent a concrete wigwam for the night, and the sadly boarded-up Bono's giant orange is an example of the roadside juice and citrus stands that used to line the highway.

With enough imagination, you can picture how weary travelers must have felt—emigrating from the 1930s dust bowl or 1950s midwest towns—when they took a sip of fresh-squeezed orange juice and knew they were close to the end of the line. They'd reached California. They were Westerners now. And they knew that if this didn't work out, they could always pack up and hit the road.

CALIFORNIA

ON THE ROAD

🔖 Donut Man

915 E Route 66, Glendora

MILE/EXIT: 42A (exit 25A from CA-57 N)

DISTANCE FROM HWY: 6.6 miles

626.335.9111

OPEN: *Daily 6a–6p*

Cash only

The first thing to know about the Donut Man is that his doughnuts aren't very good. The buttermilk bar is disappointingly dry, the raspberry cream has all the appeal of flavored yogurt, and the less said about the coffee, the better. The second thing to know is that none of this matters. Four months out of the year, the Donut Man asserts his reign over the Inland Empire with peak-of-season strawberry and peach doughnuts that inspire pilgrimages from all over Southern California. Strictly speaking, these are closer to something you'd find in a patisserie than a doughnut shop—a mountain of fresh fruit is glazed with sticky syrup, sandwiched between slices of sugary dough, and requires a fork and several napkins to attack with any sort of success. Based on his reputation, you kind of wish everything in the bakery case held up to the legend, but after all, a mediocre doughnut is still a doughnut.

🍴 The Hat

611 E Route 66, Glendora

MILE/EXIT: 38A

626.857.0017

www.thehat.com

OPEN: *Sun–Thu 10a–11p, Sat 10a–1a*

The Hat's website features a ridiculous theme song set to the tune of that 1950s chestnut "At the Hop" (you can, I'm sure, imagine the reworked chorus). It's worth a listen for the entertainment value alone—one verse includes the phrase "When you get a case of the hungries"—but the song also highlights the restaurant's tie to a time most of us only know from Beach Boys tunes and *American Graffiti*, when cruising through the hamburger stand in a little deuce coupe was a teenager's highest aspiration. Burgers are on the menu at The Hat, but it's known for its pastrami sandwich, which is frequently included on local "best of" lists. The house-cured pastrami is peppery and not too fatty, the mustard is spicy but doesn't overpower the meat, the pickle slices add a welcome crunch, and the bun's bland sweetness tempers it all. The sandwich is made even better by the unadorned interior of the restaurant, thankfully lacking the chrome-and-vinyl nostalgia overdose of the Johnny Rockets of the world.

VARIOUS LOCATIONS *in Pasadena, Upland, Monterey Park, and Lake Forest*

⑩ Graber Olive House

315 E 4th St, Ontario

MILE/EXIT: 51

800.996.5483

www.graberolives.com

OPEN: *Daily 9a–5:30p*

One minute you're driving down residential streets somewhere in the suburban wilds of Ontario, questioning your choices in life; the next you're pulling into a circular driveway lined with bougainvillea, feeling as though you've stepped back a century to a time when the surrounding split-levels were olive groves. The Graber family now trucks their crop in from the Central Valley (it has a better growing season), but production is all still done on the premises, in many cases on the original equipment that C. C. Graber invented himself. The family's original Spanish-revival home now serves as the main retail store, where you can stop in for a sample and a chat with the woman behind the counter, who has worked here for nearly 50 years and will happily explain what makes Graber olives so special. Most California ripe olives are picked green and get their signature black color from oxidization, but Graber olives are picked at peak ripeness and never exposed to air. The result is a mottled army-green fruit with a meaty texture and surprisingly mild flavor. Even my staunchly anti-olive companions admitted they "didn't hate it." Don't leave without a peek in the dusty one-room museum in a nearby outbuilding, packed high with antique olive-industry tools, crate labels, and other fascinating old junk from California's past.

KNOW: *There are picnic tables in the peaceful, fragrant main courtyard. Bring a meal and supplement it with a jar of olives.*

CALIFORNIA

TOURS: *You can call ahead and request a free tour any time of year, which will give you more information than you ever wanted to know about the role the Grabers have played in the California olive industry. But unless you visit in the fall when production is in full swing, you'll just be looking at a bunch of dormant equipment. (Sept–Nov; call for details.)*

California Ripe Olives

God help us the day the foodies discover the California ripe olive. The unsung hero of pizza toppings and children's finger food, these mild black olives are only made in California and make up 95 percent of the country's total production. Their invention was largely an accidental one. Spanish missionaries brought the first olive trees to missions around 1800, but it took nearly a century for enterprising farmers to try their hand at olive oil, at the time considered the only valuable by-product of the crop. Competition from Spanish and Italian imports was fierce, and the future of the domestic olive industry looked bleak until Freda Ehmann came on the scene in 1897. A struggling widow determined to make a living from her sole asset, an olive orchard, Ehmann decided to cure the fruit herself on her back porch using the simplest and quickest method available. Necessity is the mother of invention.

Unlike Spanish olives, which are picked green and fermented in brine for up to a year, or Greek olives, which are picked ripe and preserved in vinegar and salt, California ripe olives are soaked in lye and water for a few days to leech out their natural bitterness, exposed to oxygen to turn them a uniform black, then canned and sold immediately. The resulting olive is mild and prosaic, certainly bland enough to appeal to the unadventurous American palate at the turn of the century, when Ehmann brought their everyday consumption to the masses. Today, canned black olives account for 99 percent of the California crop; olive oil remains a boutique industry, despite a growing interest in local food.

 Mitla Café

602 N Mount Vernon Ave, San Bernardino
MILE/EXIT: 72 (then exit 44A from I-215 N)
909.888.0460
www.mitlacafe.com
OPEN: *Daily 9a–8p*

You kind of have the feeling, walking in, that no matter how high the temperature rises on the outside, it's always cool within the whitewashed walls of the Mitla Café. This 75-year-old Mexican restaurant off old Route 66 is a true roadside oasis, a place where beer comes in frosty mugs, tortilla chips are served still warm from the deep-fryer, and leisurely rotating ceiling fans set a pace far removed from the wearying grind outside. The food in such a place merely needs to be adequate, but the food at Mitla is outstanding. The chile relleno may be the best in Southern California, an island of fresh green pepper, pillowy egg batter, and oozing cheese in a sea of mild red sauce that will make you believe, however temporarily, in the existence of a higher power. Tacos and enchiladas are similarly godlike, made even better with the addition of the house hot sauce: vaguely spicy, chipotle-smoky, worth putting on everything. It's easy to imagine the relief that hopeful mid-century Midwestern transplants must have felt, settling into the cafe's big booths after a harrowing drive over Cajon Pass into the San Bernardino Valley, satisfied that here, at last, they had finally reached the promised land.

Original Mcdonald's/Route 66 Museum

1398 North E St, San Bernardino
MILE/EXIT: 72 (then exit 44B from I-215 N)
DISTANCE FROM HWY: 5.2 miles
909.885.6324
OPEN: *Daily 9a–5p*

This is the site where milk shake machine salesman Ray Kroc stumbled onto the McDonald brothers' successful burger joint in 1954 and convinced them to let him franchise it across the country, launching the fast-food nation. Well, kind of. The original building was demolished in 1971, and what remains is a strange amalgamation of memorabilia that has a distinctly homemade feel to it. (It's not even owned by the

McDonald's corporation; the museum is owned by the chicken fast-food chain Juan Pollo, and the building doubles as its corporate offices.) The lack of corporate packaging is actually kind of refreshing, and it's fun to see all the pre–Ray Kroc stuff like menus, fry press, hamburger boxes, and more, along with all the Hamburglar memorabilia and Happy Meal toys from the 1980s you could ever want or need. The museum also doubles as an homage to old Route 66, with some signage and other knickknacks. Really, it's all said in the sign that hangs above the front door: "We don't sell any 15¢ hamburgers, but we serve plenty of FREE memories!"

KNOW: *Admission to the museum is free. You can call ahead for a tour by a curator, but it's pretty self-explanatory.*

Parent Navel Orange Tree

7115 Magnolia Ave, Riverside

MILE/EXIT: 72 (then exit 61 from CA-91 W)

DISTANCE FROM HWY: 11.1 miles

This tree changed the course of history. How many other plants do you know with that claim to fame? It all started back in 1893, when a missionary in Bahia, Brazil, sent the U.S. Department of Agriculture a dozen clippings of a new species of orange tree, notable for its seedless, easy-to-peel fruit with unprecedented sweetness. Superintendent of Horticulture William Saunders sent a pair to his friend Eliza Tibbets in Riverside, where they flourished in the SoCal climate and soil and single-handedly kicked off the state's "second gold rush"—the explosion of the citrus industry and the state's resulting population boom. One of the two original Washington orange trees still thrives in a tiny park at the busy intersection of Magnolia and Arlington Avenues. (The other died in 1921, after it was transplanted to the courtyard of the Mission Inn.) The viewing experience itself is somewhat underwhelming—it is, after all, just an orange tree, albeit an impressively robust one—but it's still worth a drive-by, if only to contemplate how a single fruit has the capacity to transform an empire.

California Citrus State Historic Park

9400 Dufferin Ave, Riverside

MILE/EXIT: 72 (then exit 58 from CA-91 W)

DISTANCE FROM HWY: 15.8 miles

951.784.0456

www.citrusstatepark.org

OPEN: *Apr–Sept Mon–Fri 8a–5p, Sat–Sun 8a–7p; Oct–March daily 8a–5p*

Before Riverside County was an endless stretch of suburbs, it was an endless stretch of orange groves, the export of which made Riverside the nation's richest city per capita in 1895. (Chew on that, Manhattan.) A century later, the state created this commemorative park, which houses nearly 200 producing acres of orange, lemon, and grapefruit trees and a small museum dedicated to the history of citrus in California. The museum's exhibits are colorful and informative, if you're into that sort of thing; more importantly, to this writer anyway, the gift shop has stacks and stacks of affordable orange and lemon crate labels. (Framed, they make amazing wall art.) The park also features a walking path that winds through orange groves and palm trees and offers scenic vistas of the surrounding foothills. It's all very pleasant, and after miles of freeway overpasses and gridlock, you can almost imagine everything melting away and remember the orange blossom–scented dream that California is built on. Spot the park's entrance by the can't-miss-it farm stand in the shape of a giant orange, the likes of which used to dot highways up and down the state.

KNOW: *Visit in the beginning of April, when the orange trees are in bloom, and you'll understand why turn-of-the-century journalist and cultural booster Charles Fletcher Loomis once wrote that the orange is not only a fruit, but a romance.*

 Gless Ranch

19985 Van Buren Blvd, Riverside

MILE/EXIT: 72 (then exit 58 from CA-91 W)

DISTANCE FROM HWY: 15.8 miles

951.653.5991

www.glessranch.com

OPEN: *Daily 8a–5:30p*

CALIFORNIA

Since 1907, now in the fifth generation of the Gless family ranchers, this roadside farm stand still offers boxes of oranges and grapefruit picked daily from the ranch. It's a living testimony to a time changing—in 2009, in light of the state's ongoing water crisis, Riverside announced that it was going to open a 500,000-square-foot shopping center with a Target, McDonald's, and more on a lot of the ranch's groves. Support it while you still can and get some of the best—and cheapest—oranges you'll find anywhere.

Orange County and San Diego

City Stats

LOCAL FLAVOR: Burger stands, beachside cafes, and Mexican food.

BEST TIME: Late summer and early fall, if you want to brown on the beach.

WORST TIME: It usually rains in January, and June is beset by a period of fog and cooler temperatures that's known locally as "June Gloom."

MORE INFO: Orange County Tourism (www.visittheoc.com), San Diego Tourism (www.sandiego.com)

Once, a week before I moved from Los Angeles the second time, I drove down to Newport Beach to visit a friend and she took me to lunch at the Cheesecake Factory in Fashion Island. It was my first (and only) visit to the restaurant and I wanted to go somewhere more local—but she assured me that it would give me a taste of Orange County at its finest. And there, waiting for our table on a padded bench with million-dollar views of the ocean, it sure did.

A little blond girl in a pink polo shirt who couldn't have been older than five sat next to me. Her coiffed mother was talking into a cell phone, and the girl wanted to talk. Specifically, she wanted to show me something her mom had just bought her at the mall, and I cannot fully put into words the waves of pity and horror I felt when I saw what it was: My First Makeup Kit, complete with eye shadow, blush, and lip gloss. I felt it more than I thought it: *I will die if I don't get out of Southern California.*

Melodramatic, sure, but the point is that parts of Orange County can be just as shallow as popular culture makes them out to be. It's historically one of the country's richest, whitest, and most conservative counties. It's a place that was once nothing but orange groves, now transformed into nothing but tract homes and strip malls. An afternoon in Newport Beach is enough to restore your faith in the accuracy of reality TV. Girls really are that vacuous; guys really are that conceited. And one mustn't forget

CALIFORNIA

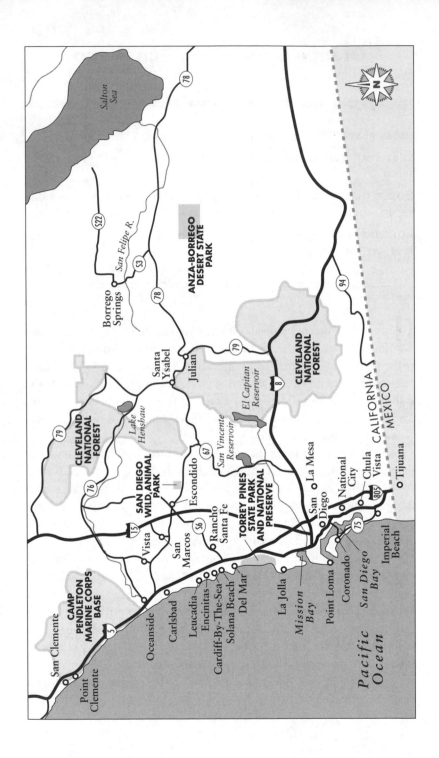

that Orange County is the home of Disneyland and the far-reaching influences of its Imagineering.

There are two sides to every story of course, and Orange County does have its moments. Westminster is home to the biggest Vietnamese population outside of Vietnam, and a bowl of pho in Little Saigon is restorative in more ways than one. A half century of surfing culture has bred boardwalks with old-fashioned burger stands and date milk shakes. Laguna Beach is still a quirky artist community under the gentrified veneer. And then there are the beaches—flat sand, perfect surf, beautiful people, gorgeous weather—that remind you why people lived here in the first place.

San Diego is just a few miles from the Mexican border, and oddly overlooked for a metropolis of four million. Part of that is because it's lodged way down in the southwest corner of the country—the only place farther is Hawaii—and it's not a city you pass through on the way to somewhere else. (Unless that somewhere else is Tijuana, and no judgment passed here.) San Diego was once a boomtown that matched Los Angeles in size and scope, but that fizzled out and it became a Navy town instead. Carb-load with the surfers in a beachy breakfast shack, and have fish tacos for lunch—no city on earth makes 'em better.

ON THE ROAD

🍴 Ruby's Shake Shack

7703 E Coast Hwy, Corona del Mar
MILE/EXIT: 27
949.464.0100
www.rubys.com
OPEN: *Daily 10a–6p*

The original Shake Shack was a legendary surfer hangout set against the sand dunes and the gently rolling coastal mountains of Newport Beach, but a 2006 takeover by the nostalgia-driven Ruby's Diner restaurant chain has stripped the original burger joint of some of its authentic glory. But it's not all gone. Ruby's kept the Date Shake on the menu—a California institution made from ground dates that's so sweet your teeth hurt while drinking it, but so delicious you don't want to stop. Ruby's also has a long menu of burgers, sandwiches, salads, and other diner favorites, along with desserts like malts, ice cream sundaes, and burgers and fries.

VARIOUS LOCATIONS *in Anaheim, Costa Mesa, Fullerton, Huntington Beach, Laguna Beach, Long Beach, Los Angeles, Malibu, and Oceanside*

Pho 79

9941 Hazard Ave, Garden Grove
MILE/EXIT: 19
714.531.2490
www.pho79.com
OPEN: *Mon–Tue, Thu–Sun 8a–8p; Wed 8a–3p*

The section of Orange County known as Little Saigon has one of the biggest Vietnamese populations outside of Vietnam, and is the best place on the West Coast to try pho, bahn mi, coffee with condensed milk, and other Vietnamese specialties. Pho 79 is a reliably good local chain that is considered one of the best pho houses in the area. Pho is all about the broth, and Pho 79's does not disappoint—it's a rousing, complex, deeply beefy bowl of soup redolent of star anise and oxtails, and filled with noodles and meat. Word to the wise: do not add too much of the house hot sauce before you know your limits. The menu also has Vietnamese spring rolls and other specialties, all in an atmosphere that's truly of the neighborhood, surrounded by representatives of the area's Vietnamese population. Toto, I don't think we're in the O.C. from the TV show anymore.

Sugar Shack

213½ Main St, Huntington Beach
MILE/EXIT: 16
714.536.0355
www.hbsugarshack.com
OPEN: *Mon, Tue, Thu 6a–4p; Wed 6a–8p; Fri–Sun 6a–5p*

Wildly popular breakfast spot in Huntington Beach since it opened in 1967. As the story goes, proprietors Pat and Mary Williams were taking a stroll down Main Street one afternoon when Mary saw the "for sale" sign in the window of a vacant restaurant. She decided she would buy it, open a restaurant, and teach her five children the value of money and hard work. It's now run by a third generation of Williamses, but still turning out massive three-egg breakfast burritos, egg combos, omelets, and pancakes to a hungry crowd of surfers and families. Make sure to put your name on the list for both the front and back patios—they're separate entities, wait-wise, and many people don't know about the back one.

 Taco Loco

640 South Coast Hwy, Laguna Beach
MILE/EXIT: 10
DISTANCE FROM HWY: 12.3 miles
949.497.1635
www.tacoloco.net
OPEN: *Mon–Thu, Sun 11a–midnight; Fri–Sat 11a–2a*

This health-conscious taco stand has been a fixture in the upscale artist community of Laguna Beach since 1987. The secret is the addictive blackened fish tacos, the brainchild of owner Gonzalo Rebollar, who wondered what would happen if he added Cajun blackening spices to the fish batter. Blackened fish options include unusual suspects like salmon, mahi mahi, and swordfish, along with shrimp, chicken, carnitas, beef, and a surprising number of vegetarian options, including mushrooms, tofu, and a mysterious protein called "vegie phish." All tacos come with a side of freshly made guacamole. The menu also includes salads, quesadillas, nachos, and—this being Southern California—herbal teas and fresh-squeezed orange, carrot, and celery juices. Eat outside on the patio or brave the restaurant's flower-power interior, and be on the lookout for celebrities—just like us, they've been known to stop in to satisfy their cravings.

 101 Café

631 S Coast Hwy, Oceanside
MILE/EXIT: 53 (from I-5)
760.722.5220
www.101cafe.net
OPEN: *Daily 7a–midnight*
Cash only; ATM on premises

Built in 1928 in the "Googie" architectural style, this coffee shop along the Pacific Coast Highway has been a popular roadside attraction since Highway 101 was the main thoroughfare through California. The road is the obsession of owner John Daley, who has several long essays devoted to it on his website, and has made it the theme of his retro diner. Menu items have cute names like "Dicey Conditions" (scramble with diced ham), "Stacked Up at the Light" (buttermilk pancakes), and "Accelerate Now" (French toast). These are standard diner breakfasts, a step up from Denny's, but the history of the place is what makes them so tasty. You can almost put yourself in the mind-set of the men and women who frequented the cafe in the early years—an entire nation of people who were unconcerned about cholesterol levels and trans fat.

Stone Brewery

1999 Citracado Pkwy, Escondido
MILE/EXIT: 51B (from I-5)
DISTANCE FROM HWY: 17 miles
760.471.4999
www.stonebrew.com
OPEN: *Mon–Thu 11a–11p, Fri–Sat 11a–midnight, Sun 11a–10p*

This North County brewer is regularly cited as one of the best craft brewers in the country, known for its giant, supercharged ales like the Arrogant Bastard (whose label warns potential consumers that they might not be worthy of it), Stone IPA, and Stone Ruination IPA (which, as the name suggests, will pretty much spoil your palate for anything else for the rest of the meal). The brewer's challenge, of course, is managing to maintain any sort of flavor in the face of the hop onslaught—your palate can only take so much, after all—but somehow Stone manages to find the balance. Enjoy a Stone brew or sample another local microbrew—there are 32 beers on tap in all—at the solar-powered pub or in the one-acre beer garden. Food is first-rate, focusing on local, organic ingredients. If you want to learn more about the hops-to-suds process, pick up a pass in the gift shop for a free tour, which leaves frequently throughout the day on weekends and Monday–Thursday at 2, 4, and 6pm.

Rubio's

4504 Mission Bay Dr, San Diego
MILE/EXIT: 23
858.272.2801
www.rubios.com
OPEN: *Mon–Thu 10a–9p, Fri–Sat 10a–10p, Sun 10:30a–9p*

Fish tacos in San Diego are a dime a dozen, but you should go straight to the source. Rubio's is where it all started in 1983, when founder Ralph Rubio returned from a long ramble in Baja California, where he'd spent his days sampling the tacos up and down the coast and delighting in their simply marinated fresh fish, crispy cabbage, and fresh corn tortillas. Today, Rubio's is such a well-known chain that it's easy to forget its important place in San Diego culinary history. The menu has since expanded to burritos, bowls, wraps, and more of what's being marketed as the "Beach Mex" cuisine, but don't let such distractions sway you—you're here for the fish taco, smothered in guacamole, Jack and cheddar cheese, and cilantro. This is the original location, a tiny taco shack where it's easy to imagine Rubio dreaming of escaping to Baja once again.

VARIOUS LOCATIONS *in Anaheim, Glendale, Los Angeles, Redlands, Temecula, Thousand Oaks, and Tracy*

El Indio

3695 India St, San Diego
MILE/EXIT: 18A (from I-5)
619.299.0333
www.el-indio.com
OPEN: *Daily 8a–9p*

So it turns out that taquitos aren't a traditional Mexican specialty, as I've believed my entire life—they were invented by El Indio proprietor Ralph Pesquiera Sr. in 1940. El Indio was a tortilla factory at the time, and during WWII, workers from nearby airplane factories began asking him to serve them a hot lunch. Pesquiera rolled meat in one of the factory's fresh corn tortillas, called it a "taquito" (for "little taco"), and culinary history was made. El Indio moved to its current Mission Hills location in 1971 and is now run by Ralph Pesquiera Jr., but taquitos are still the star of the show. They are outstanding, almost criminally greasy, and available in shredded beef, shredded chicken, and potato. The rest of the menu offers Mexican combo plates—the kind that come to the table piping hot and oozing with refried beans and melted cheese.

CALIFORNIA

(🍴) Hob Nob Hill

2271 1st Ave, San Diego
MILE/EXIT: 18A (from I-5)
619.239.8176
www.hobnobhill.com
OPEN: *Daily 7a–9p*

Husband-and-wife team Harold and Dorothy Hoersch opened their first San Diego diner together in 1944, and though they've been through many locations and iterations since, they've never lost their passion for old-fashioned American cookery and dishes made from scratch. Hob Nob's freshly baked muffins, cinnamon coffee cake and gooey cinnamon rolls are lure enough at breakfast—especially when supplemented by fresh-squeezed orange juice, strong coffee, and breakfast classics like a Belgian waffle, stack of buttermilk pancakes, or a corned beef omelet. Lunch and dinner offer American standards like meat loaf, chicken and dumplings, and roast turkey with sage dressing. Uniformed waitresses bring the food to the table with practiced skill, and the whole experience makes you nostalgic for a time when coffee shops like this used to grace every town in America.

DETOURS & DESTINATIONS

Temecula

The story of Temecula is the story of a town noticed, then forgotten, then remembered again. Said to be the only town in California still known by its Indian name, Temecula was an out-of-the-way settlement until it was chosen as a stop on the important Butterfield stagecoach route between Georgia and San Francisco. The town was made immortal thanks to a brief visit from writer Helen Hunt Jackson, who chose it as the setting for the influential novel *Ramona*, a romantic idealization of Southern California's Spanish past. Then the railroad tracks were washed out in a flood and never replaced, and Temecula drifted into obscurity until recently, when a burgeoning wine industry and an old-town revitalization renewed it to a day-trip destination for Angelenos and San Diegans. Front Street, the main drag, seems more like a Western movie set than a working town, with Wild West–style storefronts and plaques proclaiming "Kit

Carson slept here twice," but the rough-and-tumble history is toned down some by the gourmet restaurants and high-end gift shops moving in.

 Temecula Olive Oil Company

28653 Front St, Temecula
MILE/EXIT: 59/Rancho Candido Road
951.693.0607
www.temeculaoliveoil.com
OPEN: *Sun–Thu 9:30a–6p, Fri–Sat 9:30a–7p*

Good olive oil should never be tasted with bread—it should be sipped like a fine cognac, all the better to appreciate the full bouquet. At least, that's what we were told as we took a rapid series of olive oil shots at this tasting room in downtown Temecula. The family-owned company makes excellent extra-virgin olive oils and vinegars with fruit grown at their sustainable ranch in the Temecula Valley. Along with early- and late-harvest EVOO (you'd never guess three months would make such a difference), we also sampled seasonal oils with flavors like lemon, garlic rosemary, and blood orange, along with unusual vinegars like vanilla and fig balsamic. With ingredients like these, you could rule the world. The tasting room itself has brushed concrete floors and decor bordering on country kitsch, but I was so dazzled by the flavor that I even forgave a prominent sign that read, "May olive your dreams come true." And so they might—we were never given a hard sell, but we each walked away with several bottles of the stuff anyway, plotting our rise to culinary fame and fortune . . . or at least the killer salad dressing we were going to make tomorrow.

KNOW: *The store also sells jars of olives, tapenade, muffuletta, and more gourmet foodstuffs, along with olive oil soap made in nearby Marietta.*

Swing Inn

28676 Front St, Temecula
MILE/EXIT: 59/Rancho Candido Road
951.676.2321
www.swinginncafe.com
OPEN: *Daily 5a–9p*

If Old Town Temecula has made an industry of its cowboys-and-Indians past, the Swing Inn just exists, as it has since 1927, serving up good, cheap breakfasts that will set you up for a day of hard labor—or put you in a food coma, depending on your vocation. The best thing on the menu is the chicken-fried steak, which will make you regret ever wasting your time on anything less worthy. All too often the meat requires a steak knife to saw through, but this is cattle country—the beef here is tender enough to cut with a fork, and the breading is so tasty you don't even need the accompanying country gravy. Which isn't to say you don't want it. This is the Sistine Chapel of gravy, a peppery, ethereal sauce so velvety you know it can't be good for you, but it's somehow light enough to convince you it might be. The same kitchen wizardry applies to the biscuits and gravy, the heaviest item on the breakfast menu by anyone's estimation, here somehow rendered lighter than a cloud. Hanging lanterns, dark wood siding, red vinyl booths, and career waitresses complete the picture. If Kit Carson ever ate here, there certainly isn't a plaque advertising the fact.

KNOW: *The test of a good diner is its patty melt, and the Swing Inn's is the real deal—the high-grade beef patty, cheddar and Jack cheeses, and rye bread meld together into one delicious bite.*

Selected Bibliography

Alt, David and Donald W. Hyndman, *Roadside Geology of Northern and Central California* (Montana: Mountain Press, 2000).

Alt, David and Donald W. Hyndman, *Roadside Geology of Oregon* (Montana: Mountain Press, 2009).

Alt, David and Donald W. Hyndman, *Roadside Geology of Washington* (Montana: Mountain Press, 1984).

Bergon, Frank, ed., *The Journals of Lewis and Clark* (New York: Penguin, 1989).

Davidson, Alan, *The Oxford Companion to Food* (New York: Oxford, 2006).

Gulick, Bill, *Roadside History of Oregon* (Montana: Mountain Press, 2005).

Hayes, Derek, *Historical Atlas of California* (Berkeley, University of California Press, 2007).

Hayes, Derek, *Historical Atlas of the Pacific Northwest* (Seattle: Sasquatch Books, 2000).

Herbst, Sharon Tyler and Ron Herbst, *The Cheese Lover's Companion* (New York: HarperCollins, 2007).

Herbst, Sharon Tyler and Ron Herbst, *The New Food Lover's Companion* (New York: Barron's, 2007).

Jackson, Michael, ed., *Beer* (New York: DK, 2007).

Kirk, Ruth and Carmela Alexander, *Exploring Washington's Past: A Road Guide to History* (Seattle: University of Washington Press, 1990).

Kurlansky, Mark, *The Food of a Younger Land* (New York: Riverhead, 2009).

MacNeil, Karen, *The Wine Bible* (New York: G.P. Putnam, 2001).

McWilliams, Cary, *Southern California: An Island on the Land* (Utah: Gibbs Smith, 1973).

Pittman, Ruth, *Roadside History of California* (Montana: Mountain Press, 1995).

Starr, Kevin, *California: A History* (New York: Random House, 2005).

Stern, Jane and Michael, *500 Things to Eat Before It's Too Late* (New York: Houghton Mifflin Harcourt, 2009).

Stern, Jane and Michael, *Roadfood* (New York: Broadway Books, 2008).

Taylor, Judith, *The Olive in California: History of an Immigrant Tree* (Berkeley: Ten Speed Press, 2004).

Willard, Pat, *America Eats!* (New York: Bloomsbury, 2008).

Index

M

N

Y

About the Author

Anna Roth is a food writer and editor. Her work has appeared many publications including *Sunset, Seattle Metropolitan, Seattle Weekly, San Diego,* and more. Anna is currently the managing editor of *eHow Food* and previously spent two years as the Northwest editor of Citysearch, covering restaurants, nightlife, and events in Seattle and Portland. She received a national Eddy Award from Edible Communities for her 2009 essay on the history of sourdough. Anna currently lives in Los Angeles and Seattle.